# FEEDING AND LEADING

# FEEDING & LEADING

## KENNETH O. GANGEL

VICTOR BOOKS ®

A DIVISION OF SCRIPTURE PRESS PUBLICATIONS INC.
USA CANADA ENGLAND

6   7   8   9   10   Printing/Year   00   99   98   97   96   95

Unless otherwise noted, all Scripture quotations are from the *Holy Bible, New International Version,* © 1973, 1978, 1984, International Bible Society. Used by permission of Zondervan Bible Publishers. Other quotations are from *The Living Bible* (TLB), © 1971, Tyndale House Publishers, Wheaton, IL 60189. Used by permission, and the *King James Version* (KJV).

Recommended Dewey Decimal Classification: 262
Suggested Subject Heading: CHURCH ADMINISTRATION
Library of Congress Catalog Card Number: 88-62833
ISBN: 0-89693-678-3

For information, address Victor Books, P.O. Box 1825, Wheaton, IL 60189.

# TABLE OF CONTENTS

# TABLE OF ILLUSTRATIONS

To My Pastors

*Ernest Elwell*
*Herman Braunlin*
*Harold DeVries*
*Roy Hamman*
*Delbert Hooker*
*William Hadeen*
*Don Jones*
*Burge Troxel*

# FOREWORD

Enculturated Christianity has become something of a norm among evangelicals. Our music takes on contemporary styles; our theology of family adapts to a whirlwind of divorce demographics; our long-standing commitments on issues like homosexuality and the use of alcohol crumble under cultural pressures.

It is not surprising, therefore, that our understanding of leadership has undergone a subtle but dramatic shift from the meekness and gentleness of Jesus to power-brokering in the political style of the kings of the Gentiles. Biblical qualifications for elders and deacons tend to get lost in our search for people who can "get the job done" or "take charge." The current secular literature on leadership abounds with emphases on assertiveness, and has already begun to show up in the writings of evangelicals. Doubtless we will see more.

Part of the problem comes from our *misunderstanding of the concept of servant leadership*. As a pastor once complained to me after a seminar session on servant leadership, "I tried that with one congregation and they walked all over me. I'll never try it again." We have confused meekness with weakness, and attitude with act. A servant leader is characterized not by his doormat demeanor, but by the way he considers himself in relation to other members of the congregation (Phil. 2:1-5). The Scriptures abound with emphasis on this principle, but let me offer here just one dramatic verse: "For by the grace given me I say to every one of you: Do not think of yourself more highly than you ought, but rather think of yourself with sober judgment, in accordance with the measure of faith God has given you" (Rom. 12:3).

A second problem is *the confusion between the church as organism and organization*. It is, of course, both. The church is *organism* because it is the body of Christ, a spiritual and eternal entity not hinged to earthbound restrictions and guidelines. But in its local form (it is not my purpose to discuss ecclesiology in detail), the church is clearly an *organization* if the words of our language mean anything. An organization is a group of people bound together for distinctive purposes, led by appropriate officers, handling sufficient funds and budgetary commitments to carry out their tasks, owning such properties as are deemed necessary, and transacting business with other organizations. Obviously the church can be thus described and clearly falls within the boundaries of the definition.

This book has been written to straighten out some of this confusion as well as provide a practical manual for those who lead the people of God. To a great extent, we will be looking at pastoral functions; but Christian leadership in the church certainly cannot be limited to one office or even a small team of professionals. Furthermore, *feeding and leading* are tasks for those who serve in parachurch organizations as well; and though the term would rarely be used, Christian school principals, college presidents, and mission board executives are also "pastors."

Each chapter will reflect a commitment to balance. We will try to sort out differences between administration and leadership and describe how the functions of each are carried out. We will try to demonstrate that ministry and management are not contradictory concepts of Christian leadership but rather correlated approaches to what the Bible demands. We will try to balance an emphasis on the task and the people, the "it" and the "thou." As Luecke and Southard put it:

> For ministers with a sense of mission and a love for people, our appeal is to the personal satisfaction that can arise from making their administrative work serve fundamental ministry purposes. When it is integrated with the ministry they want to do, pastors can find joy in administration.[1]

Amid the plethora of problems which have surfaced in the world as the twentieth century winds down, two central issues have surfaced in the church. These are certainly not unrelated to their cultural context but they offer unique problems for the body of

Christ, for it is there these behaviors ought to be positively modeled rather than negatively mourned. The first is *family distintegration*, and the second, a *lack of leadership*.

The reader notes immediately that these problems are closely related, virtual Siamese twins of congregational life. Since leadership begins at home, breakdown and failure there will of necessity be mirrored in that larger family of families we call "church." To put it very simply, weak fathers make weak elders or deacons. It may very well be that until the church solves the problem of family disintegration, it cannot solve the problem of lay leadership development.

The product of any organization is subject to ultimate evaluation. Today educators call this "competency based" learning outcomes. The "product" of the church is *not* new believers, as important and strategic as evangelism certainly is. The ultimate product is rather a mature and equipped lay leadership able to minister to others. No modern invention of the North American church, this idea comes from the pages of the New Testament.

It was He who gave some to be apostles, some to be prophets, some to be evangelists, and some to be pastors and teachers, to prepare God's people for works of service, so that the body of Christ may be built up until we all reach unity in the faith and in the knowledge of the Son of God and become mature, attaining to the whole measure of the fullness of Christ. Then we will no longer be infants, tossed back and forth by the waves, and blown here and there by every wind of teaching and by the cunning and craftiness of men in their deceitful scheming. Instead, speaking the truth in love, we will in all things grow up into Him who is the Head, that is, Christ. From Him the whole body, joined and held together by every supporting ligament, grows and builds itself up in love, as each part does its work (Eph. 4:11-16).

It is very possible that what laymen *think* their pastors want from them is very different than what their pastors *really* want. That still leaves open the question, What do laymen want from their pastors? Walt Henrichsen and Bill Garrison have addressed these questions in a book entitled *Layman, Look Up! God Has a Place for You.* Right at the beginning of chapter 1 they refer to an incident at the Lausanne International Congress on World Evangelization at which a U.S. representative speaking on a panel argued that laymen would no longer be content with their traditional role.

He indicated that a "good" layman has traditionally been asked to do four things:

1. regularly attend all church functions,
2. liberally give money in support of the church's programs,
3. support all church programs established by the leadership,
4. and adhere to the "eleventh commandment," which is "don't rock the boat."[2]

This book is based on the premise that the genius of the New Testament is lay leadership, not brilliant clergy. Granted, the Apostle Paul was trained in rabbinical studies and offers a prototypical model of the sophisticated seminary graduate in our day. But Peter, Barnabas, Silas, Timothy, Epaphras, and a host of others who made the New Testament church work were laymen trained and built up by those able to do so. Henrichsen and Garrison are right: "In these days of unprecedented opportunity, the laity's functioning as God's servants should be affirmed and encouraged. God has called the various ministries into being to do this task."[3]

One further word calls for mention. The title of this book may ring familiar in the minds of some readers. It has certainly echoed through mine since I first read Richard Caemmerer's book of the same title published by Concordia in 1957, an experience enjoyed while studying practical theology with Dr. Caemmerer at Concordia Theological Seminary in the early 1960s. Since the Caemmerer book has been out of print for some time, Concordia Publishing House has granted the privilege of reusing the title in this present work.

---

[1]*David S. Luecke and Samuel Southard,* Pastoral Administration: Integrating Ministry and Management in the Church *(Waco, Texas: Word Books, 1986), p. 13.*

[2]*Walter A. Henrichsen and William N Garrison,* Layman, Look Up! God Has a Place for You *(Grand Rapids: Zondervan, 1983), p. 16.*

[3]*Henrichsen and Garrison, p. 13.*

# CHAPTER 1

# UNDERSTANDING ADMINISTRATIVE PROCESS

Is there a difference in meaning between the words "leadership" and "administration"? How about "administration" and "management"? The latter question can be disposed of quickly; the former offers stubborn complications.

As a doctoral student at the University of Missouri my major field of study centered in the administration of higher education; my minor field, organizational communications. The education courses were taken on one side of the campus in the School of Education, and the communications courses in the School of Business. It took awhile to catch on to the fact that education faculty used the term "administration" to describe and discuss precisely the same functions and professional skills which business faculty referred to as "management."

The title of the Luecke/Southard book mentioned in the Foreword indicates the synonymous nature of the terms—*Pastoral Administration: Integrating Ministry and Management in the Church.* Though there is no generally accepted definition of management or administration, it is invariably related to organizational goals and resources. Anderson's definition appears as good as any coming out of the secular domain: "Management is the process of defining organizational goals and making decisions about the efficient and effective use of organizational resources in order to ensure high organization performance."[1]

But how is *leadership* different from *administration* (management)? Dr. Thomas C. Stanton, the vice president for Academic Affairs at James Madison University, proposes that "leaders and managers have common foundation *abilities* but they differ with respect to their predominant *tendencies.*" Leaders, he says, tend to be goal-oriented while managers tend to be result-oriented. Managers strive for order but leaders tolerate ambiguity. Managers try to correct failures; leaders turn failures into successes. Leaders inspire people, but managers depend on systems. Managers attempt to adjust to change while leaders attempt to produce it.[2]

Whereas one doesn't want to oversimplify the distinction, Stanton may be overplaying it. Drucker for example, defines managers as those who give direction to organizations, provide leadership, and make decisions about the way the organization will use the resources it has available.[3] In other words, one of the things an administrator does is lead. Almost twenty-five years ago Louis Allen's classic book *The Management Profession* (McGraw-Hill, 1964) divided all management into four functions: planning, organizing, leading, and controlling. In several legitimate models then, leading appears as just a subcategory of administration.

Think for a moment about your favorite NFL quarterback. Picture him calling his own plays rather than having them signaled in from the sidelines. He changes the play at the line of scrimmage, waves the wide receiver inside rather than outside, and distributes helmet slaps and words of encouragement as everybody comes back to the huddle after a seventeen-yard gain. Is he a leader? Of course. Is he an administrator? Not in any of the definitions commonly linked with that word.

Now picture some fourth-level bureaucrat buried in the bowels of the Pentagon. Paper flows in and out of his office as he handles and signs hundreds of forms a week. He may even supervise a small staff in his office, but his name never surfaces above the level of his department. Is he a leader? Possibly, but not probably. Is he an administrator? Yes.

Distinctions calling for a linkage of the words *leader* with people relations and *administration* with nonhuman resources seem too neat. Generally leaders may be more people-oriented but that might just be another way of saying a given administrator tends to excel more in his leadership functions than in other areas of his task.

Perhaps the purposes of this book are best served by not making that distinction too clearly. We must state it, however, and the separation of the first two chapters demonstrates that. But here's the key: *we want leaders in Christian organizations to be effective administrators and administrators in Christian organizations to be good leaders.* In ministry, both are better than either, and both can be taught and trained (as Jesus' experience with the disciples clearly attests).

Pastor Jim graduated from seminary and eagerly began service in his first church. It was a small church of about 150 people, and Jim felt quite prepared and competent to do the job.

After about six months, however, Jim began to realize there was a great deal more to being a pastor than preparing two sermons for Sunday, a Bible study for Wednesday, and calling on sick church members. He struggled with a reasonable but flexible work schedule with a part-time church secretary. The monthly meetings with church leaders seemed to go on and on as discussion centered on problems rather than planning. Meanwhile everybody seemed to be looking to him for decisions about the budget, the Sunday School, youth group activities, music, and outreach.

The congregation certainly viewed Jim as their leader, but perhaps they did not realize how much they were pushing him to make decisions about nearly everything happening at the church. In the midst of such crisis management, Jim was forced to take a long, hard look at his ability to lead and administer. He began to think about long-range plans and goal-setting.

The model we seek in these chapters parallels the biblical model of the Christian leader as both shepherd and overseer, ministering elder and chief executive officer, team captain and supervisor. We want to resist conflict between management and ministry. In a most thorough article to which I will refer again, Agustin B. Vencer, Jr., sums up how all this comes together to advance the kindgom of Christ on earth.

> It is an organization with government. It is institutional ministry or ministerial order to administer God's work. Hence, it must maximize its effectiveness to carry out the Great Commission. This corporate operational function is a management task and the minister is called to be a manager.[4]

## FOUR TASKS OF ADMINISTRATORS

We've already taken note of Allen's fourfold approach to managerial process. Acronyms abound in the study of administration (as they do in the study of theology), and I have chosen a common one for this chapter—PLOD. The word evokes reactions of sluggish stability, so I want to build a second related function into each basic administrative task. Without doubt the second set could be studied separately and in my classrooms I teach that way. But the linkage is not forced and the value can plant in the reader's mind four basic concepts, an easy handle by which to "grab" administration.

## PLANNING AND GOAL ACHIEVEMENT

The study of administration contains almost as many clichés as acronyms, maybe more. Often, however, those clichés describe actual truisms, axioms which direct us to better leadership. And one fits right here: *a goal needs a plan to make it work.* A brilliant example surfaces as early as the first book of the Old Testament.

Joseph's interpretation of Pharaoh's dream indicated that the goal over the next fourteen years would be to keep the nation from starving. "The reason the dream was given to Pharaoh in two forms is that the matter has been firmly decided by God, and God will do it soon" (Gen. 41:32). But how? Pharaoh certainly had no ideas, so in verses 33-36 Joseph unveils the plan, and in verse 37 we read, "The plan seemed good to Pharaoh and to all his officials."

We could go on to discuss staffing, organization, and delegation from this passage, but suffice it here to say that the development of goals in a church or any Christian organization must be accompanied by the development of a plan whereby those goals can be achieved. This book provides entire chapters on each of these items so our only purpose here is recognizing this dyad as an administrative function.

## LEADERSHIP AND SUPERVISION OF STAFF

Pastor Petroff has a problem. He struggled alone as the only trained and professional staff member in his church for four years; then the church finally hired a full-time assistant responsible for youth and music. Pastor Jerry joined the staff less than a year ago and already there are rumblings from the lay leaders to release the new man. Petroff understands that the annual meeting, now less than a month away, will require either his defense of Pastor Jerry with the intent of retaining him for at least another year, or acquiescence to what seems to be the general mood of the congregation.

What went wrong? Why is Pastor Jerry's experience so common among associate staff members in evangelical churches? Some suggest the national tenure average for associates, regardless of their specialty (youth, music, Christian education, children, discipleship), stands at about eighteen months, a figure that hasn't changed much in the last twenty years.

Whatever happens to Jerry, any good guess would have to put

16

part of the blame on Pastor Petroff's desk. His Lone Ranger leadership style (partly cultivated by what he was taught in seminary) provided precious little team leadership and supervision so desperately needed by Jerry in his first year of full-time ministry. Petroff has also not done well in developing lay leadership, but we'll save that problem for later. Here let's remember that *leadership is learned behavior,* and whether Jerry goes or stays, Pastor Petroff can improve his leading and supervisory functions by reading books on church administration, attending seminars, perhaps even continuing formal education (such as a Doctor of Ministry degree program), and certainly from studying the leadership lessons evident throughout the Scriptures. Consider, for example, the life of Moses. Did anyone in history have greater leadership and supervisory responsibilities? What lessons can be observed from his life and ministry?

**1.** *He learned that leadership was impossible in his own strength* (Ex. 2:11-14). Moses' strange combination of Hebrew theology and Egyptian politics had not yet prepared him to do the work of God; in fear and apparent defeat, he ran off into exile.

**2.** *He profited from his failures* (Ex. 3:11). In the desert we encounter quite a different Moses. Whatever else maturity may do for us, it ought to make us aware of our own inadequacies and, therefore, more patient with the inadequacies of those less experienced. The haughty dogmatism which so often characterizes young church leaders tends to pass with years of experience in failure as well as success in leadership roles.

**3.** *He recognized his own call and commission from God* (Ex. 7:14-18). Moses would never have been able to endure the pressures of a confrontation with Pharaoh had he not been constantly aware that he was doing precisely what God had called him to do. Pastors, school principals, college presidents, board members, teachers, and all church leaders must be able to stand confidently before friend and foe alike in the call and commission of the Lord.

**4.** *He persevered against all criticism and adversity* (Ex. 16:1-12). Some form of the word "murmur" (KJV) appears at least eight times in this passage and was part of Moses' leadership life for forty years. And only once in all that time did he lose his patience and control (Num. 20). Every leader knows that when things go well he stands to receive plaudits from his followers; but when things do not go well, he becomes the immediate target of most complaints.

**5.** *He showed a tender and warm heart for his people* (Ex. 32:32).

Perhaps the secret of Moses' patience and perseverance lay in his genuine love for the people God called him to serve. Like the Apostle Paul, he was even willing to offer himself as a substitutionary representative for the people.

**6.** *He stayed in constant touch with God* (Ex. 34:1-9). A literal replay of Moses' friendship with God may be too much to expect in an age of grace with the completed canon of Scripture at our fingertips. Nevertheless, through prayer and constant monitoring by the Holy Spirit, we can certainly maintain constant contact with the throne room of heaven.

## ORGANIZATION AND CONTROL

Since *process* provides the focal point in our study, perhaps we ought to say organizing and controlling are two common tasks in administration. Organizing involves structuring the work of the ministry and determining relationships within that structure. Controlling deals with performance—how it is evaluated and improved.

Throughout the study of management, historic conflict has surrounded the question of organizational climate, and we will be talking about it throughout the chapters of this book. In fact, conflict analysis may be one of the best ways to study the administrative makeup of any organization, including the church and parachurch ministries. Conflict regularly surfaces in *emphasis on tasks versus emphasis on people,* technically referred to as the *nomothetic* and *idiographic dimensions* of organizational behavior. Sometimes we simply describe this as tension between roles and goals. In a classic work Amitai Etzioni claims:

> The ultimate source of the organizational dilemmas reviewed up to this point is the incomplete meshing of the personalities of the participants with their organizational roles. If personalities could be shaped to fit specific organizational roles, or organizational roles to fit specific personalities, many of the pressures to displace goals, much of the need to control performance, and a good part of the alienation would disappear.[5]

Chapter 3 picks up on this problem and explains how organization can be effectively carried out when one is committed to both feeding and leading.

## DELEGATION AND MOTIVATION

Philosophy of ministry is crucial in administrative process. I've already noted in the Foreword that servant leadership deals with attitude, the way the leader views himself in relationships to others in the organization. Theologically one makes that case from passages like Philippians 2:1-5 but functionally it comes out in how a pastor relates to elders and deacons. Does he encourage dependence, independence, or interdependence as a mutual way of relating? Does he employ manipulation or motivation in order to lead people to action?

Significant to all of us is how one sees leadership in the body of Christ. The destructive force of clericalism provides one of those cultural traps into which evangelical leaders keep stumbling. In the Vencer article mentioned earlier the author quotes Andrew Kirk's list of "six helpful principles of Christian ministry." Not all readers will agree with Kirk and Vencer, but we surely must admit that our approach to a philosophy or theology of ministry (and, therefore, how we carry out the tasks of delegation and motivation) largely depends on our acceptance or rejection of these principles.

1. No distinction either in form, language, or theory between clergy and laity was ever accepted by the New Testament church.
2. The ministry is coextensive with the entire church (1 Cor. 12:7).
3. The local church in the Apostolic Age always functioned under a plurality of leadership.
4. There are no uniform models for ministry in the New Testament; the patterns are flexible and versatile.
5. In the New Testament church can be found both leadership and authority, but no kind of hierarchical structure.
6. There is one, and only one, valid distinction which the New Testament appears to recognize within the ministry, apart from the different functions to which we have been alluding: the distinction between local and itinerant ministries.[6]

We talk a great deal today about "doing theology." Administration in the church or Christian organization is one way of "doing theology." The way Pastor Petroff (or any Christian leader) approaches these four tasks will show how he understands the Bible and whether or not he intends to activate its teachings.

Let's design a different scenario for Pastor Petroff and Pastor Jerry. This time we'll watch a senior pastor who has prepared himself and his congregation for a new staff member. The opportunity to disciple and encourage now becomes one of his primary goals.

Our new "converted" Pastor Petroff has studied the leadership style of Moses and examined the New Testament emphasis on leadership plurality. He no longer views himself as *the* head man.

So when Jerry arrives, he is treated immediately as a team member rather than a subordinate. The two pastors meet regularly to discuss the schedule of the week and the month, to plan the services, to decide on mutual responsibilities or individual responsibilities, and to pray together. In these weekly staff meetings Pastor Petroff can assess and discuss Jerry's leadership strengths, how to stay informed about the parents' expectations for their young people, and help Jerry through times of criticism which come to all leaders.

Of course there are still disagreements in methodology and procedure; Petroff and Jerry come from different generations. However, when they approach their mutual tasks with a team attitude, there is less opportunity for division. Rather than two leaders attempting to separately serve in two different arenas of ministry, what we have now is a joint mutuality, a leadership team carrying out its unified task.

# FOUR INGREDIENTS IN ADMINISTRATIVE LEADERSHIP

"Is there a leadership personality?" asks Neil Hightower in a recent article. In response he reviews five qualities described by psychologist Robert Hogan in the *Johns Hopkins Magazine*—anxiety, self-esteem, prudence, ambition, and likability. Hightower concludes that this list is helpful in determining which personal qualities one ought to develop to improve Christian leadership. He warns, "We must make sure our ambitions are entirely sanctified and subject to the control and direction of the Holy Spirit. In fact, each quality will be subject to the parameters of holy discipline described in the Word of God and established internally by the unfolding ministry of the indwelling Spirit of God."[7]

Warren Bennis, currently challenging Peter Drucker for the post of chief management guru, suggests five other traits of "super-leaders"—vision, communication, persistence, empowerment, and organizational ability. Vision, according to Bennis, is the capacity to create a compelling picture of the desired state of affairs that inspires people to perform.[8]

Just when we thought the trait approach to management study had died out, it rises again. For the Christian, the concept of "trait" relates to gifts and call. In fact, any biblical understanding of the administrative process properly coordinated with professional leadership studies focuses on at least four ingredients.

## GIFTS OF THE LEADER

After a revival of interest in spiritual gifts in the '60s and '70s, the evangelical community is currently experiencing a new focus on the leadership of the laity. Such a focus requires an understanding of gifts for a ministry. One of those gifts is the gift of administration. First Corinthians 12:28 demands center court in any study of the gift of administration. There the Greek word actually means "helmsman," the responsible decision-maker on a ship. Since I have treated this at much greater length in another book,[9] it would seem superfluous to reactivate that information here.

Let us ask, however, how Pastor Petroff could tell whether he has the gift of administration or not? One way would be to *sense how others assess his work.* Do his elders and/or deacons recognize an ability to carry out the four tasks mentioned earlier? Does his denomination regularly appoint him posts requiring administrative functions? Another signal might be if *he finds joy or interest in managerial activity.* Many pastors and Christian leaders simply detest administration, but a person with the gift of administration will find himself drawn toward directing the tasks and ministries of other people.

Finally, Pastor Petroff must yield to the Holy Spirit's witness in his life. In order to help Jerry and the church's lay leaders understand and develop their spiritual gifts, Petroff must have a grasp of his own.

## NEEDS OF THE GROUP

*Leadership doesn't work unless felt needs of the group are being met.* Out of this relationship consensus can arise. The leader reflects the collective feelings of the group much in the way James verbalized the decision of the Council at Jerusalem (Acts 15), apparently without Robert's Rules of Order or a formal vote.

The inseparability of leader and group, of leaders and followers, is only now coming to the fore in leadership studies and I'll have more to say about that. Pastor Petroff? He's been charging on without looking back, forgetting that people can only be led where they want to go while the leader "follows a step ahead." Petroff has never learned the interdependence between congregation and pastor verbalized in presidential context by Michael Korda:

> Our strength makes him strong; our determination makes him
> determined; our courage makes him a hero; he is, in the final
> analysis, the symbol of the best in us, shaped by our own spirit
> and will. And when these qualities are lacking in us, we can't
> produce him; and even with all our skill at image building we
> can't fake him. He is, after all, merely the sum of us. [10]

## DYNAMICS OF THE SITUATION

Ken "One Minute Manager" Blanchard may be right when he warns
that "our society is in the middle of a move toward autocratic
leadership." He emphasizes that *administrative leadership is situational,* governed by changing needs within the organization. We
could demonstrate this by talking about a pastor who was very
successful in a rural church, then met stubborn resistance when he
moved to a larger, urban congregation. In that illustration several
different variables affected the situation—geography, congregation
size, cultural milieu, and more. But even within that first rural
congregation there were different kinds of followers who needed
different kinds of leading.

To be sure, administrative leaders will tend toward one style or
another, and we'll discuss one of those styles in just a moment. But
Blanchard tells us that we should be flexible enough to adapt and
blend leadership styles as situations change.

> Americans must stop thinking in terms of extremes in leader-
> ship styles. Instead of gravitating to the extreme, managers
> should adopt the one best style of leadership that suits the
> people they supervise. Sometimes people need direction, and
> lots of it. Sometimes they need support and direction. And
> perhaps sometimes they just need to be left alone. [11]

## CHARACTERISTICS OF THE LEADERSHIP TEAM

In the quote above Korda is talking about presidential leadership at
the beginning of the first Reagan administration. His picture of the
leader as a composite of his followers becomes especially dramatic
when we narrow the focus of "followers" to the leadership team. In
a college, that would be the president's cabinet. In a church, the
pastoral staff and key lay leaders, such as elders or deacons. In a
Christian school, the administrator or headmaster and his im-

mediate staff of principals, business manager, and other executive officers.

What the Scripture says about the unity of the church certainly can be said of the unity of the leadership team: "From Him the whole body, joined and held together by every supporting ligament, grows and builds itself up in love, as each part does its work" (Eph. 4:16). As in most things, so in a leadership team, the whole is greater than the sum of its parts. If Pastor Petroff wants followers who are committed, loyal, involved, and sacrificial, he must first display these qualities in himself as a leadership model, and then work to develop them in the leadership team. And how he adapts his administrative style toward doing that serves as the subject of the third section of our chapter.

## TWO MODELS OF ADMINISTRATIVE STYLE

So far everything in this chapter has been narrative and linear. What we need here is a descriptive model or two, a diagrammatical approach to understanding administrative style.

*COMPLEMENTARY TYPE MODEL*

Study Figure 1 on page 24[12]. Beginning in the lower left quadrant we see the amiable administrative style. Essentially giving a free rein in leadership, the *amiable administrator* tends to sit back, talk about people and feelings, and openly show reactions and emotions everyone can see. He is warm, approachable, and likable, but a bit slow to act and undisciplined in time and procedures.

Moving counterclockwise we find the *expressive administrator* whose heavy sentiment and empathy make him a feeling personality. He speaks quickly and easily to and about people, generally wants his opinions to be accepted, and appears generally impulsive, approachable, and warm. His major abilities lie in teaching, persuading, arousing enthusiasm, and communicating new ideas.

The *driving style administrator* is the intuitive type we often associate with strong, natural leadership. Action-oriented, cool, competitive, and decisive, he wants to give the impression of being in charge and eager to lead group process. As the visionary possibility-thinker of the organization, he looks ahead, nudges the group toward things which seem impossible, and furnishes the organization with new ideas.

Finally we have the analytical or *logical administrative style*. He speaks slowly, cautiously, and often seems wrapped up in his own logic and argument. He's interested in research and rarely likes to

FIGURE 1

# COMPLEMENTARY LEADERSHIP STYLE MODEL

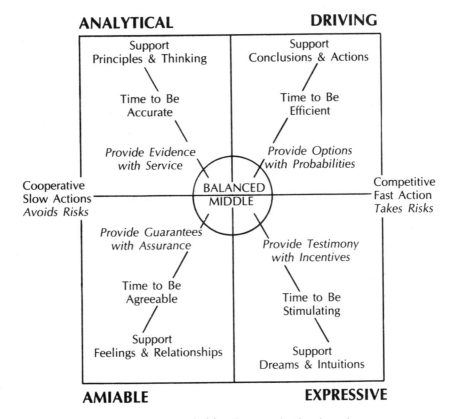

Cool, Independent, Uncommunicative (guarded)
Disciplined about Time
*Uses Facts*

**ANALYTICAL**　　　　　**DRIVING**

Support
Principles & Thinking

Support
Conclusions & Actions

Time to Be
Accurate

Time to Be
Efficient

*Provide Evidence
with Service*

*Provide Options
with Probabilities*

Cooperative
Slow Actions
*Avoids Risks*

BALANCED
MIDDLE

Competitive
Fast Action
*Takes Risks*

*Provide Guarantees
with Assurance*

*Provide Testimony
with Incentives*

Time to Be
Agreeable

Time to Be
Stimulating

Support
Feelings & Relationships

Support
Dreams & Intuitions

**AMIABLE**　　　　　**EXPRESSIVE**

Warm, Approachable, Communicative (open)
Undisciplined about Time
*Uses Opinions*

act without a strong supply of facts and data within reach. He helps us find the flaws in group thinking, likes to organize and reorganize, holds consistently to the policy handbook, and though no Christian leader likes to do it, is the most adept at firing people when necessary.

Which one is right? Depending on the group and situation, any one at different times. Which one is best? For the participation-oriented Christian leader, a constant pushing from any extreme toward the middle. This is what Blanchard emphasizes, and it offers a good reminder of the importance of balance in Christian life and leadership. Unlike the next model, where a determined motion up and right is the best alternative, this one draws us toward the center where *the balanced middle brings together the best qualities of each style.*

But even more importantly the model shows us how administrative and leadership styles complement each other. The driving-intuitive leader needs the amiable-sensitive type to keep track of details, to have patience, and to remember things that didn't seem important at the time. The expressive style is complemented by the analytical-logical style to keep things in order and guard the organization's efficiency. The amiable administrator needs a driver on his team to attack the complexities, push on in the darkness (and to explain what other driving type administrators are talking about). And finally the analytical needs the expressive to watch the organization's concern about people, to counsel, and sometimes to be a buffer between analytical leadership and emotional followership.

Maybe Pastor Petroff's problems started when Jerry was hired, not one year later. Maybe instead of trying to complement his own leadership style, Petroff allowed the church to hire someone just like him or too far off to one side or the other. Maybe no one ever taught the pastor how to lead to his strength and staff to his weakness.

## TEAM MANAGEMENT MODEL

Figure 2 offers a different look at administrative styles while suggesting five distinctive approaches.[13] Following the same explanatory pattern, let's begin at 1,1 or low-low with *impoverished management*. Here the administrative leader carries out only the minimal effort to do what is absolutely essential to keep the ministry going. He is low in both concern for people (idiographic dimension) and concern for production (nomothetic dimension).

Moving along the line to 1,9 we find the autocratic leader is heavy

FIGURE 2

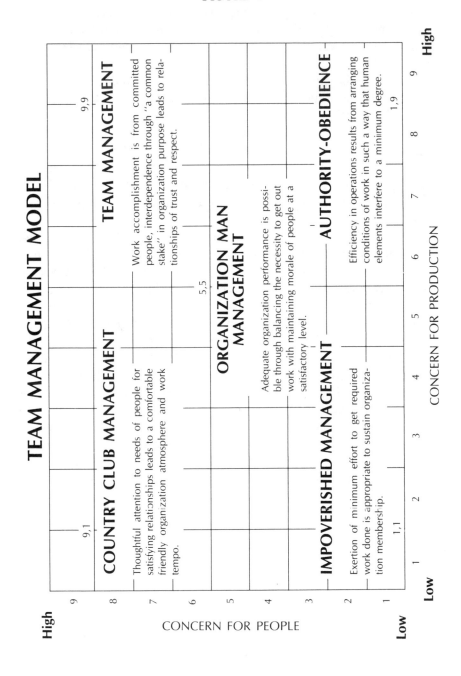

## TEAM MANAGEMENT MODEL

High

**CONCERN FOR PEOPLE**

High — 9

8

**COUNTRY CLUB MANAGEMENT**

9,1

Thoughtful attention to needs of people for satisfying relationships leads to a comfortable friendly organization atmosphere and work tempo.

7

6

5

**ORGANIZATION MAN MANAGEMENT**

5,5

Adequate organization performance is possible through balancing the necessity to get out work with maintaining morale of people at a satisfactory level.

4

3

2

**IMPOVERISHED MANAGEMENT**

1,1

Exertion of minimum effort to get required work done is appropriate to sustain organization membership.

Low — 1

**TEAM MANAGEMENT**

9,9

Work accomplishment is from committed people, interdependence through "a common stake" in organization purpose leads to relationships of trust and respect.

**AUTHORITY-OBEDIENCE**

1,9

Efficiency in operations results from arranging conditions of work in such a way that human elements interfere to a minimum degree.

**CONCERN FOR PRODUCTION**

Low    1    2    3    4    5    6    7    8    9    High

26

on *authority-obedience*. A pastor concerns himself only with what people can give to the church and insists they be there every time the doors are open. He tends to be legalistic and demanding.

His counterpart is the 9,1, called by the creators of this chart *country club management*. Picture a pastor who lovingly relates to everyone while forgetting appointments, never preparing for business meetings, and failing to develop lay leadership. People may put up with him because they love him but they understand the church's goals are not being achieved.

On this model we *don't* want to aim for the middle. To do so is to choose mediocrity. The 5,5 *organization man management* is probably a step ahead of the other three (though some would prefer 9,1) but has not achieved the highest point on this chart which is 9,9— *team management. Team leadership is the genius of the New Testament.* Exemplified first in Jesus and the disciples, it continues in the ministry of the apostles both in the early church and all of the missionary journeys. It creates what Lyle Schaller calls "ownership" in the organization. *Not* "Pastor Petroff's church" but *our* church.

How can Christian leaders improve their administrative capabilities? Robert Hahn of Harvard Graduate School of Education has developed an "inventory of general learning goals for managers." In pilot testing he came out with the following top-ten-ranked goals. The parentheses represent my attempt to theologically integrate Hahn's research. [14]

1.5 To develop ability to interact easily and productively with others (while remembering the biblical relationships described in Phil. 2:1-5, 14).

1.5 To develop ability to think critically about received ideas (while depending on the Holy Spirit to sort out right from wrong, true from false, and best from better, 2 Cor. 10:1-5).

3. To develop ability to balance conflicting viewpoints (while practicing the humble, conciliatory attitude described in Gal. 6:1-5).

4. To develop ability to listen effectively (while according the ideas of others, including subordinates, equal weight of importance with my own, Rom. 12:3-8).

5. To develop ability to communicate ideas orally (while depending on the Holy Spirit to guard against error and offense, John 16:13).

6. To develop self-confidence and self-esteem (remember the warnings of 2 Cor. 3; all competence comes from God).
7. To develop tolerance and trust in relations with others (while balancing appropriately the doctrine of original sin and its devastating effects on the mind of man with the image of God's restoration which comes through regeneration as described in Eph. 4:1-6).
8. To develop self-awareness and self-understanding (while recognizing that my ministry comes from the Lord, that I am a jar of clay, and that all the power and glory belongs to God as described in 2 Cor. 4:1-7).
9. To develop a capacity for self-evaluation (while allowing God to encourage me if I am unduly discouraged and to humble me if I am unduly proud, Phil. 2:1-5).
10. To develop a capacity for assuming responsibility (while remembering that the people I lead belong to God, not to me, and that my role is to assist them in achieving spiritual maturity as described in Eph. 4:11-16).

## STUDY QUESTIONS

**1.** Consider the differences between administration and leadership. Does this chapter adequately identify them? How is this distinction important in the church? In your particular leadership role?

**2.** Discuss (explain) the statement (p. 16), "A goal needs a plan to make it work."

**3.** Why is the average tenure of assistant pastors so short?

**4.** Review the six principles offered by Kirk regarding the evils of clericalism. How would you change the list?

**5.** As the text suggests, find a slot in Figure 1 for Pastor Petroff and describe the kind of associate he needs.

## ENDNOTES

1. David S. Luecke and Samuel Southard, *Pastoral Administration* (Waco, Texas: Word Books, 1986), p. 13.

**2.** Thomas C. Stanton, "Are You a Manager or a Leader?" Source unknown.

**3.** Peter F. Drucker, *Management: Tasks, Responsibilities, Practices* (New York: Harper & Row, 1974), p. 2.

**4.** Agustin B. Vencer, Jr., "The Ministry of Management for Christian Workers: A Biblical Basis," *Evangelical Review of Theology* (October 1982), p. 292.

**5.** Amitai Etzioni, *Modern Organizations* (Englewood Cliffs, N.J.: Prentice Hall, 1964), p. 75.

**6.** Vencer, pp. 292–93.

**7.** Neil Hightower, "Is There a Leadership Personality?" *The Preacher's Magazine* (September/November 1983), pp. 42–3.

**8.** Warren Bennis, "Vision: Key Trait of 'Superleaders,' " *Dallas Morning News* (November 23, 1982), 8D.

**9.** Kenneth O. Gangel, *Building Leaders for Church Education* (Chicago: Moody Press, 1981), chapter 21.

**10.** Michael Korda, "How to Be a Leader," *Newsweek* (January 5, 1981), p. 7.

**11.** Ken Blanchard, "The Extremes of Leadership," *Church Management—The Clergy Journal* (Nov.–Dec. 1986), p. 8.

**12.** "Check List of Practical Applications of Type Differences in Administration," *President's Letter* (September 1975), p. 6.

**13.** Developed by Robert Blake and James Mouton of Scientific Methods, Inc. and described in *The Value of People Review,* July 1981, pp. 1–2.

**14.** Robert Hahn, "An Inventory of General Learning Goals for Managers," *Dallas Morning News* (September 13, 1982), p. 20.

# CHAPTER 2

# FUNCTIONING AS A SPIRITUAL LEADER

Oswald Sanders' classic book *Spiritual Leadership* (Moody Press) still stands as mandatory reading for all who accept Christian leadership roles. The idea of spirituality, though not the content of Sanders' book, affords the focal point of this chapter as we try to understand what Christian leadership really means.

The clericalism condemned in chapter 1 stands as a chief deterrent to achieving spiritual leadership. In the New Testament Jesus pointed to the Pharisees as the supreme example of autocratic leadership evident in clericalism. They hold legitimate office, said the Lord, "so you must obey them and do everything they tell you. But do not do what they do, for they do not practice what they preach" (Matt. 23:3). Hypocrisy, false dichotomy between the clergy and laity, injustice, ostentation—these are the marks of clericalism and the reverse of spirituality in leadership. How does Jesus call for us to respond?

> But you are not to be called "Rabbi," for you have only one Master and you are all brothers. And do not call anyone on earth "father," for you have one Father, and He is in heaven. Nor are you to be called "teacher," for you have one Teacher, the Christ. The greatest among you will be your servant. For whoever exalts himself will be humbled, and whoever humbles himself will be exalted (Matt. 23:8-12).

Any definition of Christian leadership is inadequate, but to stay with our integrational goals we might describe Christian leadership as *the exercise of one's spiritual gifts under the call of God to serve a certain group of people in achieving the goals God has given them toward the end of glorifying Christ.*

In raising and answering the question, "What makes leadership Christian?" John R.W. Stott offers five distinctives—vision, industry, perseverance, service, and discipline. He warns us to avoid the traps of pessimism and mediocrity. Rather than extolling superstars and flaunting individualism Stott concludes " . . . that God has a leadership role of some degree and kind for each of us. We need, then, to seek His will within all our hearts, to cry to Him to give us a vision of what He is calling us to do with our lives, and to pray for grace to be faithful—not necessarily successful—in obedience to that heavenly vision."[1] Faithful, not successful! How out of line with today's value system; yet how utterly biblical!

Many of the metaphors in Scripture emphasize the centrality of Christ's leadership role in the church. He is the Head and we are the body (Rom. 12:4-5; 1 Cor. 12:12-27; Eph. 1:22-23; Col. 1:18). He is the High Priest and we are a kingdom of priests (Rom. 12:1-2; 1 Peter 2:9). He is the Shepherd and we are the sheep (John 10:11-18; Acts 20:28; 1 Peter 5:1-3). He is the Master and we are the servants (1 Cor. 7:22; Col. 4:1). We could talk more about cornerstone and living stones, bridegroom and bride, vine and branches, but surely the evidence already substantiates the idea.

Henry Budd reminds us that the servant must be more conscious of *responsibilities* than of *rights* (Luke 17:10): "Our contemporary mind-set, conditioned by our culture, tells us to assert ourselves—to insist on our rights. But Jesus tells us that we must consider ourselves unprofitable servants . . . the servant mind embraces responsibility and is prepared to lay aside rights for the cause of Christ."[2]

So the spiritual leader and the servant leader are synonymous. Without spirituality there is no servant leadership. Without a servant mind-set, there is no spirituality in leadership. Christian leadership might well be equated with them both to form a trinity of equals calling us to service that is biblical, Christian, and spiritual.

In a fascinating article, Donald MacLeod describes ordination as "shared servanthood" by quoting Dietrich Bonhoffer:

The church does not need brilliant personalities but faithful servants of Jesus and the brethren. The question of trust, which is so closely related to that of authority, is determined

31

by the faithfulness with which a man serves Jesus Christ, never by extraordinary talent which he possesses. Pastoral authority can only be attained by the servant of Jesus Christ who seeks no power of his own, who himself is a brother among brothers submitted to the authority of the Word.[3]

# CHRISTIAN LEADERSHIP IS BASED ON SPIRITUALITY BY DEFINITION

Linked closely with the whole problem of definition is the balance between legalism and license. On the one hand are those who jump on every opportunity, every rule or standard, to bring the church or other Christian institutions into conformity with their own views. Those at the other extreme want to push aside all rubrics, tear down all restraints on their behavior, raising the flag of God's grace anytime anyone suggests that salvation ought to produce a somewhat definitive lifestyle in accordance with New Testament teaching. Of course the biblical position, as always, provides the balanced middle between legalism on the right and license on the left. Where we find distinctly Christian leadership, there we find liberty which is clearly related to spirituality; and there we find the control of the Holy Spirit freeing the believer to serve. As Paul put it, "Now the Lord is the Spirit, and where the Spirit of the Lord is, there is freedom" (2 Cor. 3:17).

*WHAT IS SPIRITUALITY?*

Let's begin by looking at the word "spiritual" and how it is used in the New Testament. The common word for "spirit" (or "Spirit") is *pneuma*, which gives us the adjectival form *pneumatikos*. The only New Testament writer other than Paul to use the word is Peter (1 Peter 2:5), and fifteen out of the twenty-four Pauline uses are in 1 Corinthians.

Paul uses the word three ways: to describe a spiritual "something" (such as a gift, resurrection of the body, blessings, songs); to describe spiritual activities or attitudes; and to describe a spiritual person. Obviously the latter use confronts us when we talk about spiritual leadership.

Serving as elder in his church, Joe offers an example of a spiritual leader who understands his spiritual gift and how to use it effectively in the local body. Joe's outgoing personality and love for people are expressed through his gift of hospitality. Guests and members alike are greeted warmly each Sunday with a handshake and a warm smile. Everyone needing a place to stay can be sure of an enthusiastic welcome at Joe and Ann's home.

Friendship evangelism comes naturally for Joe as he shares his faith with others. When his church launched a formal evangelistic program, Joe was available to train and lead a team of believers eager to reach into their communities with the Gospel. A multiplication of spiritual leadership is reflected in his life just as the Scripture designed.

The Bible describes spirituality not as something which comes automatically at the time of regeneration, but rather a state of maturity into which one grows as the result of a vital Christian life. Paul relates spirituality to the knowledge of biblical doctrine when writing to the Corinthians: "Did the Word of God originate with you? Or are you the only people it has reached? If anybody thinks he is a prophet or spiritually gifted, let him acknowledge that what I am writing to you is the Lord's command. If he ignores this, he himself will be ignored" (1 Cor. 14:36-38).

The responsibility of leadership-modeling looms even larger when we examine Christian leadership in the light of spirituality. After washing the disciples' feet Jesus said, "I have set you an example that you should do as I have done for you. I tell you the truth, no servant is greater than his master, nor is a messenger greater than the one who sent him" (John 13:15-16). Like teachers and teaching, leaders will lead as they are led, not necessarily as they are taught to lead. If a pastor wants servant-oriented deacons or elders, he had better be a servant-oriented shepherd. If a college president (or school principal) wants servant-oriented administrators and faculty, they had better see that mentality in him.

## WHAT IS THE LINK BETWEEN SPIRITUAL LEADERSHIP AND MATURITY?

The biblical servant called to minister to others must effectively carry out certain tasks in obedience to biblical principles, in an attitude of Christlike perspective, and in the reality of spiritual power. This is not a role for children but for grown-ups—physical and spiritual adults.

One church which I served as pastor for a short time categorized developing Christian maturity into five areas.

**1.** *Unconditional love.* There is nothing you have done or will do that can make me stop loving you. I may not agree with your actions but I will love you as a person and do all I can to build you up (1 Cor. 13:1-8).

**2.** *Availability.* The mature Christian leader sacrificially puts time, energy, insights, and possessions at the disposal of the group (Acts 2:43-47).

**3.** *Vulnerability and confidentiality.* This is a tough one but maturity requires the Christian leader to be an open person who can share his feelings and struggles, his joys and his hurts in an honest way with other people (Eph. 4:25; James 5:16; 1 John 1:5-7). By the same token he must be responsible to speak the truth in love to others (Eph. 4:15) so the vulnerability and confidentiality becomes a mutual interdependence.

**4.** *Responsibility and accountability.* The mature spiritual leader takes seriously the responsibility for growth of others. In submission he makes himself accountable to God, to the body, and especially to other members of the leadership team. He avoids giving or taking a position of irresponsible dependence, knowing that such a position encourages sloth in both leaders and followers.

**5.** *Spiritual authority.* A mature spiritual leader willingly submits himself to appropriately appointed congregational authority. While recognizing the fact of fallibility, he trusts God to produce His will through them so the result in the body will be unity, harmony, and stability (Eph. 4:11-16).

To those five we might yet add *integrity*, which identifies the mature Christian leader as incorruptible, honest, and dependable. He does what he says he will do; he keeps his promises. The Parable of the Faithful Servant stares at us from the pages of Luke 12 and particularly its conclusion in verse 48: "From everyone who has been given much, much will be demanded; and from the one who has been entrusted with much, much more will be asked." Engstrom and Dayton remind us that "it often costs a great deal to maintain integrity, to keep our commitments. Sometimes it may cost the *organization* a great deal to do it *just because we said we would.* Many times it is easier to conclude that we had better let this one slip because the extra expense involved will really stress us. When that happens, we lose some of our integrity."[4]

## WHAT ARE THE KEY NEW TESTAMENT TEXTS TREATING SPIRITUAL LEADERSHIP?

The sources of biblical data in understanding spiritual leadership are essentially five, four of which relate to the New Testament. In the Old Testament we are limited somewhat to a *study of models* both positive and negative. Among the positive examples we find Joseph, Moses, David, and early Solomonic leadership. Negative examples include Eli, Samson, and Saul. There are very few Old Testament didactic portions, though one could draw inferences from verses in Proverbs and many of the prophets. Before the time of Christ, theology of leadership can be studied in the lives of people whom God used.

A second source is the *direct teaching of Jesus.* Here we are led to passages like Matthew 18:1-5; Mark 9:33-37; Luke 9:46-48; 22:24-27. In our Lord's discussion of leadership, authoritarian attitudes are condemned, control of other people is rejected, a servant mentality is commended, but most of all, a basic biblical axiom is unveiled: *leadership in the church is different from leadership in the world.*

A third source is *the example of Jesus* in leadership and here serious students will want to check two sources written exactly 100 years apart—*The Training of the Twelve*[5] by A.B. Bruce and Michael Youssef's *The Leadership Style of Jesus.*[6]

We also have *New Testament models* like Peter, a man who genuinely *learned* how to lead. The raw material may have been there all the time, but a gradual polishing process was essential before the Peter of the Galilean seaside could become the Peter of pentecostal power. But we need not limit ourselves to Peter and Paul as obvious New Testament models. God has also given us Stephen, Philip, Barnabas, Timothy, Titus, and many others who demonstrate what spiritual leadership means.

Finally, tracking down New Testament texts will lead us to *didactic passages* like Romans 12 and 1 Corinthians 12 which deal with the matter of spiritual gifts and their relationship to leadership. We learn that the spiritual servant must lead (1 Tim. 3:1-7; 5:17-18); teach (Gal. 6:6; 1 Tim. 6:1-2; 2 Tim. 2:24-26; Titus 2:1-10); serve (1 Tim. 4:6; 2 Tim. 4:5, 11; 1 Peter 4:10-11); model (Phil. 3:17; 1 Thes. 2:9-10; 1 Tim. 4:11-14; 2 Tim. 2:15; Titus 2:6-8; 1 Peter 5:2-3); make disciples (2 Tim. 2:2); build the body (Eph. 4:11-16); and evangelize (2 Tim. 4:1-5). Texts like these are the "stuff" from which a theology of ministry can be formed.

So the Christian leader is the *servus servorem dei*—the servant of the servants of God. We dare not yield that mandate to some ecclesiastical office but rather perpetuate it in the dynamic life of the church. The many passages dealing with spiritual leadership lead us to some general theological conclusions. Let me summarize five of them briefly:

1. Spiritual leadership links inseparably with identifiable spiritual gifts and a clear-cut call from God to distinctive leadership positions.

2. Spiritual leadership consists of a servant attitude patterned after the ministry-to-others demonstration of Jesus Himself.

3. Spiritual leadership places a strong emphasis on the involvement of people in participatory decision-making as opposed to autocracy and authoritarian techniques.

4. Spiritual leadership always includes the responsibility of teaching and nurturing those whom we lead.

5. Spiritual leadership requires an attitude of humility and meekness thoroughly demonstrated by Moses and Paul (among others), and not to be confused with weakness or indecisiveness.

# CHRISTIAN LEADERSHIP IS BASED ON SPIRITUALITY BY GIFT

The Christian leader (administrator) understands that he functions in order to facilitate the ministry of others. He does what he must do in order that they may do what God has called them to do. Like the slow-forming image of a painting, our picture of spirituality and leadership begins to take shape. It is inseparably linked with the knowledge of the Word and the control of the Holy Spirit, and it assumes the maturing process.

We can hardly study spiritual maturity apart from the concept of "gift" in leadership. Consider Paul's words in Romans 12:3-8. He takes up the question of how one moves from liturgy to leadership in the church. It is valuable to remember that Paul had never seen the church to whom these words were written and yet spoke so pragmatically regarding the issues involved in church leadership. Remember too that verses 3-8 spring from the first two verses of the chapter and the doxology with which the previous chapter ends. Three qualities of spiritual leadership surface in these six verses.

*SPIRITUAL LEADERSHIP IS MEEKNESS*

> For by the grace given me I say to every one of you: Do not think of yourself more highly than you ought, but rather think of yourself with sober judgment, in accordance with the measure of faith God has given you (Rom. 12:3).

Four times in one verse the apostle uses various forms of the word *phroneo*. This obvious play on words emphasizes the servant mentality of leadership we have been talking about since this book began. The apostle appears concerned that leaders be thinkers who

36

think sober judgment in accordance with the degree of serving faith (as opposed to saving faith) God has given them. The great Greek scholar A.T. Robertson suggests that Paul's frequent use of *phroneo* was designed to identify conceit as a form of insanity. Paul's experience at Corinth made him particularly sensitive to this kind of attitude in church leaders, a constant temptation to those who hold leadership posts even in the present hour.

George Wallace once stated that he had no problem with dictatorships as long as they were "pro-American." It sounds a bit like saying that one has nothing against a cancer cell as long as it is pro-health. When it comes to spiritual leadership, one finds no good dictatorships (and no healthy cancer cells). Absolute monarchy may indeed be the most efficient system the world has ever known, but we had better wait for the absolute control of the Perfect One, in the meantime resisting any pretenders to the throne.

Meekness stands in rigid contrast to the assertive politicism of modern secular leadership, however it might be disguised. Imagine, for example, a national leader who once desired to be a priest and a playwright; who exhibited great aesthetic sensitivities. Think of him as stoutly defended by the religious establishment, both Protestant and Catholic, lauded by poets and philosophers, and suggested by at least one international leader as a candidate for the Nobel Peace Prize. Do you have the picture? Don't forget it, because you are focusing on the twentieth-century figure who most represented popular charisma and least understood biblical servant mentality, a barbarian whose behavior made Genghis Khan look like a social worker. His name was Adolf Hitler!

## SPIRITUAL LEADERSHIP AS MEMBERSHIP

Just as each of us has one body with many members, and these members do not all have the same function, so in Christ we who are many form one body, and each member belongs to all the others (Rom. 12:4-5).

Paul then launched into one of his favorite analogies, the relationship between the human physical body and the spiritual body as church. These two verses contain a threefold emphasis which applies both to the physical body and the spiritual body—unity, diversity, and mutuality. Peter Drucker reminds us that the word "organization" fails us unless we understand that it means people, a helpful clue to better church relations.

37

When you look at white mice in a laboratory, you don't call them an organization. Organizations are people, human beings who are never, in modern organizations, "members." I am very careful not to use that word. I hear it all the time— "members of our company." It's the wrong term. Members by definition do not exist away from their body. You cut off a hand and it isn't a hand. People exist primarily "outside" in modern organizations. They exist as parents and Christians and Americans and members of the school board and fathers of little leaguers and what have you—ninety-nine other exposures, each of them meaningful and real. It is only through one dimension, and a very important one, but only one, that persons are also *in* the organization.[7]

Sure Drucker likes to play with words, but it's a poignant idea. Membership emphasizes the leader's relationship to others in the body and obviously the church's people. Perhaps the dehumanizing smog of selfishness must be lifted before we can find each other and practice leadership as membership.

Jeffrey Rada raises a point here relating to the matter of *decentralization* as a key to emphasizing relational "membership."

The pulpit has become the crucible of a minister's professional success. Many pastors feel torn between their teaching ministry and their other reponsibilities. How a conscious or unconscious use of the minister as part of our public image as a church, and his (frequent) enjoyment of this limelight only feeds the stress placed on his shoulders. And the mantle he took on at his ordination seems to give legitimacy to this.[8]

## SPIRITUAL LEADERSHIP IS MINISTRY

We have different gifts, according to the grace given us. If a man's gift is prophesying, let him use it in proportion to his faith. If it is serving, let him serve; it if is teaching, let him teach; if it is encouraging, let him encourage; if it is contributing to the needs of others, let him give generously; if it is leadership, let him govern diligently; if it is showing mercy, let him do it cheerfully (Rom. 12:6-8).

The diversity which marks the body also marks the ministry of its members. Seven ministry gifts appear in verses 6-8 and, though we have no time for a detailed explanation of each, I want to at least fall back on the text of one of my earlier books to identify the uniqueness of the gift which most concerns us in this present study—the gift of leadership.

> The word *prohistemi* appears eight times in Paul's writings, usually with an emphasis upon personal leading of and caring for others. A key reference is 1 Timothy 3:4, where managing or ruling one's own house or family is identified as a prerequisite for pastoral ministry (cf. 1 Tim. 3:12; 5:8, 17). Some say that the context requires us to interpret leadership as linked with gifts of "giving" and "showing mercy," which may be, they say a reference to the administration of charitable programs (Cranfield, Lagrange, Huby, Leenhardt). It seems to me that, in the treatment of spiritual gifts, one only engages in dogmatism in closure to his own peril. I prefer to think of these gifts as closely related, possibly united for some church leaders, but not necessarily dependent upon the other.[9]

The spiritual gift of leadership seems to emphasize serving others, personal care, and feeding which meets needs and encourages growth. *Spiritual leadership as ministry is not giving orders but nurturing the people of God.*

Have you noticed that the term "layman" frequently carries negative connotations? If something appears simplistic and elementary, we refer to it as being written in "lay-language." A secondary definition of the word in the *American Heritage Dictionary* sounds like this: "One who does not have special or advanced training or skills." The *Random House Dictionary* doesn't help: "One who is not a clergyman or one who is not a member of a specified profession; one who is not a member of the law or medicine." The general definition of "layman" seems obvious—a person who is unable to do certain things, a negative picture. Such a distorted concept stands diametrically opposed to biblical church order.

The first Sunday at Oak Community Church gave Carol the distinct feeling she was experiencing something new. Several different people took part in the program and at times it seemed difficult to determine who was the pastor. Throughout the service there was an obvious feeling of ownership by the people.

Several months passed before Carol could begin to assess the difference between Oak Community and other churches she had attended. She finally concluded that here was a church in which lay persons were valued, trained, and encouraged to be a part of the leadership. The pastor was unthreatened when one of the elders did the preaching and quite open about shared leadership in business meetings, conversations, or from the pulpit.

Carol immediately began to attend the membership class and was soon advanced to the teacher training class. For the first time in her adult life Carol genuinely felt a part of the ministry in a local church. She gave herself to teaching, working on the Christian Education Committee, and reaching out to ladies in her class who needed encouragement and personal warmth.

Practical implementation serves up the difficulty. We can make the theological case, but carrying it out is something else. As Francis Cosgrove reminds us, "This teaching of leading by serving continues to have an unfamiliar ring in an age that calls for us to do everything we can to climb to the top. The Bible teaches that to lead is to serve. We may recognize the truth of this concept and respond positively. The problem, however, is in doing it day to day."[10]

# CHRISTIAN LEADERSHIP IS BASED ON SPIRITUALITY BY MODEL

We tend to talk about the concept of spirituality as only a theory or feeling which cannot be measured, but apparently that notion is wrong. Paul clearly understood that certain people were spiritual and certain were not (though this does not rule out the possibility of various levels of spirituality), and deliberately wrote to those who should themselves understand their spiritual maturity. Presumably these leaders can be found in any church, and those in Galatia received the message in the sixth chapter of that book: "Brothers, if someone is caught in a sin, you who are spiritual should restore him gently. But watch yourself, or you also may be tempted" (Gal. 6:1).

Several things seem immediately apparent in a verse like this and they all deal with Christian leadership, spirituality, and modeling.

*PEOPLE WHO HAVE IT, KNOW IT*

When the letter circulated among the churches of Galatia, certain people in those congregations who read it were to view themselves (with some accuracy) as *pneumatikos* Christians. Others apparently knew immediately that the reference did not apply to them. Such an

40

understanding certainly should not advance pride or in any way negate the meekness spoken of earlier. Here again we find a recognition of gift and call, the fact that Christian leaders in any given group, especially a local congregation of the body of Christ, can be spotted by the qualities they possess (1 Tim. 3; Titus 1). I'm tempted here to review all the qualifications of elders and deacons described in these passages, but that work has been better done by others. More practical perhaps, is a list of twenty-one questions prepared by one of my colleagues for his classes. Figure 3 shows those questions in six categories.[11]

One could surely ask here whether women can exercise Christian leadership in the church, and my response would be immediately positive. It seems obvious in the New Testament that people like Priscilla (Acts 18), the daughters of Philip (Acts 21), and Phoebe (Rom. 16) held positions of general leadership. But let us not confuse *leadership* with *office*. The latter argument looms large among evangelicals in the late twentieth century. Without wandering the treacherous paths of 1 Corinthians 11, 14, and 1 Timothy 2, I am willing to affirm that there are only two areas (offices) out of bounds for women in the body of Christ—those of elder and deacon. Though she disagrees with me on the issue of deacon, Susan Foh (a woman well trained in theological issues) offers a balanced view on the question of eldership.

> If 1 Timothy 2:12 does refer to the office of elder, then the authority forbidden to women would not be authority in general but the authority to rule the church, to exercise church discipline. If Paul is only forbidding eldership to women, other jobs in the church could be opened to women. Women could have a say about the use of funds, church property, and the like; this sort of authority hardly compares to the authority (and responsibility) the minister of God has over human souls. . . . The kind of authority administrative officers have, even when it extends to the choice of programs, etc., is not the authority over individuals' doctrine and life that the minister has.[12]

Apparently women can hold distinctive leadership roles as long as they do not require ordination, are not connected with the chief ruling/teaching/eldership positions in the church, and are not improperly grasped or usurped. Their spiritual position in the body of

41

FIGURE 3

# TWENTY-ONE QUESTIONS FOR SPIRITUAL LEADERS FROM 1 TIMOTHY 3:1-7; TITUS 1:5-9

## I. GOD

*Not a new convert*
1. Can you point to definite areas in your life in which you have spiritually matured during your four years in seminary?

*Devout*
2. Does your lifestyle reveal that your highest priority is knowing and walking with God?

## II. YOURSELF

*Temperate*
3. In the everyday situations of life do you tend to react to them according to a biblical perspective? That is, are you alert to biblical teaching as it bears on your daily living?

*Prudent*
4. Are you prudent and sober minded to the extent that you can apply biblical principles to walking wisely?

*Not quick tempered*
5. Do you have a short fuse?

## III. YOUR FAMILY

*Husband of one wife*
6. Are you totally devoted to your own wife, and not distracted, even mentally, by other women?

*One who manages his own household well*
7. Do your wife and children love, respect, and obey you and are they responding positively to God?

## IV. OTHERS

*Hospitable*
8. Do you make it your practice to invite to and share your home with both Christians and non-Christian outsiders?

*Able to teach*
9. Are you able to communicate the Word of God to others in a nonantagonistic manner and able to handle those who disagree with you in a patient and gentle manner?

*Not self-willed*
10. Are you able to set aside your own preferences in order to maintain peace with people?

*Loving what is good*
11. Do you take advantage of opportunities to do good to all men (both Christians & non-Christians) and to build people up rather than tearing them down?

*Not a bully*
12. Have you overcome the temptation to use the position of leadership to bully people?

*Uncontentious*
13. Have you developed a dislike for becoming involved in quarrels?

*Gentle*
14. Are you able to handle other people in a gentle and mild-mannered way?

*Just*
15. In your relationships with other people are you able to make just decisions; that is, ones which are wise, objective, and honest?

*Above reproach*
16. Is your lifestyle above reproach when evaluated by those closest to you?

*Respectable*
17. Do others around you respect you in that your life adorns the Word of God?

*Having a good reputation with those on the outside*
18. Do you have a good reputation among nonbelievers in the way that you pay your bills, manage your affairs, and react to situations? That is, do they respect you even though they may disagree with your theological viewpoint?

# V. THINGS

*Free from the love of money*
19. Is the amount of salary you will receive in a position low on your priority list?

*Not addicted to wine*
20. Are you free from being addicted to anything that might take control of your life and cause a weaker Christian to stumble?

# VI. THE BIBLE

*Ability to use the Bible*
21. Are you able to use the Word of God to exhort people with sound doctrine and to refute those who are antagonistic?

43

Christ stands strong (1 Cor. 11:11; Gal. 3:28). Spiritual women who clearly understand the biblical teaching of ontological equality and functional subordination in the home can be greatly used of God in exercising the gifts the Holy Spirit has given them to minister to others in the body of Christ.

## PEOPLE WHO HAVE IT ALSO HAVE GREATER RESPONSI-BILITY

The responsibility of spiritual leaders is obvious from the chart in Figure 3. Here I only wish to emphasize that we dare not ignore nor take lightly the biblical command that we stick to God's qualifications when selecting spiritual leaders. The importance of the issue centers in their modeling responsibility. Let's look again at the text of Galatians 6.

> Carry each other's burdens, and in this way you will fulfill the law of Christ. If anyone thinks he is something when he is nothing, he deceives himself. Each one should test his own actions. Then he can take pride in himself, without comparing himself to somebody else, for each one should carry his own load (Gal. 6:2-5).

These verses, when added to the restoration command of verse 1, point out that *pneumatikos* Christian leaders have the responsibility for taking care of those who are having difficulties in their Christian lives—in this case, having been caught in some sin.

Responsibilities of leadership have always been obvious to those who lead. At the inaugural day service in National City Christian Church of Washington, D.C., Billy Graham preached a message on "The Spiritual Dimensions of Leadership" to more than 1,000 people invited by President Lyndon B. Johnson. Whatever one's assessment of the Johnson/Humphrey administration, the following words of Dr. Graham are precisely accurate:

> You have . . . the opportunity to lead the nation to its greatest moral and spiritual heights. Jesus Christ said, "Unto whomsoever much is given, of him shall much be required." Those who have the greatest power always need the greatest guidance. . . . No government rules except by the will of God. You are leaders, not just as a result of the greatest mandate the American people have ever given, but because there is a mandate higher than the ballot box. You not only have responsibil-

ities to all the people of America and to the peoples of the world; you also have a great responsibility to the God of our fathers.[13]

## PEOPLE WHO HAVE IT CAN LOSE IT

The state of being spiritual carries no permanence since mature Christians responsible for gently restoring sinning brothers in Galatia had to be careful of temptation which might perhaps carry them off into the same sin. This refers not to loss of salvation but rather loss of spiritual qualities which commend one for leadership. The church functions to help people understand spirituality and to teach them the Word of God. Then they can become growing, maturing Christians able to come to the place of effective faith and service based on maturity, at which point they can genuinely be called *pneumatikos* leaders. Not just people who have been to seminary. Not just people who have been ordained. Not just people who carry certain titles, such as, pastor, elder, or deacon. To His leaders the Lord warns, "But watch yourself, or you also may be tempted" (Gal. 6:1).

A chapter on spiritual leadership located so close to the beginning of this book certainly tips the author's hand. The book's primary commitment bows to solid biblical theology as the foundation for understanding administrative leadership. Nevertheless, we must also understand the Augustinian process of "spoiling the Egyptian," learning all we can from the past research of secular leadership studies and adapting it theologically to the service of Christ and His church.

Not everyone shares this viewpoint. The article on "Spirituality" in the *Evangelical Dictionary of Theology* lists the current interest in administration as one of the primary reasons for the "dearth of spiritual leadership and direction in the evangelical world" today. W. Ward Gasque disagrees and argues for the integrational principle I have repeatedly emphasized.

Christians do not cease to be human when they commit their lives to Christ. Rather, they share a common humanity with all people. Therefore, it is not surprising that they should learn truth from people who are not themselves believers. The church has done so in the past, to its everlasting benefit, and will doubtless do so in the future. This will come as no surprise to anyone who believes in the biblical doctrine of creation.[14]

45

It seems to me that the development of Christian leadership (spiritual leadership) in the church and Christian organizations of all kinds requires us to understand what God wants in His administrative leaders, and then, by His grace and in the power of His Holy Spirit, to become just that.

# STUDY QUESTIONS

**1.** Review the Stott quote on page 31. Has he described a real problem? Do Christian leaders in our day give in to pressures to be successful rather than faithful?

**2.** Consider the five qualities of Christian maturity listed on pages 33–34. Are they satisfactory goals for church lay leadership development? What would you add or delete? How does your life presently measure up?

**3.** Study carefully the five general conclusions on pages 35–36. Do they reflect *your* view of spiritual leadership? With which one(s) do you disagree? Why?

**4.** Write a paragraph describing your understanding of spiritual gifts for today's church, especially as they relate to leadership.

**5.** Review Figure 3—the twenty-one questions related to church leadership. Rate yourself and the lay leaders in your church according to the list.

# ENDNOTES

1. John R.W. Stott, "What Makes Leadership Christian? *Christianity Today* (August 9, 1985), p. 25.

2. Henry Budd, "Servant Leadership," *The Gospel Message* (1984, Num. 2), p. 8.

3. A. Donald MacLeod, "Ordination As Shared Servanthood," *Crux* (June 1983), p. 19.

4. Ted W. Engstrom and Edward R. Dayton, "Integrity," *Christian Leadership Letter* (August 1983), p. 3.

5. A.B. Bruce, *The Training of the Twelve* (New York: Harper, 1886).

6. Michael Youssef, *The Leadership Style of Jesus* (Wheaton,

Ill.: Victor Books, 1986).

**7.** Peter F. Drucker, "The Role of the Organization," *At the Edge of Hope*, Howard Butt and Elliott Wright, eds. (New York: The Seabury Press, 1978), p. 152.

**8.** Jeffrey R. Rada, "Restoring New Testament Church Leadership," *Seminary Review* (September 1982), p. 108.

**9.** Kenneth O. Gangel, *Unwrap Your Spiritual Gifts* (Wheaton, Ill.: Victor Books, 1983).

**10.** Francis Cosgrove, "The Disciple Is a Servant," *Discipleship Journal* (Issue Thirty, 1985), p. 35.

**11.** John Best and Gary Carter, Unpublished class notes, Dallas Theological Seminary, 1985.

**12.** Susan T. Foh, *Women and the Word of God* (Grand Rapids: Baker, 1979), pp. 24, 29.

**13.** Billy Graham, "The Spiritual Dimensions of Leadership," *Christianity Today* (February 12, 1965).

**14.** W. Ward Gasque, "The Church in Search of Excellence," *Christianity Today* (February 15, 1985), p. 55.

CHAPTER 3

# CULTIVATING A BIBLICAL
# LEADERSHIP STYLE

As the twentieth century edges toward a close, there seems to be a growing anxiety about the availability and quality of leadership in the world at large, as well as in the Christian community. Several current books on the subject depict corporate leaders as teachers, mentors, exemplars, and forgers of values, but there is no agreement as to the solution of the leadership crisis. In their very popular book *Leaders: The Strategies for Taking Charge,* Warren Bennis and Burton Nanus complain that, as in 1648, leadership again "hath been broken into pieces."[1] Today's world is characterized by a chronic crisis of governance—a pervasive incapacity of organizations to cope with the expectations of their constituencies.

As a consequence of the obvious need, leadership studies are on the rebound all around the country. In one sense this is good news for the church of Jesus Christ. We have learned to spoil the Egyptians, to borrow eclectically what the world has done, run it through the grid of biblical understanding, and apply it in ministry. Essential to that process, however, is the recognition that the Gospel has always been countercultural in every age and in every place.

Part of the problem we face in the current study is definition. More than ten years ago R.M. Stogdill perused 3,000 books and articles on leadership, only to conclude that:

Four decades of research on leadership have produced a bewildering mass of findings. Numerous surveys of special problems have been published, but they seldom include all the studies available on a topic. It is difficult to know what, if anything, has been convincingly demonstrated by replicated research. The endless accumulation of empirical data has not produced an integrated understanding of leadership.[2]

So the obscurity of definition in the world of research, and the countercultural nature of Christianity, force us to look at leadership studies both negatively and positively. Negatively we must analyze and steer around cultural corruptions. Positively we must renew again what the Scripture has to say about leadership.

But before we do that, there may be merit in identifying some of the contemporary eruptions or distortions through which the Christian must make his way if he is to find a genuinely biblical view of leadership. One is our present love affair in many segments of the evangelical community with what might be called the *American success syndrome*. We have capitulated almost completely to the measurements of society in distinguishing "successful ministry" from "unsuccessful ministry." A missionary, caught up in the Indonesian revivals some years ago, returning home to report several hundred converts in six months, is clearly a "success." A missionary in Saudi Arabia, however, who might labor for several terms seeing virtually no converts and only a minimal amount of interest in the Gospel is quite obviously "unsuccessful."

One author reminds us quite wisely that "leadership which is evil, while it may succeed temporarily, always carries with it the seeds of its own destruction. . . . Misleadership is something false coming through a strong personality, and the stronger the personality, the worse the ultimate crash."[3]

A second corruption is our *compulsion to imitate*. When one leader is "successful" another can become successful by following the same procedures or methodologies. We tend to franchise Christianity, though there is no evidence that Antioch tried to be like Jerusalem, and Ephesus like Antioch, or Smyrna like Philadelphia. Certainly modeling leadership development is a valid principle but there is a vast difference between that and crass secular imitation of techniques and methodologies.

Still a third corruption is our *infatuation with bigness*. Typically, this leads to autocratic leadership styles as Peter Wagner clearly demonstrates.

Some congregational-type churches oppose strong pastoral leadership on principle. Congregationalism was developed along with American democracy, and strong pastoral authority seems undemocratic to some Christians. Where this feeling persists, it will be overcome if the church wants to move into a pattern of growth.[4]

Lyle Schaller commits the same error when he puts these words into the mouth of his vignette hero Pastor Jerry Buchanan: "When anyone unites with the congregation where I am the pastor, they play by the rules that go with that game."[5]

Still a fourth pitfall is the *corruption of assertiveness*. Psychologist Bruce Baldwin, head of *Direction Dynamics*, offers an article entitled "Miseries of the Mild-Mannered Manager" which he subtitles "The Meek Are Emotional Victims with Many Excuses." His closing line in the article is typical of the assertiveness school: "Blessed are the meek. They always get out of the way before you have to push them! So it is with the ways of the world . . . unless you are willing to teach a different lesson."[6]

Consider also the *corruption of political clout*. Leaders who lead by political control end up cloning subordinates rather than developing new leaders. They draw unto themselves people like themselves and reproduce graven images. They say, "Agree with me, think like me, dress like me, act like me, and you too can be successful in ministry." Evangelicals once said to the world, "What we say is true because the world despises us and disdains our message and membership." In the late twentieth century, however, one consistently hears the opposite: "Look at us, you can tell that what we say is true because so many people are signing up or applauding us and we are finding more favor in the national arena."

But 2 Corinthians 10:4 won't go away: "The weapons we fight with are not the weapons of the world." Competition and comparison are enemies of a biblical leadership style because they focus on the wrong battle—conflict with people rather than unrighteousness. Servant leadership is an attitude which governs managerial functions. It describes how we think about ourselves in relationship to God and other people and it runs in direct opposition to the thinking of the contemporary culture.

## HOW CAN WE DEVELOP A BIBLICAL ANALYSIS OF LEADERSHIP?

There are essentially five steps in the process of developing a biblical understanding of any discipline or field of study—exegesis, hermeneutics, theology, philosophy, and methodology. The first three are inseparably related to a study of the biblical text. Exegesis has to do with an uncovering of the original words, sentences, and paragraphs of special revelation; hermeneutics deals with the interpretation or meaning of those passages; and theology has to do with the formulation or systemization of the truth which we have claimed through the spade work of exegesis and hermeneutics.

Obviously it is impossible in this chapter to go through the procedures. Limitations require a narrowing to merely identifying sources of scriptural data useful in acquiring an understanding of leadership.

## OLD TESTAMENT MODELS

Of the five sources of biblical data we will consider, the biographical examples of Old Testament leaders represent the first and most obvious information about God's understanding of leadership. Of consequence is the fact that the Bible records the history of the ancients precisely the way it unfolded without glossing over the errors and problems of Israel's leaders. As someone has suggested, there are no heroes in the Bible except God.

Very few Old Testament didactic portions deal directly with leadership. One could draw inferences from certain recitations of the Law and the Prophets and multitudinal guidelines from Proverbs and poetical literature. But none of these really represent didactic description of godly leadership. Like much of the theology of the Old Testament, a theology of leadership is learned by the study of the lives of people whom God used.

## NEW TESTAMENT MODELS

Space and time do not permit the treatment of all the leadership models of the early church. Let me just select two, one of whom dominates the Gospels and the early chapters of Acts while the other serves as a central figure in the rest of the New Testament.

One example of Peter's leadership style emerges in Acts 6 where a question arises about the welfare program for the Hebrew and Hellenistic widows. Could Peter or one of the other apostles have solved this problem with executive mandate? Undoubtedly. But they model participatory involvement by turning the matter back over to the people.

Some have suggested that the New Testament leadership style is not democratic in view of the fact that elders were appointed. For this reason (among others) I prefer the word "participatory," a style which is certainly reflected here in the selection of the "deacons."

When we come to the model of Paul, we see varieties of style appearing throughout Acts and then his epistles. One significant passage is the second chapter of 1 Thessalonians which contradicts first-century pagan understandings of leadership precisely in the same way that a true biblical picture of leadership contradicts cultural corruptions in our day. In the first six verses of the chapter Paul identifies what he *did not* do at Thessalonica. Verses 7-12 then describe a process of nurture and family care in which the apostle depicts himself as a nursing mother, a patient school teacher, a mother bird, and a loving father.

## EXAMPLE OF JESUS

Here we come to the clear-cut positive model. With frequency Jesus admonished the disciples to follow His example and thereby learn what Christian leadership is all about. And what was that example? Humility, patience, consideration, long-suffering, concern for individuals, and the distinctive servant motif demonstrated in John 13 and described in Matthew 11:25-30.

## TEACHING OF JESUS

In addition to His continuous modeling, Jesus frequently taught His disciples about leadership because that was precisely their task in the early church. Numerous passages can be identified in the Gospels but the teaching seems to culminate in those final hours in the Upper Room, a high watermark appears in the 22nd chapter of Luke.

> Also a dispute arose among them as to which of them was considered to be greatest. Jesus said to them, "The kings of the Gentiles lord it over them; and those who exercise authority over them call themselves benefactors. But you are not to be like that. Instead, the greatest among you should be like the youngest, and the one who rules like the one who serves. For who is greater, the one who is at the table or the one who serves? Is it not the one who is at the table? But I am among you as one who serves (Luke 22:24-27).

Numerous inferences can be drawn from this passage, all important. The disciples were not to be like the kings of the Gentiles, says Jesus, and emphasizes it with a strong four-word negation— "But you, not so."[7]

## TEACHING OF OTHER NEW TESTAMENT WRITERS

God has not left us in the dark as to what the Christian leader should be in home, church, and society. An exegesis of key words like *kubernesis, prohistemi,* and *huperetes* is basic to the task. Tracing down words like this leads us to key passages which I have enumerated in an earlier chapter. Only when we have analyzed these passages in the light of what the New Testament models understood them to mean, in an effort to follow the example of Jesus, based on the direct teachings of our Lord, in fulfillment of the Old Testament models, are we ready to draw some theological conclusions about leadership and ministry, and that is the intent of the next section of our chapter.

## HOW DOES LEADERSHIP RELATE TO PHILOSOPHY OF MINISTRY?

The phrase "philosophy of ministry" describes our understanding of how to serve effectively within the context of whatever ministry God has given us. A philosophy of ministry for a church, for example, might be different from the philosophy of ministry for a mission field or a Christian college. Nevertheless, there are some commonalities which pervade all biblical ministry, and those are particularly true on the issue of leadership style.

One could ask, for example, where is ministry carried out? How is ministry accomplished? What is its nature? For whom is it done? It is not inaccurate to suggest that those four questions are all answered in John 17:4: "I have brought You glory on earth by completing the work You gave Me to do." And the work of Jesus was carried out through His disciples, who not only served with Him but continued that ministry after He went back to the Father.

It seems clear that biblical ministry is more than one person can do, regardless of the size of the church. The wise pastor can be an effective leadership trainer as he learns the basic components of leadership development, prioritizes lay training, shows visibility in educational ministries, refuses to allow the pulpit to lord it over other ministries of the church, and when he has developed lay leadership, genuinely recognizes it. Steve Swayne talks about "the pastor as boss" and asks the question, "Can the same person be tender shepherd and tough supervisor?" He concludes that it is not only possible but necessary—"They are two separate roles, but with a little thought and compassion, one person, guided by the Holy Spirit, can fulfill both functions."[8]

More could be said about the various aspects of the philosophy of ministry and the kind of components involved. Crucial to our intent, however, is the centrality of leadership in philosophy of ministry.

53

How we see ourselves as leaders will distinctively determine how we carry out the whole of ministry. In many ways we could focus on how biblical leadership is developed but I choose to emphasize the model of Christ.

## INVITATION TO CHRISTLIKE LEADERSHIP

As always for the past 2,000 years, the key to learning is learning *from* the Lord, and the key to learning to lead is learning to lead *like* the Lord. Consider the following passage:

> At that time Jesus said, "I praise You, Father, Lord of heaven and earth, because You have hidden these things from the wise and learned, and revealed them to little children. Yes, Father, for this was Your good pleasure. All things have been committed to Me by My Father. No one knows the Son except the Father, and no one knows the Father except the Son and those to whom the Son chooses to reveal Him. Come to Me, all you who are weary and burdened, and I will give you rest. Take My yoke upon you and learn from Me, for I am gentle and humble in heart, and you will find rest for your souls. For My yoke is easy and My burden is light" (Matt. 11:25-30).

In this familiar passage the Lord offers an invitation to Christlike leadership. Who should respond? According to the text, weary leaders and burdened leaders. Weary leaders need to grasp the biblical axiom that the way up is down. Jesus teaches that those who deny themselves will be exalted by the Lord, but those who exalt themselves will be denied by the Lord. How do leaders get weary? Sometimes just in the daily battles they face and sometimes from struggles within their ministries. People tend to forget that biblical leaders are recognizable, responsible, and accountable. Elders, deacons, and pastors are recognizable by the character of their lives and the general consent of the body. They are responsible for the flock and for each other, and they are accountable for the ministry and for the people under their leadership (Heb. 13:17).

Burdened leaders must also learn Christlike leadership—those for whom the tasks of ministry have grown too great because they have tried to carry them alone through the darkness of crisis and heartbreak. Jesus says to bring your burdens to Him and don't blame God for what has happened in your church, in your family, or in your life. Our problems come on us because of the inadequacy of our spiritual and theological foundations, not because God has abandoned His servants. So we learn to work and work hard in ministry to exert faithfulness over the various tasks God has given us to do (1 Thes. 5:12-13).

Charles Mylander offers a series of questions to consider whether or not a new task (opportunity) can be added to an already overweight ministry. He derives these from the experience of Nehemiah, and they apply not only to pastors and professional and church leaders but to lay leaders as well.

Is there a crying need for something to be done? Does the Bible suggest that God wants it done? Will this task help God's redeemed people? Is there an inner urging from the Holy Spirit to do something about it?

If one answers these questions affirmatively, "the Nehemiah principle" is activated. God will help His leaders to relieve the pressures, resolve the problems, and finish the task. Nehemiah and his team of unpaid volunteers got the job done.[9]

## QUALIFICATION OF CHRISTLIKE LEADERSHIP

The Lord tells us that His leadership was "gentle and humble in heart" and those who take on that kind of yoke will find rest for their souls (Matt. 11:29). When did our culture ever suggest that we look for gentleness and humility as qualities in leadership? Scripture calls for shepherds while culture calls for cowboys who can round 'em up and head 'em out.

Two other times in Matthew the Lord's gentleness is emphasized. He says, "Blessed are the meek, for they will inherit the earth (5:5); in chapter 12 we read, "Here is My Servant whom I have chosen, the One I love, in whom I delight; I will put My Spirit on Him, and He will proclaim justice to the nations. He will not quarrel or cry out; no one will hear His voice in the streets. A bruised reed He will not break, and a smoldering wick He will not snuff out, till He leads justice to victory. In His name the nations will put their hope" (vv. 18-21). Gentleness is a biblical mark of the Christian leader.

Add to that the quality of humility which, in biblical context, describes a right view of ourselves in relation to God and others. Matthew tells us Jesus demonstrated humility by spending time ministering to children (19:13-15). In Philippians Paul tells us humility is attained by renouncing position rather than striving for it. And

James encourages spending time with lowly people as a means of gaining humility (James 4:4-6).

Five hundred years before the birth of Christ, Dao Teh Ching offered a classic Chinese philosophy:

> A leader is best when people barely know that he exists, not so good when people obey and acclaim him, worse when they despise him. Fail to honor people, they fail to honor you; but of a good leader, who talks little when his work is done, his aim fulfilled, they will all say, "We did this ourselves."

## EDUCATION FOR CHRISTLIKE LEADERSHIP

How do we learn gentleness and humility? Jesus said, "Take My yoke upon you and learn from Me. . . . For My yoke is easy and My burden is light." How interesting that these words of our Lord in a context of personal gentleness and humility coincide so closely with modern concepts of participatory leadership. First of all, it is necessary to *learn to take the yoke*. Leadership is learned behavior only partially affected by personality.

Certainly many churches define the idea of organizing around the charismatic personality of the pastor an attractive option. But is it biblical? It seems to me that the mutual commitment to a biblical philosophy of ministry on the part of both pastor and people offers the best option.

Taking the yoke means that leaders are to lead in accordance with what the Scripture shows us. They lead willingly, not by compulsion, but by calling (1 Peter 5:2). They lead with eagerness, not for material profit, but ministerial pleasure (v. 2). They lead exemplarily by life, not law (v. 3).

Servant leadership is a foundational axiom in this entire process. We have declared it and described it. "But," asks Lorne Sanny of The Navigators, "How do you know when you have a servant attitude?" His answer? By how you react when you are treated like one. Longing to take the yoke of leadership is one side of a two-sided coin. It speaks to responsibility, accountability, duty, productivity, achievement, and all the good things we would tie to the kite of dynamic Christian leadership.

The other side requires that we learn to *share the burden*. Taking the yoke without sharing the burden leads to burnout, frustration, and even bitterness with God and people. Sharing the burden without taking the yoke leads to irresponsibility and confusion in the church and in Christian organizations.

Evangelical leaders following the gentleness and humility of Christ recognize they are neither the single nor final authority; they decentralize decision-making and develop the leadership qualities of their colleagues. The pastor is the coach, not the general manager, and certainly not the team owner.

During June of 1986, forty-five false killer whales beached themselves on the South Florida shore. In attempting to come up with answers, scientists checked out parasites and pollution, both to no avail. Their final conclusion was that the whales have such a strong instinct for following their leader, they do so even when he's lost.

# HOW DO WE CREATE A CLIMATE FOR LEADERSHIP DEVELOPMENT?

Pastor Peter Jackson is struggling to keep the frazzled ends of his congregation together. The constitution calls for seven deacons but the church is currently operating with five. Two Sunday School classes are being taught by students from a nearby Bible college who will not be available in another month when summer vacation begins. Vacation Bible School, once a thriving summer ministry, provides only a memory, a smile or two from slides taken more than three years ago. By his own admission, Jackson faces trouble and his trouble has a name—lack of lay leadership. Forced into crisis management the once vibrant pastor now rushes from place to place putting out fires. Meanwhile, the central problem continues to smolder because with each passing week, Jackson's congregation offers a less and less satisfactory climate for leadership development.

What can he do? More to the point, what should he have done five or six years ago when he first came to the church? In this last part of our chapter we want to try to offer four answers to that pressing dilemma which currently troubles so many pastors.

*SEE THE CHURCH AS BOTH ORGANISM AND ORGANI-ZATION*

In most of my books on leadership I have raised this point because it is so frequently misunderstood. Since few readers bother with forewords, I emphasize the issue again here. Of course the church is organism—the body of Christ—living, changing, and supernatural in its very being. But it is also organization or the English language means nothing. Pushing either one of these to the exclusion of the other leads to a denial of the reality of the church. This body of

Christ, this living dynamic organism, functions as a group of people who operate according to bylaws, write objectives, own property, elect officers, and prepare budgets. By any definition of the word, the church is an organization.

The problem that we face is the problem of offering organismic answers to organizational problems, and organizational answers to organismic problems. It may very well be that Pastor Jackson's problems are both organismic and organizational: that is, problems of a spiritual nature and problems dealing with leadership functions. In order to be the church as organism, Jackson's congregation must understand who and what they are in New Testament patterns. They need to go back to Acts 2 and analyze how the believers related to one another in the very first congregation (Acts 2:42-47). Marlene Wilson says it well.

> The reason Christians come together as that body is to receive the power of the Spirit promised to us, not that we might be just an effective organization, but that we might be the *church*. And not the church stacked neatly in a row on every other block in towns and cities but the church in the everyday lives of real people along the hiways and byways of life. That brings us back again to that word *theology*—the why of Christian involvement. [10]

But the problems might also be organizational. Is it possible that Jackson doesn't know how to recruit and train lay leaders? Is it possible that his own leadership style takes place in a vacuum? Might he be unaware of the needs of other people, unaware of their potential for ministry? Did his seminary or Bible college prepare him to work with congregations or to function well in what we are fond of calling "strong leadership"? That actually leads us to a second answer to our question.

## UNDERSTAND TYPES OF LEADERSHIP STYLE

Consider the traumatic demonstration of Barnabas at Antioch in Acts 11. Totally free from the crushing burden of defensiveness, willing to be vulnerable in order to see the work of the Lord advanced, Barnabas trudged off to Tarsus to bring back a new assistant pastor—Rabbi Saul. All this happened early in his first year as a senior pastor, and we surely must understand that Barnabas grasped the significance of what he was doing; namely, bringing onto the staff one more gifted than himself. But his leadership style

had freed him from "macho-management." Even the secular literature understands how flagrantly such a position defies everything
we know about genuine leadership.

In her book, *Changemasters*, Rosabeth Moss Kanter lists ten
surefire ways a manager can stifle innovation:

1. Regard any new ideas from below with suspicion.
2. Insist that people who need your approval first go through
   several other levels of management.
3. Get departments/individuals to challenge each other's
   proposals.
4. Express criticism freely; withhold praise; instill job
   insecurity.
5. Treat identification of problems as signs of failure.
6. Control everything carefully. Count everything in sight—
   frequently.
7. Make decisions in secret and spring them on people.
8. Do not hand out information to managers freely.
9. Get lower-level managers to implement your threatening
   decisions.
10. Above all never forget that you, the higher-ups, already
    know everything important about the business.[11]

These insights remind us of Paul's teaching in 2 Corinthians 3.
There he delivers us from the pressures of the ministry by showing
us that *we serve from a position of common weakness and humanity*
with the people whom we lead. The adequacy comes from above,
not from within. The passage surely seems to say that we are *not*
like Moses who put the veil over his face not so that people would
not be stunned by the magnificent reflection of God, but to keep
them from seeing that fading reflection in the return of their great
leader to ordinary humanity. Paul claims that our leadership style
should be different. We don't put veils over our faces, but allow
people to see that Christian leadership is equal-to-equal.

## COMMIT TO THE TEAM PRINCIPLE

One could argue that we see the team functioning as early as the
deacons in Acts 6 and certainly a pastoral team at Antioch in Acts
11. But in Acts 13 the team concept of leadership so central to New
Testament ecclesiology really surfaces. Yes, the Apostle Paul was
the leader of the team but he never functioned in isolation. He
remained accountable to the other members of the team and they to

him. For the rest of the Book of Acts only one time does Paul minister alone, and that was "by accident." He planned to wait at Athens for the rest of the team to catch up (Acts 17) but was so overcome by the blatant idolatry, he was drawn into debate and proclamation before they arrived. Paul was not in error, for God did bless the ministry in Athens. The point is that the notable exception stands in opposition to everything the great apostle did in team ministry.

All the evidence we have indicates that wise leaders, even those who are not believers, must be constantly on the alert with respect to the use of power and influence which attends the leadership role. William Barclay wrote in his autobiography, "The greatest peril of the ministry is that a man is his own master." Even the recognition of accountability only to God is a corrupt view of Christian leadership. We stand mutually accountable to each other, even to subordinates. Commitment to team ministry can deliver the leader from individualism, isolation, empire-building, and burnout. Stott suggests three reasons for the importance of team ministry.

> First, team members *supplement* one another, building on one another's strengths and compensating for one another's weaknesses. No leader has all the gifts, so no leader should keep all the reins of leadership in his own hands. Second, team members *encourage* one another, identifying each of their gifts and motivating each other to develop and use them.
>
> Third, and finally, team members are *accountable* to one another. Shared work means shared responsibility. We listen to one another and learn from one another. Both the human family and the divine family (the body of Christ) are contexts of solidarity in which any insipient illusions of grandeur are rapidly dispelled. "The way of a fool seems right to him, but a wise man listens to advice" (Prov. 12:15).[12]

## CHOOSE DECENTRALIZATION OVER CENTRALIZATION

Pastor Jackson is more than the preacher for his congregation. He chairs the official board, directs the activities of the Sunday School superintendent (and, therefore, the Sunday School), and serves as moderator at all church meetings. In short, Jackson is mired in the muck of centralization—everything passes over his desk. He could take a significant step toward the development of lay leadership by pushing decisions down to the people who must live with them.

Biblically we see a good demonstration of this in Acts 15 as James allows everyone at the council to participate and requires the group to listen to all the varying viewpoints. His final summary is not an independent autocratic determination of what should be done. Christian leaders should recognize that decentralization is biblical but it may be helpful to know that it stands the test of research as well. In 1981, Yukl reviewed the literature of management science and made conclusions about participatory leadership styles.

1. Under participatory management, subordinates understand and accept decisions better.
2. Participation leads to greater identification with decisions and a greater commitment to implement them.
3. Participation increases understanding by subordinates of both objectives of decisions and plans to achieve them.
4. Task motivation is increased by participation because through participation subordinates understand that efforts will be rewarded and that lack of effort will lead to negative outcomes.
5. Participation is consistent with the needs of mature subordinates for autonomy, achievement, self-identity, and psychological growth. Because autocratic leadership does not meet these needs it tends to cause frustration, resentment, and apathy.[13]

So now we are three chapters underway and the bias of the book has been displayed. Developing leadership begins by cultivating a biblical leadership style. Rugged frontier individualism may look exciting on old John Wayne reruns but is opposed to interdependence in the church. Mahlon Hillard reminds us of our goal.

The first item to consider might be helping the layman realize he has a gift in ministry to be developed and used before God. To train in *this* manner is not once-a-year message presentation. Rather, this teaching must be a major part of a pastor's emphasis. Many know this basic Bible principle but it must be stressed continually for results. Many have been tutored but only a few really minister, and it takes time to overcome this thinking. People's thought patterns can change—and the most thrilling change is to see a layman realize *he* is a minister and has a gift to be used of God.[14]

## STUDY QUESTIONS

**1.** In spite of the "obscurity of definition," try your hand at a one-sentence definition of "leadership."

**2.** The author lists five "cultural corruptions" of leadership. List them in the order you would consider to be decreasing danger.

**3.** In what specific ways does the second chapter of 1 Thessalonians contradict first-century pagan understandings of leadership?

**4.** List several ways in which "leadership in the church is different from leadership in the world."

**5.** Review again the Mahlon Hillard quote at the end of the chapter. How strongly do you agree or disagree with his description of lay ministry? What is currently being done in your church to develop the ministry gifts of lay leaders?

## ENDNOTES

**1.** Warren Bennis and Burton Nanus, *Leaders: The Strategies for Taking Charge* (New York: Harper and Row, 1985).

**2.** R.M. Stogdill, *Handbook of Leadership* (New York: Free Press, 1974), p. vii.

**3.** B.L. Montgomery, *The Path to Leadership* (New York: Putnam, 1961), p. 37.

**4.** C. Peter Wagner, *Your Church Can Grow* (Glendale, Calif.: Regal, 1976), p. 62.

**5.** Lyle Schaller, *Getting Things Done* (Nashville: Abingdon, 1986), p. 39.

**6.** Bruce A. Baldwin, "Miseries of the Mild-Mannered Manager," *Pace* (April 1986), p. 17.

**7.** For a detailed treatment of Luke 22 and 1 Thessalonians 2 see my *Building Leaders for Church Education* (Chicago: Moody Press, rev. 1981), chapter 6.

**8.** Steve Swayne, "The Pastor as Boss," *Leadership* (Winter 1987), p. 120.

**9.** Charles Mylander, "The Nehemiah Leadership Principle," *Eternity* (February 1982), p. 42.

**10.** Marlene Wilson, *How to Mobilize Church Volunteers* (Minneapolis: Augsburg, 1983), p. 12.

**11.** Quoted in Chambers Williams, "Macho-Management: It Has No Place In Today's Business," *Phoenix Business Journal* (July 7, 1986), p. 4.

**12.** John R.W. Stott, "What Makes Leadership Christian?" *Christianity Today* (August 9, 1985), p. 27.

**13.** Quoted in David R. Powers and Mary F. Powers, *Making Participatory Management Work* (San Francisco: Jossey-Bass, 1983), pp. 205–06.

**14.** Mahlon Hillard, "Mark Twain and the Leadership Church," *The Standard* (May 1, 1973), p. 27.

# CHAPTER 4

# ORGANIZING YOURSELF AND YOUR WORK

The mid-sixth century B.C. was a time of gloom for the people of God. Most were still in captivity in Persia, though God's servant Zerubbabel had returned in 538 after the decree of Cyrus followed by Ezra's trip in 458 B.C. The report from this second trip reached Nehemiah in the castle of the Persian King at Susa.

> They said to me, "Those who survived the Exile and are back in the province are in great trouble and disgrace. The wall of Jerusalem is broken down, and its gates have been burned with fire." When I heard these things, I sat down and wept. For some days I mourned and fasted and prayed before the God of heaven (Neh. 1:3-4).

We know nothing of this servant before the opening of the book which bears his name, but immediately we learn that God's Word has introduced us to a leader with both servant heart and supervisory hands. The Book of Nehemiah teaches us that spiritual leadership does not scorn proper administrative principles, particularly the principle of organizing one's work. After clear emphasis on *prayer* (1:4-11), a clarification of *priorities* (2:1-5), and quite specific *preparation* for his task (vv. 6-10), Nehemiah unfolded his *plan* for the development of the walls in the city (vv. 11-18). In chapter 3 we see his organizational commitment to two very crucial principles: *decentralization of responsibility* and *delegation of work and authority*. As a leader Nehemiah had identified with the people, initiated a workable solution for their problems, and led them in invoking the faithfulness of God on the project. This 2,500-year-old model stands before us today.

"Organizing," as we use that word within the context of this book, means to *arrange, acquire, and allocate adequate resources in order to achieve clear objectives.* Perhaps it would be useful to briefly review several key principles of organizing, though I have dealt with them in an earlier work.[1]

1. Organizing serves no end in itself: We do not create organizational machinery just so we can say we are organized. Machinery does not constitute ministry and can become a barrier rather than a blessing. In any organization the possibilities for failure are greater than those for success, even though the emphasis of modern-day literature focuses almost exclusively on the latter. So wise leaders allow for failure, forgive it, and even plan for it by always organizing "Plan B" as a backup for organizational strategies.

2. Organizing should always grow out of need: The selection of the original "deacons" in Acts 6 provides a beautiful biblical example. Until the need arose for food distribution to the Hellenistic widows, no organization in the church carried out that function. Organizational frameworks in churches and Christian organizations tend to outlive the needs which gave them birth.

At the end of the twentieth century, any church which believes that the old "youth group" of the past will function with similar success in the present era has simply not kept up with the necessity of organizing from need. Churches of any size soon discover (or should) the necessity of some kind of ministry to single adults apart from whatever high school or college age-groups are currently in place.

More adults are staying single longer, becoming single again through separation, divorce, or death of a spouse. The needs of this group are not only different from other groups in the churches but often different from other members in the group. General programming by age-group or topic will not get the job done.

In the church we might very well consider an adoption of zero-based budgeting which requires every ministry to justify its existence and contribution to the overall mission of the congregation before we allocate funds for the coming fiscal year. Added to that, we might want to consider (at least in conference if not in actuality) an approach to zero-based programming which assumes no perpetuation of current programs but asks annually how these programs contribute to the objectives of the ministry.

3. Organizing depends on decentralization: Decentralization moves decision-making to the lowest possible level. Sunday School departmental superintendents should not decide what could be decided by teachers; general superintendents should not decide what could be decided by departmental superintendents; and the church board should never see agenda items which could be cared for more adequately and effectively closer to trench-line ministry experience. Obviously this also leads to maximal participation in the ministry, one of the biblical goals toward which leaders must be striving all the time.

4. Organizing should be flexible: Organizational variables abound in every program of ministry—immaturity of the people it serves; differences in culture even within the same country; changes in time and people; and changes in needs which call for different kinds of ministries than we initiated ten or twenty years ago.

The life of an organization offers an interesting theological study in itself. Ministries invariably start with some human need identified by one or more persons. The need is met and an organization is formed (consider how virtually every Christian college came into existence). Leadership is determined, resources identified, membership recruited, tasks assigned, and goals set. As the years go by the organization carries out its function and the surrounding environment either responds or does not respond, in some cases deciding whether the organization will live or die.

Many Christian colleges face precisely this problem in the late twentieth century. Curriculums and academic programs designed thirty or forty years ago may not be meeting the needs of contemporary young people and, therefore, drastic changes need to be made in order to bring the institution into conformity with the clear definition of organizing mentioned above—the achievement of objectives. The ministry that can't flex with the changing needs and times faces serious trouble, especially with financial resources at a premium.

5. Organizing works best with wide participation: Since the body of Christ consists of a universal priesthood of believers, involvement in the ministry is crucial for every member of the congregation. Lyle Schaller calls this a spirit of "ownership," productively contrary to the spectator mentality we so often find in local congregations and parachurch ministries.

6. Organizing requires records and reports: Planning depends on available data, and the more comprehensive and accurate the data,

the better the planning process can proceed. Reports from various committee chairpeople, department heads, and other leaders will provide a valuable body of information for the ongoing of the ministry in decades ahead. Remember too the legal requirements to keep accurate minutes of board meetings and other important gatherings.

In their very helpful *Christian Leadership Letter* Engstrom and Dayton bring out the importance of the corporate or collective nature of the body of Christ as a basis for proper organizing.

> The will of God for the organization is not the sum of the parts of His will for individuals. We should begin where the Bible begins, which is with the *organization*, with people in relationship. . . . We should look at the individual through the lenses of the organization, rather than look at the organization through the lenses of the individual.[2]

# COMPONENTS OF THE ORGANIZING TASK

Several aspects or principles of organizing make possible its actual practice, and though there is no magic number, at least five critical components seem worthy of explanation at this point.

## ORGANIZATIONAL CHARTS

An organizational chart is a pictorial or diagrammatic presentation of the organization. Anything else we will talk about in this section depends on a clear organizational chart. The various boxes describe different positions in relationship to one another while the lines show the flow of authority. The solid lines indicate direct authority and the dotted lines, indirect authority. Organizational diagrams (work charts) need not be detailed to be helpful but there is no organization so small that it cannot be charted in some form. Figure 4[3] contains five simple organizational charts. Study them carefully, and then we'll talk about several lessons in organizing which jump out at us from the charts themselves.

## LINE-STAFF RELATIONSHIPS

A well-drawn organizational chart shows how people stand in line-staff relationship to each other. The first chart clearly points out the pastor's accountability to the congregation and that of the minister of music to the pastor. We call that *line* relationship. Each of the four associates in ministry, however, all equally accountable to the pastor, are in *staff* relationship to one another. They do not supervise each other, cannot delegate to one another, and are not responsible for evaluating each other's work. The organizational chart

FIGURE 4

# ORGANIZATIONAL CHARTS

## 1. Congregationally Governed Larger Church

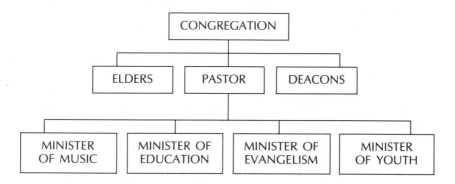

## 2. Elder Governed Smaller Church

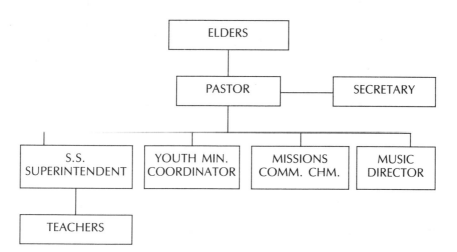

# 3. Organizational Chart for a Parochial School
## PARENTS

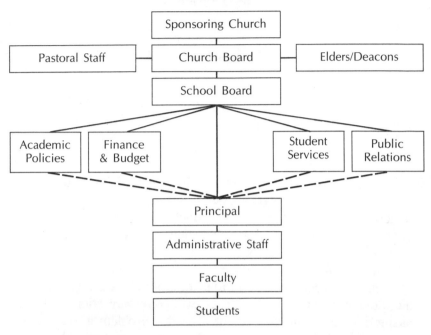

# 4. Organizational Chart for a Parent-Society School
## PARENTS

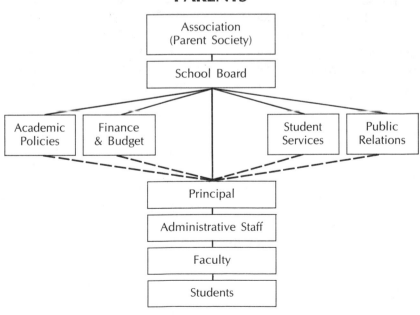

## 5. Christian Liberal Arts or Bible College

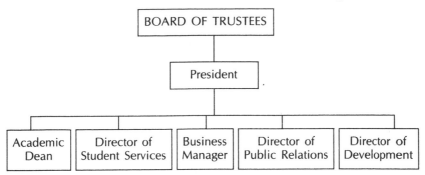

immediately shows staff relationship by the position of the boxes just as it shows the line relationship by the way the boxes appear one above another. A good organizational chart describes a "people system," showing us a great deal about the arranging of human resources in the organization.

*It is always dangerous and sometimes fatal to violate line relationships.* Imagine a Sunday School teacher from chart 2 bypassing the superintendent and the pastor (two levels of organization) and complaining directly to an elder about a certain problem in the Sunday School. The only wise response on the part of a mature elder would be to send that teacher immediately back to his superintendent for a response. By the same token, the college board member (chart 5) doesn't bypass the president and the dean to communicate directly with a faculty member regarding his dissatisfactions or complaints about something on campus. The system works when we work through the system. It teaches us responsibility and oversight; everyone in the organization should understand to whom and for whom he is responsible.

*SPAN OF CONTROL*

This simple phrase describes the number of people over whom a leader holds supervisory responsibility. We're not talking about pastoral ministry or counseling, advice or general relationships, but supervision for administrative outcomes. In short, how many people answer to you? Here secular management has given us a marvelous rule of thumb: *your span of control should never be in double digits.* To put it another way, even the best administrator cannot effectively supervise more than nine people, and four or five sets up a better arrangement.

Look again at our organizational charts in Figure 4. In chart 1, the

pastor with four assistants has a comfortable span of control. In chart 5, the president supervises five vice presidents or institutional officers. These are wise organizational arrangements because they allow the leader to genuinely guide, oversee, develop, and teach his subordinates rather than rushing to and fro among twelve or thirteen people just putting out fires (crisis management).

To be sure, the span of control will vary with the maturity of the subordinates (a Christian school principal could much more easily supervise nine veteran teachers than six first-year teachers) and will also be influenced by the nature of the tasks. Generally supervisors at lower levels in the chart can supervise more people than chief executive officers. The reason is that the CEO must have discretionary time for long-range planning and visionary leadership lest the organization degenerate into a survival mode.

How do you know whether you're trying to supervise too many people? Ask yourself some key questions:

Do I really have control of my job?

Am I really fulfilling the objectives laid out for me by my superiors?

What is my level in the organization—supervisor, chief executive officer, or other?

How much of my time is spent actually supervising subordinates directly?

Reducing the overload provides distinctive advantages to the leader in the Christian organization. Engstrom and Dayton mention three.

1. It gives the previously overloaded executive room to grow, time to learn new things.
2. It gives room for others to assume responsibility.
3. It permits flexibility in the organization, thus allowing the organization to grow.[4]

The visionary leader, the kind of person who really helps Christian organizations reach their God-ordained destinies, works through other people to achieve those destinies. We could say he is person-centered rather than task-centered; challenged by long-term goals rather than crisis management; practices administrative skills rather than manipulating people through the power of his own personality; and he works from a plan agreed on by the leadership team rather than "winging it" day to day according to his own intuition.

## JOB DESCRIPTIONS

Job descriptions, as much as they sound like bureaucratic machinery, are extremely practical and helpful in the Christian organization. A one-page job description can include the title of the job; qualifications of the person who should fill it; a brief description of duties (preferably in list form); an identification of the person *to* whom this worker is responsible; and an identification of the persons *for* whom he is responsible (Fig. 5). Every worker in the organization should have a job description, though some may share the identical job description (for example, all Sunday School teachers could use the same job description whereas the descriptions for the Sunday School superintendent and departmental superintendents might differ somewhat). Additional job description information might add something about purpose, describing how the goals of each particular ministry fit in with the overall objectives of the mission of the church. Also, identification of committee responsibilities would be helpful.

FIGURE 5

# SAMPLE JOB DESCRIPTION OUTLINE

_____ (organization name) _____

_____ (job holder name) _____

JOB TITLE:  
JOB QUALIFICATIONS:  
JOB PURPOSE: (end result of task-goal achievement)  
JOB DUTIES: (brief but descriptive paragraphs)  
 1.

 2.

 3.

 4.

ORGANIZATIONAL RELATIONSHIPS:  
 Supervision Received From:  
 Supervision Given To:  
COMMITTEE RESPONSIBILITIES:  
JOB GOALS—19__:

Appended to each job description (and reviewed annually for purposes of revision and updating) should be a set of annual goals for each major leader in the organization. In actuality the goals are reviewed by the worker and his immediate supervisor several times during the year, but the management team can come together to compare notes on goal achievement at least two or three times a year. You can see how the use of job descriptions in relationship to the organizational chart can help every servant of the Lord find his or her specific role in the ministry and know better how to carry it out to the glory of God.

Job descriptions provide essential tools for evaluation because they are inseparably related to management-by-objectives. In fact, we could honestly observe that any personnel evaluation without an effective job description would be unfair both to the employee and the supervisor.

## CHANNELS OF COMMUNICATION

Jeff Sloan is a youth director just completing his first year. And Jeff Sloan wants to quit. Though warned repeatedly by his seminary professors before graduation, Jeff was so excited about the ministry opportunities at Central Baptist Church that he asked few questions during the interviews. He saw no organizational chart, learned nothing about Central's line-staff relationship, was never told to whom he would be responsible, and does not know if there is a job description to guide him in his work.

Though it's too late, Jeff intends to ask about these things at a board meeting next week. For almost a year he has been practicing crisis management, totally frustrated in trying to satisfy teenagers, parents, board members, and the general congregation—often neglected by the senior pastor whose responsibilities in sermon preparation, counseling, and community activities leave little time for direct supervision of his fledgling youth director. From the start Jeff's problem has been a breakdown in communication.

Since he didn't understand the chart of line-staff relationships, he had no framework for communication up or down the organization. He may have heard it in seminary and put it down in his notebook, but he never learned how to practice the reality of formal and informal communication, oral and written communication, and the general principle that smooth-flowing, two-way communications tend to reduce conflict in almost any kind of organization—including the church of Jesus Christ.

Jeff communicates well enough with the teenagers but he has not communicated with their parents; he gets along just fine with the pastor (when he sees him) but struggles to explain what he's doing to members of the church board. Jeff needs to learn that "competence in personal communication skills, and desire to use the best of the ever-changing communication tools will distinguish the competent leader."[5] Until he practices and masters that principle, he will continue to struggle—if he survives the board meeting next week.

*Communication is a process, not an event.* It reflects the relationship Jeff has with his pastor and other leaders in his church. One management expert calls this kind of relationship the heart and core of everything we do in leading.

> . . . a sharing of formal authority, the scope and form of internal participation of governance, and the vertical distribution of authority should be characterized by full and open consultation with an emphasis on joint endeavor. Consultation and joint effort should be built on a high degree of trust. Trust can be encouraged by an emphasis on process.[6]

## KEYS TO EFFECTIVE TIME MANAGEMENT

*The first step in effectively managing your time discovers how you use it now.* To do that you must log a time chart for a reasonable period of time, preferably a month. Pick the most "normal" month in the year and block it off into half-hour segments. One shortcut to keeping such a log is to identify a common activity such as commuting to work by a simple letter or number. Commuting could be indicated by a "C" or perhaps by a "1," Bible study by a "B" or "2," prayer by a "P" or "3," etc. Whatever code you choose, put it right on the sheet so you can use it immediately. That will save time in writing out each activity. Some experts suggest recording the time in 15-minute blocks, but I find this too burdensome for accurate record-keeping.

The goal is to identify ways you use or misuse your time before you move into a program of time management. The literature of management science has indicated many lists of time wasters, and the one which follows is actually a compilation of lists rather than the result of a specific survey. These suggestions reflect secular businessmen as well as pastors and others in Christian leadership positions.

Lack of planning
Lack of prioritizing
Crisis management
Overcommitment

Undue haste
Paperwork and reading
Interruptions by phone or in person
Meetings
Indecision
Failure to delegate

Quite a list isn't it? You may not identify with all the items or you might choose a different order to describe how they plague you, but most of the common time wasters are covered somewhere in the list. The big question is, What do we do about it? Here are eight practical steps you can take to manage your time effectively and, therefore, do a better job in whatever leadership role God has called you to fill.

## CONTROL YOUR TELEPHONE

You don't want to be interrupted by a phone or anything else in the middle of writing a report, preparing a sermon, or doing something else that takes deep mental concentration. Trying to get jobs done between phone calls is both annoying and counterproductive. Essentially you control your phone by letting your secretary take incoming calls, make judgments on items sufficiently crucial to bother you during a "no interruption" time, while at the same time making the caller understand that you will give him your complete attention as soon as possible.

Of course, some pastors and Christian leaders don't have secretaries, so it may be necessary to simply "pull the plug" in order to have some study time, privacy with your family, or even essential rest and relaxation. Obviously you need some kind of emergency backup system whereby people can reach you if a genuine crisis arises. Quite frankly, however, most of the interruptive calls we struggle with do not approach crisis dimensions.

## LEARN TO SAY NO!

For some reason most of us in Christian work find that answer difficult. Even when we do turn down some new task or speaking engagement we feel compelled to give a number of reasons or excuses. But we stand under no obligation to serve people who are not a part of the specific organization or ministry God has placed us in. Even within that primary arena of service there may be exceptions to what we should do. So it becomes important to say no without giving reasons. Many of us just try to do too much. We forget that God isn't impressed by what we *do* as much as by what we *are*. The more we focus on what God wants us to be, the more time management will fall into place.

Peter Drucker's distinction between *effectiveness* and *efficiency* is helpful here. The efficient leader, he says, *does things right* and, of course, we all favor that choice. The effective worker, however, *does the right things,* and that could hardly include everything we're asked to do. *Saying no may very well be a spiritual discipline cultivated after we understand the objectives and priorities of the ministry to which God has called us.* Narrowly speaking, among evangelical leaders those priorities are: (1) a personal relationship to God; (2) a productive relationship with our families; and (3) a positive relationship to the ministry. God always wants us to put first things first.

## ORGANIZE YOUR WORK AREA

By "work area" I mean your desk, the equipment on and around your desk (typewriter, computer, dictating equipment, reference books, etc.), and whatever you might need to work comfortably and effectively in a given place. I maintain an office at the seminary and a study at home. I call them by different names because I do different things in those rooms. I don't try to study at the seminary since 40–50 percent of my time is given to administration and the rest to teaching. By the same token, I don't administer from my study at home. The work areas have similar characteristics, but they differ slightly to accommodate what happens there. A pastor's sermon preparation area will be quite different from the desk at which his music director works. The work area of the church librarian looks not at all like that of the church custodian. You have to do what works well for you.

## USE PROPER EQUIPMENT

Again "proper" means what works well for you. Some readers will be surprised to know that in the writing of my books (this is the twenty-fifth) I have never used a word processor. The reason? I don't type manuscripts but rather dictate them on portable dictating machines. Changing to a word processor would slow me down measurably and for me, therefore, it would be *improper* rather than *proper* equipment. As a leader you have to determine what equipment will help you function effectively. It might be something as expensive as a copying machine in the church office or as simple as an up-to-date dictionary on your desk.

## ORDER A LARGE WASTEBASKET

Somebody has called this function practicing "wastebasketry." Some leaders suggest we should deal with every piece of paper only once. That may be a bit idealistic since the letters and memos may have to be handled more than once, and certainly the reading could give rise to clipping, making copies of certain pages, sharing of key articles with colleagues, and other important but delayed responses.

But let's focus for the moment on the "toss" action. Junk mail, brochures, flyers, contests in which somebody just can't wait to give you a million dollars, and such items fill up that big wastebasket in a hurry. I like the basket just the right distance from the desk, up against the wall where I can get a good bank shot "off the glass" through the hoop. Junk mail gives me the opportunity to brush up on office basketball skills.

## FILE PROPERLY

*The key word here is "retrieval."* Anybody can put things in a folder, put the folder in a file drawer and close the closet door. The question is, can you find it again when you need it? Filing needs to be related to the kind of ministry you do (filing for a pastor varies from filing for a school administrator), suited to the person who carries out the filing function (you, your secretary, your spouse), and subject to instant retrieval when the need arises (we can assume the person who files will also be the person who retrieves).

My preference is to use the expanded Rossin-Dewey system at home for biblically related materials and subject matter headings at my office, usually arranged by topics or class titles in my teaching field. Arrange correspondence alphabetically within monthly and annual folders. Use one or more folders for "A," placing within those folders items to/from correspondents whose last names begin with "A." At the end of the calendar year those materials, still alphabetically arranged, can be removed to some archival location.

## HANDLE MAIL ADEQUATELY

We have already talked about tossing junk mail; now we're discussing how you handle the real stuff. A competent and experienced secretary can become an administrative assistant answering a number of letters for you either over her signature or even over yours. Sometimes you might find it helpful to have certain basic form letters already prepared, allowing your secretary to adapt and sequence appropriate paragraphs.

Here again grouping similar tasks is important. Have a time for answering your mail, however you do it — secretary instruction, dictation, prearranged form letters — and try to keep other kinds of interruptions away from the mail-handling time segment.

Pastors are notorious for not answering their mail or answering it unconscionably late. Break that pattern by determining that first class mail will get your attention, a response and a return envelope on the way within a reasonable boundary of time, such as three or four days, or at the very latest a week.

*DELEGATE WHENEVER POSSIBLE*

We have a whole chapter coming up on this, so I will just touch on it briefly here. *Every time you do a job that someone else can do, you sacrifice work that only you can do. Delegation does not call us to do everything we can and then give away the overload, but to hand out everything we possibly can and only retain what we absolutely must do.* That might just give you time to be an effective leader rather than a custodial manager. As I said, more on that later.

## ANALYSIS OF ACTIVITIES AND PRIORITIES

How do pastors misuse their time? Charles Reimnitz, after extensive study on that question, suggests that the number one culprit with a "weight" factor of 100 (indicating the number of times the response is given in relation to other responses) is *personal disorganization*. It beats lack of planning two to one and going to meetings almost four to one. He urges the application of the DOE formula to get Christian leaders organized and functioning—Delegate, Organize, and Eliminate.[7]

That's essentially what I'm suggesting in offering the following priority grid which provides a model for analyzing our activities according to four different measures. Figure 6 shows the chart and the following paragraphs contain the explanation.

*ACCORDING TO IMPORTANCE*

Day-by-day tasks can be analyzed according to their intrinsic importance. Notice that the chart offers four selections using the letters A, B, C, and D. Most of us understand how to move crucial activities up into the 1A category. But we often fail to recognize what ought to be placed in a 1D category, cut off, and forgotten. Such items can hang like an albatross around the neck of a busy leader, creating guilt feelings in an already stressful life. Do you really need to write an article for the denominational magazine? Maybe not. Maybe that's a 1C or even a 1D item. The day you decide it should move to the right of the chart on line 1 you can forget about it and no longer torment yourself for not having started your manuscript.

*ACCORDING TO URGENCY*

Though sometimes used in a negative sense, we use the word here to describe time constraints. Some items must be labeled 2A—they

FIGURE 6

## ACTIVITY ANALYSIS GRID

| | A | B | C | D |
|---|---|---|---|---|
| **INTRINSIC IMPORTANCE** | | | | |
| I. Very Important | Absolutely MUST be done | Important Should be done | Of Small Importance May be useful | Unimportant Can be eliminated |
| **URGENCY** | | | | |
| II. Very Urgent | Must be done NOW | Urgent Should be done soon | Not Urgent May be done later | Time Not a Factor May be done anytime |
| **DELEGATION** | | | | |
| III. Must Be Done by Me | I am only person who can do it | Can Be Delegated to A | Can Be Delegated to B | Can Be Delegated to C |
| | Associate or Secretary | | | |
| **PERSONAL CONTACTS** | | | | |
| IV. | People I Must See Each Day | People I Must See Weekly | People to See Regularly | People to See Infrequently |

must be done now. Please note that just because an item merits 1A it does not necessarily have to be 2A. Preparation of the annual report is clearly 1A, but if you function on a calendar year and it is now March, you have a 1A-2C item. Obviously the farther right an item can be pushed on the chart, the less likelihood exists that you should be doing it at all. The farther to the left on the chart you place it (after thoughtful consideration), the more importance it radiates; stop procrastinating and get the job done.

## ACCORDING TO RESPONSIBILITY

The issue here is delegation, something we simply can't seem to separate from being organized. But here the choices differ from A through D. We simply decide whether a given item "must be done by me—I am the only person who can do it," or whether it can be delegated to someone else, such as, an associate, an assistant, or secretary. Once you can determine that an item is not 3A, determine who should assume responsibility for it.

## ACCORDING TO PERSONAL CONTACTS

Since interruptions waste time, it becomes important for leaders to sort out how to use their available time for people who "come calling." Ask yourself the key questions:

Whom must I see each day? Certainly your secretary and possibly close associates in ministry, such as, an assistant pastor.

Whom must I see at least weekly? If you're a pastor, probably the chairman of the board or one or more of the elders/deacons. If you're a school principal, the school superintendent, perhaps administrators or curriculum director.

Whom must I see regularly? Depending on what "regularly" means, a missions executive might answer by naming regional directors he supervises from the central office. A youth director might say "the parents of the teenagers I serve." A college president might name the chairman of the board of trustees or regents.

Whom must I see frequently? Don't think of this as a negative category; emphasize the fact that you *must* see these people albeit not on a regular basis. The college president mentioned above might want to see some of the school's major donors from time to time, while the pastor of a large and busy church might meet with the Sunday School teachers or pastors of branch churches. The contact must be made but time is not the prime criterion.

Like learning to drive, it may be necessary to think through each step on this analysis grid during the early days of use. Soon, however, it will become second nature and you'll be able to make wise

FIGURE 7

# CHARACTERIZING YOUR MANAGEMENT EFFECTIVENESS

| | ALWAYS | GENER-ALLY | ABOUT EVEN | USUALLY NOT | NEVER |
|---|---|---|---|---|---|
| 1. Our organizational development is achieved by managing potential. | 5 | 4 | 3 | 2 | 1 |
| 2. We apply a developed theology and philosophy of management to decision-making. | 5 | 4 | 3 | 2 | 1 |
| 3. Policy is determined by planning not by expediency. | 5 | 4 | 3 | 2 | 1 |
| 4. Our board is involved in a continued justification for the existence of the organization. | 5 | 4 | 3 | 2 | 1 |
| 5. We are able to come up with the right people for the right jobs. | 5 | 4 | 3 | 2 | 1 |
| 6. Our organization constantly reevaluates its basic goal in relationship to our mission field or outreach. | 5 | 4 | 3 | 2 | 1 |
| 7. The vision of our organization is expressed in terms of outcomes rather than methods. | 5 | 4 | 3 | 2 | 1 |
| 8. Our chief executive relates effectively to the board. | 5 | 4 | 3 | 2 | 1 |
| 9. We achieve our activity-oriented goals principally through the management of people. | 5 | 4 | 3 | 2 | 1 |
| 10. We know where we have been as an organization, where we are, and where we want to go. | 5 | 4 | 3 | 2 | 1 |

choices of priority based on new behavior patterns you've learned. *Remember to do difficult and distasteful tasks first; to design some system and follow it; to understand the reason for each task you do; and to build in conscious time for rest and recreation.*

In an article now almost a quarter of a century old, John W. Gardner suggests "how to prevent organizational dry rot." He suggests that most ailing organizations have developed a functional blindness to their own defeats and advises that they bring in outside consultants, encourage internal critics, put new blood into key positions, and rotate personnel among parts of the organization. Gardner says, "Organizations must have built-in provisions for self-criticism, an atmosphere where uncomfortable questions can be asked. For those in power the danger of self-deception is very great. . . . The organization must have some means of combating the process by which men become the prisoners of their procedures. The rulebook grows fatter as the ideas grow fewer."[8]

How does your organizational index stack up? Start by testing yourself on some kind of assessment chart like the one which appears in Figure 7.[9] Check it right now and take just a few minutes to run through the test. A perfect score is 50 and as Ed Neteland says, if you score 50 you're probably kidding yourself. If you're really honest with the test and have been doing your very best in increasing your administrative effectiveness, look for a score in the high 30s or low 40s. Find the weaknesses and start working on them as soon as possible.

# STUDY QUESTIONS

**1.** Review the definition of organization in the Foreword and list five ministries in the church which fall under or exemplify this leadership function.

**2.** Draw an "organizational chart" for your church or organization through at least three levels below the board.

**3.** Ask yourself the four questions on page 71. Answer honestly and decide what administrative changes need to be made.

**4.** Write a sample job description for some lay leadership position in the church, incorporating all the components mentioned in the chapter.

**5.** Review the time-saving suggestions and list them in priority of your personal needs. Now begin to work on them one at a time.

# ENDNOTES

**1.** Kenneth O. Gangel, *Building Leaders for Church Education* (Chicago: Moody Press, 1981).

**2.** Ted W. Engstrom and Edward R. Dayton, "The Basics of a Biblical Organization," *Christian Leadership Letter* (January 1983), p. 2.

**3.** Charts 3 and 4 are from Kenneth O. Gangel, "Who Controls Christian Schools?" *Christian Education Journal* (Autumn 1986), pp. 7–8.

**4.** Engstrom and Dayton, "Span of Control," *Christian Leadership Letter* (June 1983).

**5.** Roger Gray, "Generating Co-operation Is Leading," *Hillsdale College Leadership Letter* (vol. 10, no. 3), p. 2.

**6.** K.P. Mortimer and T.R. McConnell, *Sharing Authority Effectively: Participation, Interaction and Discretion* (San Francisco: Jossey-Bass, 1978), p. 275.

**7.** Charles Reimnitz, "How Clergymen Use (Misuse) Their Time," *The Clergy Journal* (March 1975), pp. 14–5.

**8.** John W. Gardner, "How to Prevent Organizational Dry Rot," *Harper's* (October 1965).

**9.** Ed Neteland, "Religious Organizations Are Well Managed . . . Or Are They?" *Christian Executive* (January 1976), p. 2.

# CHAPTER 5

# SETTING AND ACHIEVING GOALS

Grace Church has a long history of living and ministering from year to year without adequate goal-setting and planning. There is some effort to look ahead as nominating committees meet in preparation for the annual meeting; youth parties and social events are scheduled enough in advance to secure adequate facilities and promote the event; and Pastor Petroff does project his sermon preparation at least a month ahead so the music director can plan choir anthems and other special music. Once, when the new educational wing was built seven years ago, the church actually had to look two years into the future and plan its educational activities around the developing building and the confusion such a project always creates.

But if you were to ask the people at Grace Church about goals or objectives, they would spiritualize the concept and talk about "serving the Lord," "fulfilling the Great Commission here in our community," or "bringing glory to God through our ministry." These are all noble phrases and every evangelical church ought to be engaged in all of them all of the time. But none qualify as goals and none will help Grace Church aim its ministry beyond the next week or month.

*Yet the primary characteristic of administrative leadership is purpose.* When one looks at films of Roger Bannister running the four-minute mile there seems to be nothing particularly spectacular, just another race among milers of similar abilities who stay extremely close throughout the run. But when that final inner command told Bannister to start his kick, he moved out ahead of the pack, reached the finish line, and fell exhausted. It seems as though he had measured his energy to the last foot to achieve his goal. One is reminded of the final achievement statement of the Apostle Paul in his very last letter to a friend. Writing from the Mamertine prison in Rome he said, "I have fought the good fight, I have finished the race, I have kept the faith. Now there is in store for me the crown of righteousness, which the Lord, the righteous Judge, will award to me on that day—and not only to me, but also to all who have longed for His appearing" (2 Tim. 4:7-8).

Engstrom and Dayton talk about goals as "signs." They correctly point out that the real evidence of effectiveness in administrative leadership rests in achieved goals.

> Of course, this assumes that in the very beginning of the job you staked out some goals for yourself and for the organization, and made them known to the degree that they needed to be advertised. You must frequently evaluate your progress and see to it that some of these goals are now past events; they have been accomplished; you are moving on to new things.[1]

## THREE ASSUMPTIONS ABOUT ALL ORGANIZATIONS

Well known in the literature of administration, these assumptions have appeared in my own writings[2] and I have seen them numerous times in the writings of others. We handle them differently here by applying them specifically to the church and parachurch organizations and by building in that theological integration we have talked about so frequently.

### ALL ORGANIZATIONS HAVE GOALS

In many churches and other Christian groups crisis management appears to be the order of the day—every day. The leadership seems to focus exclusively on problems, rushing from one aspect of the work to another to "put out fires." When I talk about this kind of thing in leadership seminars, there is an immediate and highly visible display of recognition. Sly smiles appear, betraying a knowing guilt at living one's leadership life in such a manner.

Nevertheless, all organizations have goals. They may not have them spelled out. People in the organization may not know about them. Leaders may vary in their understanding of those goals. But the very existence of the church or organization indicates that somewhere, sometime, somebody thought about goals.

In my leadership classes I teach students to ask questions about goals when they go to that first candidating situation or move from ministry to ministry. In some cases they find a well-developed set of goals with an accompanying job description demonstrating how that ministry to which they are being invited will assist in goal achievement. In others, practically nothing exists.

But how does a church go about clarifying goals and objectives? The third part of our chapter deals with that in detail, but let's emphasize here that any given congregation must understand the nature and purpose of the church.[3] The questions asked should reach beyond those generalizable purposes with which every evangelical congregation ought to be concerned (worship, evangelism, missions, etc.). They should identify the precise kinds of things God expects of *your* congregation in *your* location at this time in history.

North Americans are great imitators and we quickly fall into the trap of franchising Christianity as though we were handling Big Macs or Whoppers. But the New Testament gives us no hint of that kind of thinking. Antioch did not model itself after Jerusalem, nor did the churches of Asia model after Antioch. *Each congregation designed a ministry unique to those goals and objectives for which God brought it into existence. Key ministry questions of the first century were not how, but what and why.* American pragmatism has all but drowned out the *why* questions as we concentrate to a fault on improving our methodology.

## ALL ORGANIZATIONS HAVE SOME STRUCTURE TO FACILITATE GOAL ACHIEVEMENT

Even Grace Church, with its shallow understanding of goals and objectives, has a structure. The official board consists of the pastor, the elders, and the deacons. Each of the elders chairs one of the major committees of the church—Christian education, music, missions, evangelism, membership—while the deacons supervise care for the needy and maintenance of the physical plant. Actually, the organization seems quite clear, and the structure fits rather well the size and type of congregation Grace Church has become. The problem lies in its inability to relate *form* to *function*. The form is in place, well established by constitution, bylaws, and policy handbooks. The function (how we go about achieving specific goals) struggles and vacillates all along the way.

Three crucial elements surface here and their implementation will become clearer as the chapter proceeds. Setting and achieving goals must take into consideration the importance of *sequencing*, *priorities,* and *deadlines. Sequencing* refers to the stages in the process of goal-setting and achievement. *Priorities* refers not necessarily to time, but importance. *Putting first things first may mean doing a number of lesser things earlier since they pave the way for the more important steps down the road.* When we discuss *deadlines* we talk about when certain goals will be achieved in the progress toward achieving our ultimate purpose.

## ALL ORGANIZATIONS HAVE SOME ADMINISTRATION TO ACCOMMODATE THE STRUCTURE

Administration happens at Grace Church. Though not specifically trained for it, Pastor Petroff administers the church with the help of the elders and deacons. That's good. But their administrative *activity* has so far failed to achieve ministry *productivity*. That's bad.

Administration is simply a tool which, when properly used, can produce significant benefits for any congregation or organization. It can help that organization to be *effective* as well as *efficient*. For the Christian, administration also takes on the form of a spiritual gift, a ministerial activity which serves as a means and not an end. When administration becomes an end, it closes in on itself. The result? Bureaucracy! Within its proper role as means, administration facilitates the structure that leads to goal achievement. Consider the following questions for your ministry:

1. Can you state your objectives? Remember hyperactivity is no substitute for decision-making and planning.

2. Have you chosen what God really wants for your ministry or what seems attractive in similar ministries of your acquaintance? Compromise may always be necessary to some extent simply because of limited resources. But choosing and doing the right thing rises above the value of doing things right.

3. Does your entire staff understand and agree with your goals and priorities? That's probably too much to ask of the entire congregation or constituency, but certainly the staff of the church, school, college, mission, or whatever Christian organization you serve should be in tune with a mutually determined set of goals and priorities.

4. Do you bring others into the decision-making process? We'll treat this at greater length in a later chapter but here it has to do with who names the goals. Setting and achieving goals demands adherence to a basic axiom: *People are more likely to be committed to those goals in whose preparation they have had a significant role.*

5. Will you know when to abandon certain unachievable goals? Just like automobiles, institutional goals and procedures seem to

have built-in obsolescence. The effective administrative leader tends to constantly review and revise objectives lest the organization achieve a certain level, plateau there, and fail to move forward.

6. Do you help people toward accountability for the institution's goals? The wise leader assigns people to results, not posts. It may just be possible that our failure with volunteers in the church today centers in substandard requirements of qualification and achievement. Administrative leadership enables people to work together toward goal achievement in the organization.

In order to answer all the above questions satisfactorily the following characteristics need to be present in your ministry:

1. Each administrative leader must find and understand his role in the organization.

2. Each administrative leader must give himself unreservedly to the achieving of goals in his area and the overall objectives of the organization.

3. Each administrative leader must understand his responsibility to and for others and their mutual ministry.

# GOAL-ORIENTATION AND PROBLEM-ORIENTATION

One doesn't have to be around the congregation of Grace Church very long before he can sense an atmosphere of negativism and pessimism. This is brought about not by spiritual problems of the people, though those certainly exist. No, the problem is not primarily *organismic*, but *organizational*. The administrative style practiced by Pastor Petroff and the lay leaders gives the impression they are constantly solving problems (crisis management) rather than achieving objectives. Sound familiar? Such a tendency can be measured and corrected.

*HOW TO TELL IF YOUR MINISTRY IS PROBLEM-ORIENTED*

Four questions can give you some definitive clues; you need not guess nor offer subjective opinions.

1. *How often do we initiate change?* The Apostle Paul was a master innovator. Virtually every aspect of his ministry was characterized by some new way of handling a challenge in order to achieve his goals. Remember the dramatic paragraph in 1 Corinthians 9 in which Paul describes how it was sometimes necessary to follow the law and other times to condemn it? Sometimes necessary to relate to the weak and sometimes even to be like a slave? He ends with

the words, "I have become all things to all men so that by all possible means I might save some. I do all this for the sake of the Gospel, that I may share in its blessings" (1 Cor. 9:22-23). Always difficult, in some Christian organizations change can be downright agonizing! As one pastor once told me, "In my church change is sin and we sin as little as possible."

2. *What has stimulated recent changes in our ministry?* Some organizations change because others force change on them. In my opinion, that explains why most seminaries today offer the Master rather than the Bachelor of Divinity degree. A few schools, mostly in the liberal domain, made the changeover, and then the pressure was on. Most graduate schools of theology have been forced to change to a Masters degree.

But forced change doesn't count as objective-orientation. As a matter of fact, if you have to admit that recent changes in your ministry have come about because of pressure (either internal or external), you may be describing problem-orientation. Ministry-by-objectives has not only demonstrated strategic changes in recent years but can show that those changes came from creative thinking within the organization.

3. *Do we have room for the "free thinker"?* Not a theological radical but one whose leadership ideas differ from the way we have always done things. He may just be the person who stimulates that new idea we so desperately need. True, we might have to put up with months of unworkable, far-out notions before he comes through with that terrific brainstorm, but good leaders have the patience to wait. The objective-oriented organization designs an open system in which all members can have significant voice.

4. *How do we spend the time in our business meetings?* This question can be answered on a quantitative basis. Without warning, sneak a stopwatch into the next elder, deacon, or board meeting. While the group talks about problems let the watch run. During discussions about objectives and plans for future ministry, cut it off. Then measure the difference. The problem-oriented meeting spends an inordinate percentage of meeting time just solving problems. To put it another way, *formal business meetings of such an organization will reflect its administrative style.*

## HOW CAN A PROBLEM-ORIENTED ORGANIZATION BECOME GOAL-ORIENTED?

As chairman of the elder board, Bill Thompson had the responsibility of planning the agenda and leading the monthly meetings. As he

89

evaluated each meeting month after month, he felt more and more a failure and considered resigning the chairmanship.

For example, last month 80 percent of the meeting time was spent talking about financial problems of the church: bills were not being paid, the missions budget was running several months behind, and the financial secretary had been forced into interfund borrowing. Bill decided to plan the next meeting's agenda around positive goal/purpose items rather than negative problem items. Each elder reporting on his specific area of responsibility would be asked to present a realistic plan of action leading to a particular set of goals.

But the financial situation still had to be dealt with. Bill determined that the elders, creatively working together, could come up with some strategic ways to inform the congregation of the present financial situation along with plans to improve the cash flow.

What kinds of things did Bill do in those elder meetings? Since we looked at four questions earlier, let's offer four suggestions here— four ways to develop an objective-oriented ministry.

**1.** *Decentralize the decision-making process.* To decentralize means to push down from the top and, therefore, to involve more people, preferably those who are closest to the actual functions influenced by the decision. But here someone will surely say, "Shepherds do not ask the sheep which direction they want to go." That's right, but shepherding offers only one of the many leadership metaphors in Scripture.

The husband certainly should consult with the wife, and the coach with the team. Study the Book of Acts and note how *decentralized decision-making dominated the early church.* In the first chapter they select an apostle to replace Judas. God makes the choice but everyone has a voice. In the sixth chapter they decentralize the selection of seven "deacons." In chapter 13 the church ("they") deliberates in the sending out of missionaries. *An objective-oriented ministry steers away from autocratic dominance because it knows that God speaks through people, not just pastors.*

**2.** *Ask God for a change in the people.* Changing people is more important than changing things because if you change things and God doesn't change people, those people will change the things back the way they once were. Problem-oriented people cannot become objective-oriented people unless they change. And problem-oriented people can never produce an objective-oriented ministry. Bruce Powers relates changing people and decentralized decision-making.

90

It is the role of leaders therefore to sever gradually the dependency relationship that has been established. Through judicious use of reinforcement and training and gradual withdrawal from involvement in decision-making, leaders can assist followers in assuming responsibility for and deriving benefits from changes introduced. In effect, stabilization of change requires a withdrawal of the support system that has birthed the new life. That which is left is a part of the ongoing system, perhaps not even belonging to those whom have first envisioned it. The greatest compliment for the life-giving introducer of change comes after the dependency relationship is severed, when the people say, "Look what we did."[4]

**3.** *Eliminate timidity throughout the organization.* This correlates with the third question. If we really have room for the free thinker, the one who is out of step with the popular wisdom of the present leaders, then we need to let him and others know that we want his voice to be heard. Such two-way communication encourages subordinates to speak to leaders, assuming the willingness of leaders to listen.

**4.** *Program both administration and meetings for goal achievement.* The key here is the agenda. If we prepackage the agenda with numerous front-loaded problem issues we have arranged a problem-oriented meeting. Then, two or three hours after struggling with all the horrible problems the church faces, we make our way to discussions of future planning and goal achievement. By then everyone is tired, anxious to go home, and that portion of the agenda gets brushed over very lightly. We have affirmed that we really want to give priority attention to problems and if we still have some spare time for objectives, that's fine.

I am suggesting the reverse of that. Front-load the agenda with specific goal/planning items and take the problems in the appropriate time. The available business meeting time could also be divided so that at a certain hour the group stops talking about one and gives its attention to the other.

HOW CAN WE APPLY MBO PRINCIPLES TO MINISTRY?
Many Christian leaders have told me of their hesitancy to apply management-by-objective principles to the church. Yet we have no problem with management, and we certainly should have no problem with objectives. Putting them together means that we begin to think about our ministry in terms of its overall purposes, objectives,

and goals. As I hinted earlier, the concept of "ministry-by-objectives" may be more palatable. Definition and principles of MBO are very simple—the application takes a great deal of work.

> MBO is the philosophy and process of managing based on identifying purpose, objectives, and desired results; establishing a realistic program for obtaining these results; and evaluating performance and achieving them.[5]

Can we identify specific steps that a church or other Christian organization can take to conform with this ministry-by-objectives approach? Indeed we can, and they all relate to an understanding and mutual agreement of goals and objectives on the part of everyone in the organization, especially the leadership team. Pastors, for example, can take ten specific steps toward employing a ministry-by-objectives pattern in the church.

1. *Define the church's purpose and mission.* Who are you? Why are you there? What does God expect of you?

2. *Realistically assess the church's strengths and weaknesses.* What about location? Denominational affiliation? Lay leadership? Pulpit ministry? How do these advance or detract from goal achievement?

3. *Write specific and measurable objectives for the church's key ministry areas which spring from its purpose.* Involve as many people as you can in the writing, soliciting opinions from leaders and followers alike.

4. *Work to obtain a general agreement on your objectives.* We've not yet reached long-range planning, so the objectives might just cover one year of ministry (though five would be better). In the last step we asked people as *individuals* to contribute their views of where the church ought to go. Now we're talking to the body as a *group* attempting to refine our objectives to arrive at a plan which really represents the body's "call."

5. *Strive to attain job control as quickly as possible.* In a major leadership post, that may take a year or more.

6. *Develop strategies on how to use available resources to meet your objectives.* Resources include such things as money, buildings, time, equipment, and yes, even people.

7. *Determine to practice accountability.* Goals must be claimed by people. Every member needs to see where he fits and how he relates to the total picture.

**8.** *Design long- and short-range plans to meet objectives.* We'll have more to say about this later, so here we'll just review the axiom that *a goal needs a plan to make it work.*

**9.** *Be willing to change or modify objectives, plans, or strategies as the situational variables may require.* If one of your objectives calls for hiring a minister of Christian education within three years, and for some reason that occurs in the first year, you will probably need a modification of all plans related to Christian education. On the negative side, if certain objectives were keyed to the receipt of financial contributions which did not appear, restructuring might be required.

**10.** *Measure progress all along the way.* A good leadership team evaluates itself and builds in a system for monitoring progress through formal reviews, mutual accountability, and examination of achievement levels.

## FOUR STAGES IN THE PROCESS OF GOAL-SETTING

Up to this point I have been using the terms "objectives" and "goals" synonymously. They can also be confused with the word "purpose" because in casual conversation we hardly make any distinction among these three words. Now we must alter our thinking. In administrative process, the words are not the same.

Any organization serious about setting and achieving goals will give itself to a careful sorting out of four steps or levels in that process. They look like this, and Figure 8 gives you a visual idea of how they relate to one another.

FIGURE 8

# FOUR STAGES OF GOAL-SETTING

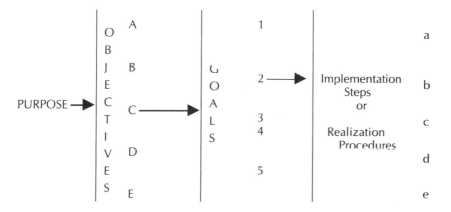

## PURPOSE/MISSION STATEMENTS

The traditional word "purpose" is now being replaced by the term "mission statement." For example, in these days of financial retrenchment, Christian colleges are rethinking their "mission statements." What are these schools intended to do? How do they differ from other colleges? In what way or ways are they unique? A purpose (mission statement) is not usually measurable but it describes the general direction of the organization using phrases like "fulfilling the Great Commission in our community," or "bringing glory to God." A mission statement should be tightly packaged in one or two paragraphs, accurately describing the ministry over which it flies like a flag on a castle. Consider this sample mission statement for a small independent church pastored by a friend of mine.

> The purpose of Chapel in the Woods Bible Church is to glorify God through ministering primarily to people in Southern Dallas County by: (a) evangelizing the lost, (b) discipling the saved.
>
> It is the Chapel's purpose to glorify God through Christ's Great Commission as given in the Gospels. This Commission involves leading lost people to a saving knowledge of Christ and leading saved people to spiritual maturity through worship, prayer, instruction, and fellowship.

You can see how almost any evangelical church could subscribe to those two paragraphs; mission statements are notably broad based.

## OBJECTIVES

While the mission statement has a somewhat singular focus, objectives must be multiply focused. Specificity begins to build as we now spell out precisely what it will take to achieve the purpose of the organization. For example, a church (maybe even Grace Church) could write objectives which might look something like this:

1. To increase the accuracy and efficiency of reports about the church's financial status.

2. To decrease the amount of time spent discussing financial matters in board meetings.

3. To renew our commitment to the teaching of stewardship in Sunday School.

4. To provide for revision of and greater adherence to the yearly budget.

Even though the mission statement might not have said anything about finances, such resources are obviously necessary to do the kind of things any church purposes to do. Therefore, financial objectives must be spelled out. Similar objectives could be written in other areas common to all churches, such as, attendance, Christian education, evangelism, fellowship, leadership development, missions, and membership, to name just a few. School or college objectives would deal with issues, such as, new academic programs, improving the quality of instruction, increasing the enrollment in certain grades or majors, etc.

The value of setting objectives for any organization lies in the process of moving from general to specific concepts. Goals become the avenue by which we reach the point of meeting needs.

Look again at the objectives for some financial changes which need to take place in order for the general mission statement to be accomplished. Folks on the Finance Committee of Grace Church now have a clear understanding of their task. In the future they should be more careful about record-keeping, obtaining accurate information for important business meetings, and keeping the congregation informed. Individual ministry heads should make every effort to stay within the budget and the Christian Education Committee may discuss the need for some kind of class or learning experience on Christian stewardship.

## GOALS

Get ready for even more specific thinking (as Fig. 9 shows). Just as a single mission statement has multiple objectives, each objective has multiple goals. It seems futile just to say that goals differ from objectives by being more specific, so let's look at an example. Under the general category of leadership development, a church I recently pastored developed an objective which read, "To recruit and train new leaders for boards and committees." How might that be broken down more specifically into multiple goals? We wrote them like this:

1. Through elevating the privilege of serving the Lord in leadership.

2. Through service activities as assistants and committee members.

Not very sophisticated you say? To be sure—it was this church's first attempt at a five-year plan with specifically developed levels of objectives. But do you agree that the goals serve the objective and that the objective stays in line with what most evangelical churches would want to achieve? Planners work hard to keep from staying general too long (so that goals still sound like mission statements) and to keep from getting specific too soon (so that objectives look like realization procedures). So let's add this fourth component and get the full picture.

*REALIZATION PROCEDURES (IMPLEMENTATION STEPS)* Now we have moved to describing actual activities carried out to achieve the goals. No longer should we use words like "to" and "through" but rather statements which can be evaluated by simple yes or no responses. Think about the area of leadership development. We can identify an objective which says we will seek "to increase the spiritual quality and practical effectiveness of all our church leaders, both pastoral and lay staff." One of the goals for that objective might read, "Through planning and carrying out effective monthly meetings of the governing board." Here are the implementation steps for that goal:

1. We will meet monthly with an agenda prepared in advance.

2. We will concentrate on planning and progress rather than problems.

3. We will distribute, read, and act on minutes within one week after the meeting.

Notice how we could answer yes to all of those items. Did we meet monthly during the past year? Was the agenda prepared in advance? Did we concentrate on planning rather than problems? Did we distribute and act on the minutes within one week after the meeting? Evaluation only becomes possible when we get down to the level of realization procedures. *It is impossible to evaluate mission statements.* They are so subjective and elusive that different opinions will measure them in multiple ways.

So far I have shown you pieces and patches of the four stages in the process of goal-setting. Figure 9, however, puts them all together (notice, however, there is only *one* objective and in the broad plan, objectives would be multiple). I use this one with my students since every seminary student could generally agree with the purpose and has chosen seminary studies precisely to achieve the stated objective. Remember Figure 9 represents only one general area in a life-planning format. This would be repeated in multiple pages with multiple objectives seeking to bring about that single general purpose.

Essential to everything we have said about setting and achieving goals is the issue of *accountability*. In an organization, goals cannot be set and achieved by one person or even by a small leadership

FIGURE 9

# PLANNING YOUR LIFE

**Purpose:**     To be as effective as possible in Christian life and ministry

**Objective:**     To be an intelligent, widely read, alert Christian leader

GOAL 1:     To be constantly well-informed on contemporary theological issues

*Realization Procedures:*

A. I read *CT* fortnightly
B. I read one theological quarterly
C. I read at least one theological book per month

GOAL 2:     To be constantly informed on current events

A. I read *Time* every week
B. I analyze newscasts in biblical perspectives
C. I attempt to relate current events to my preaching/teaching

GOAL 3:     To specialize my knowledge in the Synoptic Gospels

A. I read through the Synoptics every month
B. I purchase one new commentary on the Synoptics each month
C. I am building an organized file

task force. Yes, the vision needs to originate somewhere and the initiative for carrying out the planning process may indeed come from the pastor or a small group of staff leaders. But ultimately we must develop accountability throughout the organization.

In the Pastoral Epistles Paul calls Timothy and Titus to *be* accountable to their people and to *hold* their people accountable. Accountability demands mutual commitment which does not attach itself automatically to offices in the church. Sometimes accountability lags because people don't understand what we're trying to do. Nothing in this chapter is "operational" unless people make it work.

The *Christian Leadership Letter* offers an excellent issue on accountability in which its authors claim:

If your church or Christian organization does not have clear, concise, measurable goals, you will have a great deal of difficulty placing or accepting accountability. *Accountability assumes an ability to measure.* If there are no goals, there is nothing against which to measure progress. . . . The function of leadership is to lead. Leadership needs to lay out broad purposes and directions. But effective leadership will bring in as many people as possible to refine purposes into goals and work out ways not only to meet those goals, but to measure progress (to be held accountable) along the way.[6]

Implementation of this chapter on setting and achieving goals could revolutionize your church or ministry. How eloquently Paul put it when he wrote, "Brothers, I do not consider myself yet to have taken hold of it. But one thing I do: Forgetting what is behind and straining toward what is ahead, I press on toward the goal to win the prize for which God has called me heavenward in Christ Jesus. All of us who are mature should take such a view of things" (Phil. 3:13-15).

# STUDY QUESTIONS

**1.** Write five clear and specific goals for your present ministry. For purposes of simplicity, limit them to one year.

**2.** Review and list here all the administrative "axioms" of the chapter, most of which appear in italics. Do you understand each one? Can you apply it in your ministry? Can you rephrase it in your own words?

**3.** Identify one specific project or area of ministry in your organization (e.g., a family life seminar planned for six–eight months from now). Write a single purpose for the event or ministry, several objectives, several goals for *one* of the objectives, and several implementation steps for *one* of the goals. This exercise is to help you understand the difference.

**4.** Name some specific ways we can develop mutual accountability in the church and Christian organizations.

**5.** Review the mission statement of your ministry. Consider any need for revision or refinement. If there is none (or if you can't locate it) write one in accordance with the guidelines found in this chapter.

# ENDNOTES

**1.** Ted W. Engstrom and Edward R. Dayton, *60-Second Management Guide* (Waco, Texas: Word Books, 1984), p. 32.

**2.** Kenneth O. Gangel, *Building Leaders for Church Education* (Chicago: Moody Press, 1981) in which chapter 1 deals with "The Nature of the Church."

**3.** Gangel, chapter 1.

**4.** Bruce Powers, *Christian Leadership* (Nashville, Tenn.: Broadman Press, 1979), p. 57.

**5.** "MBO: Blue Collar to Top Executive," Bureau of National Affairs, 1231 25th St., NW, Washington, D.C. 20037

**6.** Engstrom and Dayton, "Let's Be Accountable," *Christian Leadership Letter* (December 1973), p. 2.

CHAPTER 6

# SHORT- AND LONG-RANGE PLANNING

One would be incorrect to say that Pastor Petroff never plans. Every year he and his wife "plan" a family vacation, and some years (like the time they went to Hawaii) the trip requires careful and detailed planning. They have also been "planning" financially so their children can go to college in a few years, and two years ago, he convinced the church board to sell the parsonage so he could purchase his own home. In that instance he "planned" his arguments to the board, the specific home they would purchase, the date they would move, and how this change would affect his family. At the church he has "planned" an annual missionary conference and twice been involved with the "planning" of interchurch activities in his community.

Somehow, though, none of this has translated into any long-range planning for the church. Specific projects, yes. Major events and socials, sure. But a long-range plan describing where Grace Church will go for the next five years? Not a thought.

Nor have any of his lay leaders taken the initiative in planning. This should perplex us even more since some of them are engaged in heavy-duty planning projects for the companies which employ them. To apply those same practices to the church, however, seems to most of them to be a secular imposition, an intrusion into the freedom of the Holy Spirit. They pray, they dream, and to some extent both pastors and lay leaders have a "vision" for what Grace Church ought to be. But up to this point, it all looks like a big painting on the back of their minds and doubtless a different picture in each mind.

100

In this chapter we will talk about *short-range planning as being anything up to a year and long-range planning any time period beyond that.* As I noted in chapter 1, most churches need to start with a one-year plan, work up to multiple years, and eventually work on at least a five-year plan subject to revisions on an annual basis. Other Christian organizations, particularly schools, colleges, and missions, need to be planning ten and even fifteen years ahead. Many of our failures, particularly failures in achieving goals, are due to either poor planning or a total lack of planning. Where do we commonly go wrong?

1. Often our objectives never get cleared up; they remain unrelated to a quality mission statement and, therefore, unable to give birth to legitimate goals.

2. Sometimes planning fails because we don't involve people. Even if the pastor and board carry out the planning function, actual realization of the goals must involve a much wider group of people. Engstrom and Dayton write:

> What many organizations do not realize is that planning can be a very useful way of involving many people in considerable depth. The act of asking individuals or groups to consider alternate or optimum ways of reaching their goals, or the act of asking them to propose specific goals against the higher purpose of the organization can be the trigger for a series of events. It cannot only give people the feeling of having participated in the organization, but can stimulate a host of new ideas. [1]

3. Effective planning depends on identification of legitimate resources. When we think only about finances (and many churches limit their planning to this dimension), we cripple the planning process—all resources essential for goal achievement must be spelled out.

4. Just as planning can fail because of poor objectives, it can fail because of poor goals. *Goals must be specific, measurable, and realistic.* Even then not all planning succeeds, but at least we give it a chance.

5. Planning sometimes fails because the planning group either did not understand the mission, objectives, goals, and implementation steps of the organization, or, if charged with creating these, did not understand the process of goal-setting (see chap. 5). Such a group

will often build into the plan projects or ideas which do not relate to the objectives of the ministry.

6. Since planning is based on evaluation, the process requires a clear-cut assessment of the previous year (or years). Fuzzy evaluation leads to fuzzy planning, causing future fuzziness in evaluation, and on it goes—*planning and evaluation form an inseparable cycle.*

# FOUNDATIONS FOR EFFECTIVE PLANNING

In this chapter we need to discuss how to actually design a plan. Toward the end, I'll treat the question of whether planning denies faith and represents unbiblical activity. But from what I've already said you can see the question will be somewhat rhetorical. The models of Joseph in famine relief; Moses in desert survival; David in military strategies; Solomon in massive building projects; and Paul in missionary itinerating should lay to rest any suspicion that long-range planning is unbiblical. Before we get into process, however, let's talk about principles one more time.

## PRINCIPLES OF THE PLANNING PROCESS

1. *Planning is an investment, not an expenditure of time.* The housewife who writes out a list of tasks to be accomplished on a morning outing in town does not *spend* time by prioritizing those tasks in relation to geography, opening and closing times of certain businesses, and the urgency with which they must be achieved. A fifteen-minute *investment* in such analysis might pay off three- or fourfold on the trip itself.

2. *Planning requires careful attention to immediate choices because immediate choices greatly expand or narrow future options.* The college student who plans to be a doctor better pay attention to undergraduate premedical preparation. Selection of a major in sociology or English literature will not move him toward medical school.

3. *Planning is cyclically based on evaluation (as we noted in the introduction to this chapter).*

4. *Planning demands acting objectively toward goal realization.* Remember our axiom? A goal needs a plan to make it work. Likewise, *a plan needs clear-cut objectives and goals to give it any reality or meaning.* Only when those objectives and goals are *owned* and acted on does planning become a process rather than a blueprint.

5. *Planning helps us note the relationship between determining what we want to do and realizing that end.* To put it another way, a direct and strategic ratio exists between the planning of an event and its occurrence. Let's go back to our college student and this

time let him choose that major in English literature. He'll never graduate in that or any other major unless he follows the prescribed plan the department has laid down to fulfill requirements for the degree. Playing smorgasbord with the curriculum for four years might produce some exciting learning experiences, but not a diploma.

**6.** *In planning, specificity increases as the event draws near.* Even in short-range (up to one year) planning (sometimes called project planning) we can see this principle at work. A Sunday School teacher training retreat slated for next August may be talked about in general terms in September, but needs to take on very specific form as we head into the late summer of next year.

**7.** *Planning requires maximum participation.* We have emphasized this repeatedly throughout the last two chapters.

**8.** *Planning demands that the effort applied be commensurate with the results desired.* The more careful the planning, the more likely the results (goal achievement). The more careless the planning, the less likely that those dreams and visions will translate into goals and actually come to pass.

## EVALUATION AND ANALYSIS IN PLANNING

When a representative or consultant from Church Data Services visits a church and employs that organization's "Church Development Survey," he analyzes a number of areas: demographic data, spiritual demography, Christian education profile, church effectiveness, family evaluation, individual problems, and Sunday School. He wants to find out where the church's strengths and weaknesses lie. Why do people attend the church and why do they leave? What are the areas in which the congregation needs help but perhaps would not ask for it openly? What causes most problems among the families? These are evaluative questions dealing with an analysis of what is and has been. We want to know what we did, how we did it, and eventually how we could have done it better.

Analysis is twofold: looking in the mirror and looking out the window. The more data we collect, assuming they are accurate, the better the planning process. Sometimes the evaluation stage is painful as we dig up things we would just as soon forget.

That's why planning becomes more difficult in a new church or one in which poor records have been kept. The shaky data base reduces the analysis and evaluation to guesswork. Even then, however, we must gather all the information we can, using the best possible tools.[2]

103

## ASSUMPTIONS IN THE PLANNING PROCESS

After gathering all the data we can, internally and externally, we make some "assumptions" regarding what will happen in future years. Don't miss the important distinction between analysis and assumption. The former deals with the past and the latter with the future. *Such "forecasting" builds a scenario of future trends on an extrapolation of the past.* Assumptions are constructed on the basis of analysis and interpretation of what appear to be valid trends.

The planning which follows the forecasting must initially focus on analysis of mission, clearly defining the role which the church or institution plays in its current setting. As we look out the window (external analysis), we want to be able to say something intelligent about the economic environment of our ministry, the demographic environment (demography has to do with population shifts numerically, geographically, and in other ways), certainly the moral/religious environment, and possibly the political and educational arenas.

The assumption then becomes a pivot point in the planning process. On the one hand, we look back and review our evaluation to make sure that our assumptions have been correctly drawn from an accurate analysis. Then looking toward the future, we build our objectives, goals, and realization procedures on the basis of our assumptions.

Warning! Many organizations fail right at this point. They carry out effective evaluation, write valid assumptions, and then go on to develop goals which are unrelated to what they know about the past and the future. We must always be thinking, "Since we have assumed that such-and-such will take place, Grace Church should. . . ."

Still foggy about what an assumption looks like? Here are some examples drawn from a fifteen-year planning project I worked on a few years ago.

American households in the $25,000–$50,000 income bracket will increase from the present 17 percent of the total to 25 percent by 1990 (economic).

By 1990 the over-65 age-group will surpass 31 million while the teenage population drops to 23 million (demographic).

Anti-American terrorism will increase and the unpopularity of the West in the United Nations and throughout the Third World will worsen (political).

Scandalous moral problems, such as, homosexuality, drug abuse, child abuse, divorce, premarital sex, and alcoholism are already out of control and will reach national epidemic proportions within this century (moral).

The balance of students in public and private colleges which favored private institutions by an 80 percent to 20 percent ratio in 1900 reversed those figures by 1980 and will drop to a 10-90 balance by 1990 (educational).

Not all of the above will relate to every local church but they offer samples of the kinds of information you want to plug into your assumption list. Obviously this kind of information does not come from a single source but can be located with minimal research and is often available in condensed form throughout the popular literature.[3]

## FIGURE 10

# GRAY'S VISIONARY PLANNING BOX

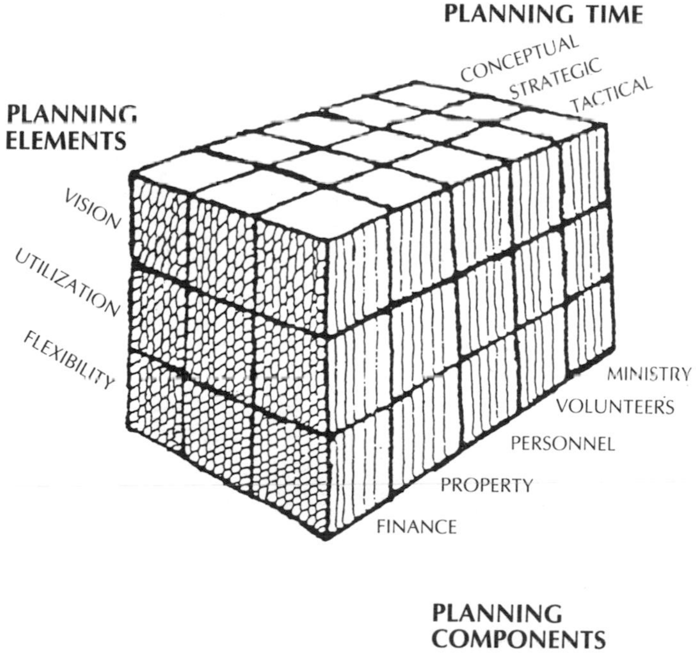

**PLANNING TIME**

CONCEPTUAL
STRATEGIC
TACTICAL

**PLANNING
ELEMENTS**

VISION
UTILIZATION
FLEXIBILITY

MINISTRY
VOLUNTEERS
PERSONNEL
PROPERTY
FINANCE

**PLANNING
COMPONENTS**

## FIGURE 11

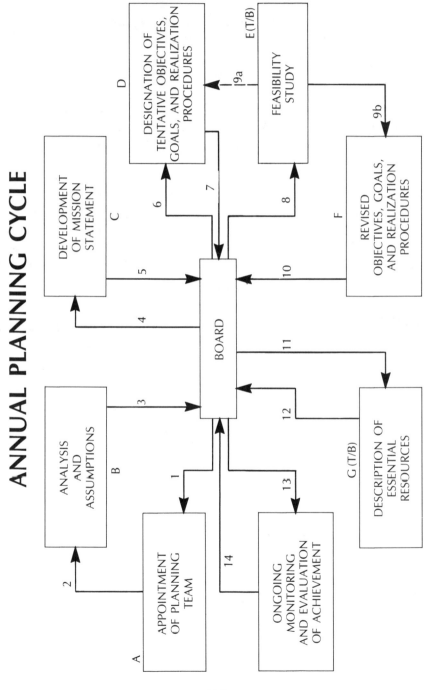

ANNUAL PLANNING CYCLE

# TOOLS FOR EFFECTIVE PLANNING

An assistant pastor in charge of adult ministries is planning a retreat for singles. Some of the tools he must use in that planning process include time, people, equipment, and location. In a very real sense, all planning starts with time. Time is required to visualize what we want to accomplish on the retreat; to decide on the location and the date; to consider the program costs and other activities.

A wise leader recognizes he cannot carry out all these plans himself, so he turns to his next tool—people. Some type of committee or task force will be needed to carry out the activities, supply the equipment, see that food is prepared and served, plan and oversee the program, and deal with both finances and publicity for the retreat.

Communication represents yet another tool for successful realization of goals. In our present illustration, the assistant pastor more than likely supervises the activities of the committee either as chair or consultant. Communication enters the process right from the beginning as he explains to the committee why this retreat is important, as he listens to their input on every phase of the program, and then as he and the committee together present the idea to the people it is designed to serve.

Obviously the kinds of literature we have already talked about represent tools, but now we want to look at some planning models which actually direct us through the procedure of planning. These are better visualized than discussed, so let me offer two with minimal explanation.

The first model is called by its designer "Gray's Visionary Planning Box." The model (Fig. 10) includes the three dimensions of "planning components, planning time, and planning elements." I'll let the author explain the only difficult dimension in the box, the time factor, which connects the "plan-as-vision" with the "plan-as-reality."

A most helpful tool is the implementation of continuum of time. *Tactical plans*, those that are the most immediate carry detailed procedures for their actualization within three months. *Strategic plans* (three months to eighteen months) are still in the skeletal stage, but are firmly entrenched within the organizational mechanism and will continually gain substance as implementation nears. *Conceptual plans* (eighteen months to infinity) may be only reasonably tangible objectives, with little structure. They offer direction for the church by being the fence posts toward which to plow.[4]

Another model tracks the process flow of planning group activities from their initial appointment to evaluation of the plan. This works better in a one-year planning cycle than a long-range plan.

The only thing confusing about the annual planning cycle (Fig. 11) is the number of arrows. They indicate actions by the board to appoint or approve some decision or recommendation of the planning team. Sometimes feasibility studies link with description of essential resources but I have divided them on the assumption that the board might negate certain objectives, goals, or realization procedures even apart from the cost of resources. This builds in a two-level control and forces a revision of objectives, goals, and realization procedures. Let's review the fourteen arrows by number.

1. The board appoints the planning team.

2. The planning team designs analysis and assumptions.

3. The planning team reports to the board.

4. The board approves analysis and assumptions.

5. The team presents the board with a mission statement.

6. The board approves the mission statement.

7. The team presents the board a document of tentative objectives, goals, and realization procedures.

8. The board approves in general and orders a feasibility study.

9a. Feasibility study demonstrates that the original document must be reworked.

9b. Feasibility study indicates that the original document is sound and the process can proceed.

10. The planning team presents the board-revised objectives, goals, and realization procedures.

11. The board approves the revised document and authorizes a description of essential resources.

12. The team adds resource needs to the original document.

13. The board approves and all systems are go.

14. The team carries out ongoing monitoring and evaluation of achievement. (Note that both steps E and G are mutual exercises of the team and the board.)

## PROGRAM EVALUATION AND REVIEW TECHNIQUE (PERT)

All the previous models lend themselves more to short-range planning than long-range. True, any one of them could be extended over a longer period of time, but the premiere long-range planning model is PERT, the design by which the Polaris submarine program was developed. This relates closely to the critical path method (CPM) used by the DuPont Corporation.

Both techniques involve identifying the jobs needed to complete a project, developing estimates of the time needed to complete each job, and determining the right sequence of the individual jobs. In particular, it is important to determine which jobs must precede, must follow, or can be done at the same time as other jobs in the sequence. PERT/CPM techniques involve creating a format called a *network diagram*, which shows the order and time estimates for jobs in a project. PERT/CPM techniques make it easier both to identify the critical jobs in a project and to manage a project effectively when resources are scarce.[5]

The concept of critical path describes the sequence of jobs which must be performed before any project can be completed. It represents the longest path in time (the shortest time in which the project can be finished) and it contains the critical control points for the project. All the critical jobs lie along the critical path and are considered "critical" because any delay will hinder the completion of the project. PERT forces us to consider all the ingredients (and relationships between ingredients) in the planning project. One could consider it a special kind of flow chart which displays events, sequences, and time frames in a systematic manner to demonstrate the necessary flow from start to finish.

In the sample PERT chart (Fig. 12), the circles represent events and the numbers within the circles simply label them (they are not time references). Arrows represent the flow of activities and tasks and connect the sequences. The top triangle of the diamond describes the work of the long-range planning team and the bottom triangle (shown by a dotted line) represents the response of the governing body, such as, the official board. At first it looks complicated, but careful study of both the chart and its explanatory detail can launch you on a similar PERT project, a procedure many have found extremely helpful in long-range planning.

## PROPER ALLOCATION OF THINKING TIME

The task of feeding and leading requires time to think. Its purpose stands among the major tasks of chief executive officers; the projec-

FIGURE 12

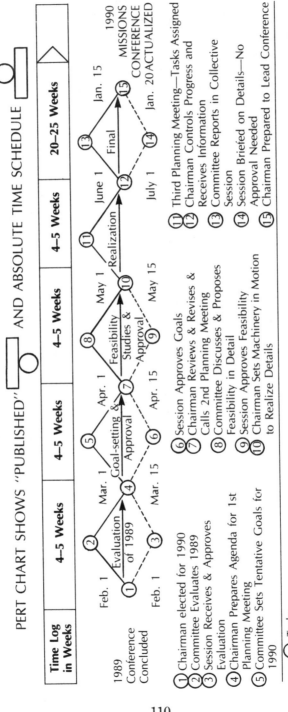

**PERT = Program Evaluation and Review Technique**

**Task = Local Church Missionary Conference:  Target = January 28-31, 1990**

PERT CHART SHOWS "PUBLISHED" AND ABSOLUTE TIME SCHEDULE

| Time Log in Weeks | 4–5 Weeks | 4–5 Weeks | 4–5 Weeks | 4–5 Weeks | 20–25 Weeks |
|---|---|---|---|---|---|

① Chairman elected for 1990
② Committee Evaluates 1989
③ Session Receives & Approves Evaluation
④ Chairman Prepares Agenda for 1st Planning Meeting
⑤ Committee Sets Tentative Goals for 1990
⑥ Session Approves Goals
⑦ Chairman Reviews & Revises & Calls 2nd Planning Meeting
⑧ Committee Discusses & Proposes Feasibility in Detail
⑨ Session Approves Feasibility
⑩ Chairman Sets Machinery in Motion to Realize Details
⑪ Third Planning Meeting—Tasks Assigned
⑫ Chairman Controls Progress and Receives Information
⑬ Committee Reports in Collective Session
⑭ Session Briefed on Details—No Approval Needed
⑮ Chairman Prepared to Lead Conference

◯ Tasks
——► = Main Planning Network Led by Missions Committee Chairman
◇ = Main Planning Group—Missions Committee
〈〉 = Correction/Balance Planning Group—Session

110

tion of thinking time beyond the immediate is essential. The chart and percentages in Figure 13 have been reproduced exactly as they appeared in a business magazine article thirty years ago.[6] I have changed the designations on the left to conform to church, Christian school, college, and mission board positions rather than those in business and industry. The figures may seem a bit idealistic but the principle is sound: *The higher your position in the organizational chart, the more long-range must be your thinking.* To put it another way, if the pastor and assistant pastor (president and vice president) do not think five to ten years ahead, nobody will.

We can only activate Figure 13 thinking when we learn to avoid overcommitment. We've already talked about establishing priorities which requires asking about the importance of each task in relation to the long-range objectives of your life and ministry. Again, we find help in the ever-practical *Christian Leadership Letter.*

One helpful approach to time management is to think about each of your commitments as a project in itself. For example, if you are committed to a meeting in another part of town or in another city, make a list of all the things that are going to take your time in order to meet that obligation. Think about the extra phone calls that you will have to make in order to make arrangements. Think about your own preparation. Note down travel times. (Allow enough time to get lost!) After you've done this, lay out the preparation times in your appointment book. If your best estimate is that it's going to take you three hours to prepare a presentation, schedule a specific time when you're going to work on that.

Schedule *all* of your time. By this we don't mean that you should be busy every minute. Rather, we would suggest that if you block out a time for all the parts of life, including recreation, family time, vacation time, work time, and so forth, you will keep yourself from double scheduling your time.[7]

## COMMON QUESTIONS ABOUT
## EFFECTIVE PLANNING
### SHOULD CHRISTIANS PLAN LONG-RANGE?
As we've already seen, God's leaders throughout history have done so with His apparent blessing. Sometimes theology (particularly eschatology) gets in the way, but only because we think "wrongly."

111

FIGURE 13

# PLANNING REQUIRES AN APPORTIONING OF THINKING TIME

| POSITION | TODAY | 1 WEEK | 1 MONTH | 3–6 MONTHS | 1 YEAR | 2 YEARS | 3–4 YEARS | 5–10 YEARS |
|---|---|---|---|---|---|---|---|---|
| President (Pastor) | 1% | 2% | 5% | 17% | 15% | 25% | 30% | 5% |
| Vice President (DCE) | 2% | 4% | 10% | 29% | 20% | 20% | 13% | 2% |
| Works Manager (S.S. Supt.) | 4% | 8% | 15% | 38% | 20% | 10% | 5% | |
| Superintendent (Div. Supt.) | 6% | 10% | 20% | 43% | 10% | 9% | 2% | |
| Dept. Manager (Dept. Manager) | 10% | 10% | 25% | 39% | 10% | 5% | 1% | |
| Section Super. (Teacher) | 15% | 20% | 25% | 37% | 3% | | | |
| Group Super. (Teacher) | 38% | 40% | 15% | 5% | 2% | | | |

One can believe in the imminent return of Jesus Christ and yet recognize any kind of date-setting as unbiblical nonsense. Paul clearly taught this view, yet urged in all his letters that the churches develop "long-range Christians" whose spiritual lives would build toward maturity.

To the Galatians Paul wrote, "Let us not become weary in doing good, for at the proper time we will reap a harvest if we do not give up" (Gal. 6:9). The apostle spoke quite frequently of planting, watering, and reaping. There has never been a farmer who reaped a harvest without some kind of planning. The soil must be prepared at just the right time of the year, the seeds planted after the danger of frost has passed, and the young plants given water and warmth. The skillful mind and hands of the farmer must plan every phase from planting to harvest.

The analogy certainly applies to all phases of Christian ministry. Without proper planning for all phases of ministry, we cannot expect the kind of harvest God promises from the seed of His Word. Teachers who are adequately trained to plant, water, and reap can change a lackluster traditional Sunday School program into a dynamic Bible-teaching and evangelism center.

## ISN'T PLANNING A DENIAL OF FAITH?

On the contrary, that question betrays little understanding of biblical teaching on leadership. It strikes me as being similar to the question of why we should spend any time studying for preaching or teaching when the Holy Spirit is perfectly capable of giving us precisely what we should say as we stand up to speak. Without doubt; but the Scriptures emphasize that the Holy Spirit activates us in the study process as well as in the speaking process. The tone of the Pastoral Epistles urges Timothy and Titus to be students of God's Word so that by careful instruction they could bring to naught the words of false teachers.

Likewise, the role of faith and hope can be as active in the planning process as in the realization process. Meeks writes:

It is much more difficult for us to comprehend the reality and necessity of hope, and this is partly so because hope and planning look so much alike. Both hope and planning are in love with the *future* . . . they are unwilling to accept what exists as if it were eternal finality. Rather they are fascinated with the *possible*. . . . Thus hope looks not for the future which it can engender, make, or put at its disposal but rather for the future which God puts at its disposal. Hope expects the future which God promises.[8]

And again:

Planners and managers should serve the ordering and organization of the church for its life of liturgy and mission in the world. Planning presupposes the church commissioned to mission in hope. Planners who do not expect the presence and power of the Holy Spirit in the world will seek something other than God's righteousness as the source of life. Persons in the Spirit who do not plan for the conditions which serve God's righteousness forsake the Holy Spirit's fight against the demonic spirits of our society and world.[9]

## WHO SHOULD BE A PART OF THE PLANNING TEAM?
Good question. Not everybody in the church or Christian organization holds adequate qualifications to serve on the planning team. People who do not believe planning is biblical will hardly make good members. Negative, pessimistic people who constantly explain why things can't be achieved would only slow down the process. Legalistic types who feel bound by all traditions of the past feel uncomfortable and threatened struggling with the potential of the future.

Biblically, we can see a marvelous contrast in mind-set between the Pharisees and the early missionaries, particularly Paul. The former were landlocked in the past and determined to preserve it in the present. The latter were grateful for the past, dissatisfied with the present, and eager for what God had in the future.

But we need not be so subjective about this question. Judson Press has published a superb *Local Church Planning Manual*[10] which should certainly adorn the shelf of every pastor. It includes a questionnaire entitled, "Will You Need Assistance in This Planning Process?" which can be used by members of your planning team.

## WHY DO PLANS SOMETIMES FAIL?
Earlier we talked about how we fail at planning; now we're talking about why, after we have planned, those plans do not develop. Consider these problems expounded in a book by Jeffry Timmons under the heading "Why Plans Fail."

1. No real goals—a goal statement that does not describe an end state is not a goal.

2. No measurable objectives.
3. Failure to anticipate obstacles—actually a plan should be flexible enough to handle obstacles, whether anticipated or not.
4. Lack of progress review—these provide corrections in direction, pace, and reality.
5. Lack of commitment—the unwillingness to see a plan through to its completion.
6. Failure to revise objectives—this links up with number 3 and calls again for flexibility in the plan.
7. Failure to learn from experience—we need to listen to feedback and with every obstacle ask, "What did we learn this time?"[11]

We've noted earlier the experience of planning in the lives of Bible characters. Let's close the chapter by citing some helpful planning proverbs and a planning prayer.

Do not those who plot evil go astray? But those who plan what is good find love and faithfulness (Prov. 14:22).

Plans fail for lack of counsel, but with many advisers they succeed (Prov. 15:22).

Commit to the Lord whatever you do, and your plans will succeed (Prov. 16:3).

And for all those who read this chapter and share the tasks and burdens of planning, here is the prayer of David: "May He give you the desire of your heart and make all your plans succeed" (Ps. 20:4).

## STUDY QUESTIONS

**1.** Name three examples of short-range planning and three of long-range planning.

**2.** Explain the statement, "A plan needs clear-cut objectives and goals to give it any reality or meaning."

**3.** Explain the difference(s) between analysis and assumption in the planning process.

**4.** Evaluate the three models described in the chapter, understanding how to use at least one of them in your present ministry.

**5.** Consider any hesitation you might have regarding the doctrinal correctness of planning. Do you agree that it does not deny faith nor quench the Holy Spirit? Can you argue that case with others who do not agree?

# ENDNOTES

**1.** Ted W. Engstrom and Edward R. Dayton, "Planning As a Process," *Christian Leadership Letter* (May 1976), p. 2.

**2.** Good planning tools are becoming more available. Two good examples for the evaluation phase are the "Church Development Survey" conducted by Church Data Services (Denver Seminary, Dallas Seminary, and other affiliate institutions) and Fuller's "Community Analysis" (P.O. Box 989, Pasadena, CA 91102).

**3.** See periodicals such as *Emerging Trends* published by the Princeton Religious Research Center; books like Davis and Clapp, *The Third Wave and The Local Church* and Naisbitt's *Megatrends*; and occasional helpful articles in *Time, Newsweek, USA Today* and *U.S. News and World Report* (e.g., "10 Forces Reshaping America, *USNWR*, March 19, 1984).

**4.** Gary M. Gray, "A Long-Range Growth Plan," *Church Management—The Clergy Journal* (February 1987), pages 32–3.

**5.** Carl R. Anderson, *Management* (Dubuque, Iowa: Wm. C. Brown, 1984), p. 499.

**6.** "Company Planning Must Be Planned," *Business Month* magazine, (April 1957).

**7.** Engstrom and Dayton, "On Getting Overcommitted," *Christian Leadership Letter* (August 1982), p. 3.

**8.** M. Douglas Meeks, "Hope and the Ministry of Planning and Management," *Anglican Theological Review* (April 1982), pp. 153–54.

**9.** Meeks, p. 157.

**10.** Richard Rusbuldt, Richard Gladden, and Norman Green, *Local Church Planning Manual* (Valley Forge, Pa.: Judson Press, 1977), pp. 101–05.

**11.** Adapted by Rusbuldt, et al., p. 231 from *New Venture Creation* by Jeffry A. Timmons, Leonard E. Smollen, and Alexandria L. Dingle, Jr. (Homewood, Ill.: Richard D. Irvine, Inc., 1977), chap. 6.

CHAPTER 7

# Assessing Needs, Gifts, and Call

Just one year before I sat down to write this chapter, *Education Week* published an issue which contained an editorial by Albert Shanker, President of the American Federation of Teachers. Shanker dealt primarily with the Carnegie Report and the national debate on public education, but more specifically with what he called "a better use of human resources." Toward the end of his article he threatened:

> Our schools are about to experience a massive teacher shortage. We have to ask ourselves what sort of incentives we will have to offer to make enough of our better college graduates want to become teachers. . . . [We must] boldly reconstruct our schools to promote collegiality and liberate the best energies of our teachers. It's a lot better way of using our human resources.[1]

Shanker's article made me think of the church. We're facing a leadership shortage too—a real one. And we have at least partially created the crisis by an inadequate use of human resources. In fact, that's partly what this book is all about.

Long before we think about training and placement, even prior to the process of recruitment, we must grapple with what I have chosen to call assessment—*an analysis of the present situation with special focus on needs, gifts, and call.* Stratton Associates, an executive search consulting firm in California, advertises, "We help our client get clear about what he really needs instead of what he thinks he needs. We'll take the responsibility for giving you the best man. We will help you to identify needs within your organization." That's where lay leadership development starts.

In a very real sense, this chapter links inseparably with earlier discussions regarding a philosophy (theology) of ministry. In the spiritual framework of the body of Christ, God calls the biblical servant to minister to others, and he must effectively carry out that ministry in an attitude of Christlike perspective and the reality of spiritual power. In order to do so he needs help in understanding the *needs* which require the ministry, the *gifts* which respond to the ministry, and the *call* which places him in ministry. Certain qualifications and characteristics mark effective lay leaders. An effective lay leader must:

1. Be wholly dedicated to God's glory (Eph. 1).
2. Understand the principles and practice of God's grace (Acts 20:24).
3. Have a burden and concern for the entire body (1 Cor. 12; Eph. 4:11-16).
4. Stand firmly for reconciliation (2 Cor. 5:11-21).
5. Model godly living in his own family and the body (Phil. 3:17; 1 Thes. 2:9-10).
6. Lead in accordance with biblical principles (Luke 22:24-27).
7. Serve others willingly (1 Peter 4:10-11).
8. Endeavor to make disciples (Matt. 28:18-20).
9. Reproduce himself in new leadership (Acts 11:19-30).

Obviously all of these and more apply to professional staff but this is not a chapter about professional staff except as they bear responsibility for the development of lay leadership. James Garlow in his very helpful *Partners in Ministry* describes "Travis trainer-of-ministers."

Travis has been the pastor of our church for ten years now. He could call himself a minister—and he is. But he prefers to think of himself as a "trainer-of-ministers." He frequently tells us that we are not a group of 300 people with one minister. Rather we are a group of 300 ministers with one "enabler" or *pastoral* minister. Pastor Travis has helped all his parishioners to understand their gifts and how they can be involved in ministries. He also makes us aware of our service to God in our occupations. Funny thing . . . our church sure has been growing since Pastor Travis came.[2]

# EFFECTIVE LAY LEADERSHIP BEGINS WITH NEED ASSESSMENT

One of the surveys implemented by the Win Arn Church Growth Center uncovered "Ten Questions Most Often Asked by Church Leaders." They spotlight the importance of our subject in this chapter.

1. How can I see more members involved in sharing their Christian faith with others?

2. How can we help our present members to be more open to newcomers and make them feel a part of the fellowship?

3. How can we involve more members in the ministry of our church?

4. How can our new members find a place of belonging in their new church home?

5. How can we train a task force in developing a successful lay ministry program?

6. How can our evangelism program be more effective in reaching unchurched persons in our community?

7. How can we build a strategy in placing members in positions that enhance their spiritual gifts?

8. How can I help our members discover that evangelism does not mean tight collars, stomach butterflies, and sweaty palms?

9. How can we close our "back door" so the people who join our church don't become inactive in the first year?

10. How can we keep our church staff and lay leaders at the "cutting edge" of effective growth and ministry insights, and all pulling together toward the same common goals?[3]

At best we can respond to this vast area of need assessment by breaking it down into a broad-narrow focus for ministry which begins with the world and ends at a specific point of service.

## NEEDS OF THE WORLD

A discussion of lay leadership in the local church must treat the wider subject of volunteerism, a major issue of public concern in America today. President Reagan argued for eight years that the nation should pay less attention to government and more attention to volunteerism. Early in his first administration he told a story about a high tide and storm-generated surf in Newport Beach, California.

All through the day and cold winter night, volunteers worked filling and piling sandbags in an effort to save those homes. Local TV stations, aware of the drama of the situation, covered the struggle. It was about 2:00 A.M. when one newscaster grabbed a young fellow in his teens, attired only in wet trunks. He had been working all day and night—one of several hundred of his age-group. No, he did not live in one of the homes they were trying to save. He was cold and tired. The newscaster wanted to know why he and his friends were doing this. The answer was poignant, and so true it should be printed on a billboard. "Well," he said, "I guess it's the first time we ever felt like we were needed."[4]

Just a few years later a Gallup Poll showed that Americans are volunteering more than ever. Fifty-two percent of the population is involved in some voluntary action and 31 percent in organized, structured volunteerism on a regular basis. Interestingly, the largest percentage of volunteers serve in religious activities (19 percent).

We live in a needy world and the response of the church must be more than sandbagging floods and handing out food baskets. The fulfilling of the Great Commission in the broadest sense requires the enlistment of many volunteers on a level unprecedented since the first and second centuries of the life of the church. In the entire world there are just 60,000 missionaries from North America. But one Protestant denomination (Southern Baptist Convention) counts 100,000 of its members living overseas, each a potential lay witness, even in countries where missionaries are denied entry.

NEEDS OF THE NATION

At the end of the twentieth century, America reels like a drunken sailor staggered by multiple blows to the head. Consider just a few of the horrifying statistics.

There are about 2.22 million unmarried-couple households in the United States, up from 1.198 million last year.

Fourteen million children are living in poverty in the United States.

More than one half of the children in America now live with one parent.

The school dropout rate is 25 percent overall and 50 percent for blacks and Hispanics.

Thirteen million Americans have drinking problems, and for every person who suffers from alcoholism, another four people are directly affected.

An estimated 23,500 people are killed annually in alcohol-related traffic accidents and 700,000 more are injured.

In New York City the 1985 revenues from marriages were $779,420; for annulments and divorces, $3,690,750.

Nearly half a million births occur to young girls each year as well as 400,000 abortions and 134,000 miscarriages.

The body of Christ may be an unheeded voice crying in the midst of anarchy and chaos, but that voice must at least be heard. This chapter argues that it cannot be properly heard without a revival of lay leadership involvement.

## NEEDS OF THE COMMUNITY

Recently I ministered in a small rural church which is the only congregation in its community. The members all know each other apart from church activities; the children and young people all attend the same schools; and community life seems to be a seamless garment. Obviously this offers both opportunities and difficulties for that congregation; but it does establish a basis for identifying the uniqueness of ministry in that place. We talk a lot about leadership vision and the concept is sound. But the vision must inseparably relate to needs, and as far as that congregation is concerned, the needs of the community are strategic.

An assessment of community needs in a large urban congregation would be very different from a small church. But needs assessment must be made. As an educator I think constantly in terms of objectives and goals but I must remind myself that goals and objectives derive from a proper understanding of needs.

Part of that vision on the part of pastoral staff must be a commitment to the development of lay leadership and volunteerism. I like the way Menking deals with the issue of pastoral vision.

To be held responsible for the realization of this vision seems

121

unfair. It is easier for you to say, "The laity did not see," than to confess, "I did not enable them to see." There is no doubt you may resist this. You do not have control over other people's responses. Lay people are free to reject the vision. In your heart you know this does not relieve you of the responsibility to have, to share, and to work for a vision of ministry. This is the burden and the challenge of your labors as an institutional leader.

Visions take time to realize, and therefore require patience and persistence. For that reason these two questions always have to be asked:

How long will it take to translate this vision into a ministry?

Will I be here long enough to be the midwife for this vision?[5]

## NEEDS OF THE CHURCH

Too many pastors trap themselves into crisis management, rushing about week by week just trying to hold the place together a little while longer. Ministry opportunities deteriorate to frantic dilemmas as we practice *ex post facto* recruitment (desperately searching for someone after the vacancy is apparent). In large measure such activity reflects failure in long-range planning, goal-setting, and delegation.

Before we can *announce* needs we must be *aware* of needs—not only present but future. Self-evaluation questions help us in this kind of process.

1. What percentage of the church's total budget is allocated to education, missions, evangelism, worship, etc.?

2. How do we keep and use records?

3. Is there a properly designed organizational chart?

4. Do all ministry positions have job descriptions?

5. Is there provision for effective leadership training?

6. Do we have a strategic plan for reaching out and assimilating new members?

7. What is the process of decision-making in our church?

8. How are people appointed or elected to positions?

9. When was the last time we did a gift or talent search?

10. When was the last time we did a community or prospect survey?

11. How much do we understand about the various age-groups in our congregation, their needs, and what are we doing to meet these needs?

12. What opportunities do we anticipate in new ministries over the next three years?

One of the needs may be more professional staff. Failure to develop lay leadership may suggest that the pastor (assuming he is the only full-time staff member) gets so overloaded with general pastoral duties he has no time and perhaps no training to carry out this strategic ministry. It might be time for that church to bring a minister of Christian education on staff.

A minister of education is a person who has felt the call of God to focus on the education ministry of the church. The role of the minister of education is in the truest sense that of an enabler, or in terms of Ephesians 4:12, an equipper. This minister brings to the church knowledge of resources, expertise in administration, and personal gifts of ministry to help the church fulfill its mission. The minister of education does not replace the Sunday School director or any other program director but enhances the work of the entire force of volunteer leaders. The minister of education is a key person to help implement shared ministry.[5]

## NEEDS OF THE SPECIFIC MINISTRY

Dangerous as it may be for a local church lay leader to miss the forest because of the trees, he or she must also learn to focus with clarity on one particular tree. We have a tendency to spread volunteers so thin across the ministry that they are unable to achieve satisfactory effectiveness in any role. A Sunday School teacher, for example, needs to grasp precisely the needs and characteristics of the age-group he teaches. An elder or deacon needs in-depth analysis of biblical responsibility and ministerial accountability for those important roles.

To be sure, a great deal of this takes place in the training process and we will come to that later. Here it may be helpful for us to grasp some of the reasons why we have been ineffective in recruiting volunteers in the local church and, therefore, why those volunteers do not serve satisfactorily in ministry. Marlene Wilson suggests five areas of breakdown that can occur in recruiting volunteers.

Most volunteer ministry jobs in the church are not clearly defined; job descriptions are almost never written.

Tradition often squelches new and creative ideas and approaches.

Time and talent sheets have helped officially reject people's gifts every year.

Clergy and lay leaders alike are often very poor delegators.

The jobs to be filled often receive more attention than the people filling them.[7]

I'm particularly concerned about the last one. The author goes on to say, "Churches have lists of 'slots to fill' and often recruit more on the basis of 'taking turns' rather than sharing gifts." *Members of the pastoral staff, confident of their own gifts and call, must design a deliberate strategy to assist every believer in the congregation to discern, develop, and deploy his or her spiritual gifts in ministry.*

## EFFECTIVE LAY LEADERSHIP CENTERS IN SPIRITUAL GIFTS

No one is more aware than I that we venture at this point into a very controversial aspect of evangelical doctrine. My personal opinion is that just as the old time "holy rollers" frightened mainline evangelicals away from a solid emphasis on holiness, so modern charismatics have frightened us away from the biblical commitment to spiritual gifts. When we refocus the task of ministry away from the exercise of spiritual gifts in the power of the Holy Spirit by means of God's grace, we have forgotten our organismic base and function only as an organization. Walter Ungerer warns:

> Too many times, the pastor, as a shepherd of the flock, ignores the fact that we, the people of God, are enabled by the Spirit in order to carry out the tasks God has given the church. For a pastor or lay people to believe that such undertakings, whatever they might be, can be accomplished for any length of time without Spirit empowerment is to misunderstand what it means to be the body of Christ.[8]

### SPIRITUAL GIFTS CAN BE DISCERNED[9]

Pastors who want lay leadership to center in spiritual gifts must approach their preaching and teaching with the assumption that people can ascertain their own spiritual gifts. Christian ministry does not have to become a neurotic compulsion to duty, but rather joy. Serving Christ can proceed on the basis of what Les Flynn calls "the delight criterion."

> How wrong to assume that because we enjoy some particular service that ministry cannot be God's will for us. Or to deduce that because something is distasteful, it must be God's plan for us. Wouldn't God more likely assign us gifts the employment of which bring pleasure, not misery? Like Jesus, in doing the Father's will we should find delight, not drudgery. [10]

That gives rise to the first important question—what do you enjoy doing? The second helps us as well—what service has God been blessing? Do you see fruit from your teaching? Are people trusting Christ as a result of your evangelism? Help people in your congregation understand God's blessing on their ministry as an affirmation of spiritual gifts.

Still a third question might be worded this way: How have others encouraged you? God gives us parents, pastors, teachers, and friends to help us in making key decisions—and this is certainly a key decision. Churches should probably be taking more initiative to assist members in identifying spiritual gifts.

But the most important question asks, what has the Holy Spirit told you? The inner witness of the Spirit cannot be limited to confirming our salvation. He wants us to know our gifts and how to use them. Spiritual gifts can be discerned.

## SPIRITUAL GIFTS CAN BE DEVELOPED

A spiritual gift is not a full-blown power to perform. Once a believer recognizes his spiritual gift(s), development becomes the next step. Spiritual gifts serve the body of Christ, its upbuilding and its ministry. They are geared to the way we serve people. We teach people; we help people; we lead people. In the church we must recognize the mutuality of the body. A spiritual gift does not belong to its recipient; it is Christ's, and each of us becomes His steward (Rom. 12:3-8). Mark Senter warns against a modern malaise.

> A strange mind-set has infected the church in recent years related to the use of spiritual gifts. Instead of accepting gifts as a means to serve other Christians, many people in the local church have assumed a showcase mentality, placing their spiri-

125

tual gifts on display for other people to see, but they are not touched by them. There is much more talk about spiritual gifts in some churches than there is of using them for serving the body of Christ.

The object of spiritual gifts, to build up the body of Christ, was evident in the early church as it was built up in both numbers (quantity) and in spiritual maturity (quality). Today, the Holy Spirit is just as anxious to produce these same results in the local church through the ministries of Spirit-filled and gifted people.[11]

Philosophies of life and ministry are crucial here. Selection Research, Inc., of Lincoln, Nebraska has conducted extensive studies in an effort to identify specific leadership talents. Their findings identify "life themes."

Such life themes are formed early in one's personality pattern. Hence, persons come into administrative positions, into professional schools, and into religious congregations already formed. It is clear, therefore, those who choose persons for such leadership positions are shaping the character of their organization, determining the direction of the entire congregation and its future.[12]

## SPIRITUAL GIFTS CAN BE DEPLOYED

Our leadership studies first treat the role of the pastor, particularly an understanding of his administrative functions. Only when that issue has been clarified, when professional staff members in the church are confident and effective in their leadership roles, only then can lay leadership development be realized. The deploying of spiritual gifts depends not only on their being discerned and developed, but also on the entire leadership climate in which a layman finds himself. Once again Menking is helpful.

The biblical theological consensus about the ministry of laity serving others has not completely permeated the consciousness of the laity. Many lay people feel they lack a call, training, and authority. They help others, but this is not viewed as ministry. Some laity believe the pastor is paid to do this. Where ministry is still perceived as what a pastor does, it is a challenge to share the ministry dimension of helping others.[13]

But here we face a problem. When spiritually gifted laymen are recruited, trained, and enlisted, the deployment of their spiritual gifts often threatens the pastoral staff. What happens then offers a sad indictment on the contemporary church—pastors unwilling to share the ministry. Listen again to Menking.

When you decide to help laity help others, the first thing you realize is that this decision requires you to prepare yourself before you can help the laity. There are, of course, costs and benefits. The primary cost will be time—in this case, time to prepare to guide the laity into a lay service ministry. No promise can be made that deciding to help laity help others will mean you will always have less to do. It may mean that what you do is different. On the benefit side there is the possibility that more will be done for others and laity will have a significant and meaningful way to exercise their faith commitment. When that happens, you will feel good about your ministry.[14]

When that happens, you will be functioning as a biblical leader.

## EFFECTIVE LAY LEADERSHIP REQUIRES CLARITY OF CALL

The whole issue of "call" has been a battleground since the publication of *Decision-Making and the Will of God.* In that significant book Gary Friesen argues for less attention to specific calls and more attention to general service according to biblical principles and common sense.[15] I have no taste here to argue either case or even to enter the discussion. Let us assume that in some way, at some time, God calls believers to ministry in general, to ministry in a specific organization, and to ministry at a specific task. Let's take those one by one.

*CALL TO MINISTRY IN GENERAL*

I like *The Living Bible* treatment of 1 Peter 4:10 11.

God has given each of you some special abilities; be sure to use them to help each other, passing onto others God's many kinds of blessings. Are you called to preach? Then preach as though God Himself were speaking through you. Are you called to help others? Do it with all the strength and energy that God supplies, so that God will be glorified through Jesus Christ—to Him be glory and power forever and ever. Amen.

From teaching in Sunday School to tentmaking in Bangladesh, God calls His people to service. The variety of spiritual gifts indicates a variety of ministries available and those ministries do not all need to be designed and programmed by the local church. We need to help lay people understand the importance of self-initiated ministries which God directs them to undertake. Engstrom and Dayton talk about "the intentional lay person."

> We believe that encouraging men and women of all ages to understand themselves as people whom God can use as part of His kingdom is the first step. Where does one go for such insight and counsel? Certainly, we begin with God's Word. Understanding the biblical concept of being *one body* and that the work of Christ is done by the body of Christ, rather than individuals, is an important concept. This means that there needs to be a group of men and women who have committed themselves to encourage one another and encourage themselves as a local church to understand their individual and corporate vocational tasks.[16]

## CALL TO MINISTRY IN A SPECIFIC ORGANIZATION

Understanding God's call need not be viewed as some mystical revelation-in-the-night experience. It's probably more like an inner confirmation from the Lord that He wants one of His people in a certain kind of ministry. The words "specific organization" in this context could refer to service with one mission board rather than another; membership and ministry in one local church rather than another; giving one's life to the military chaplaincy rather than to a local church pastorate; evangelizing teenagers with Youth for Christ rather than Young Life; or choosing to work in a Tuesday night club program rather than in children's church on Sunday morning. These are not accidental or unimportant decisions. Lay people need to understand God has gifted them and called them first to ministry, and then to a certain kind of ministry.

I agree with Friesen that sometimes God may leave an open door, allowing us to choose within the "circle" rather than narrowing us to the "dot." But what a tragedy to enter the insurance business if God has called you to serve in Central Africa, or to run off to Central Africa if God wants you in the insurance business. Such decisions are made by spiritually mature, growing, committed believers—not baby Christians.

## CALL TO MINISTRY AT A SPECIFIC TASK

Jim Stone sells computers. At thirty-five he is considered a successful businessman with a salary in the $50–$60,000 bracket. Each day he commutes from their suburban home into the city and each night returns to his wife and two children, Harold, thirteen, and Heidi, ten. The Stones attend Bethel Church where Jean teaches the Primary 3 Sunday School class (third-graders), and Jim heads up Evangelism Explosion on Thursday evenings. If you talked with Jim and Jean about their respective ministries you would grasp immediately that they believe they are serving precisely where God wants them. Jim used to teach Sunday School and did very well; but when confronted with the opportunity to head up E.E., he prayed about the change, discussed it with the family, and sensed that this was what God wanted him to do at that particular point.

Jean is a committed early Primary teacher. If you asked her to leave her third-grade class and move into a junior high class, she would laugh and politely decline. She senses that her gifts and talents lie in teaching, but more specifically, teaching that age-level. Let's make the proper distinction here. Jean does not have the gift of teaching *Primary* Sunday School; age-group ministry is not a spiritual gift. She may very well have the gift of teaching and a call from God to use that gift with third-graders. That is why we have spent so much time in this chapter discussing gifts and call separately.

Ray Syrstad, Pastor of Lay Ministries at Lake Avenue Congregational Church in Pasadena, California, talks about "God's appointment to ministry."

> We all have many important things to do but none of them can be more important than the ministries to which Jesus Christ has appointed us. Years ago when my wife and I entered the ministry, we claimed this promise: "Faithful is He who calls you, who also will do it" (1 Thes. 5:24). God never calls us to a task without also promising to supply all that we need to accomplish that task. That's the innate beauty of God's appointment to ministry . . . and that's why we can say with the Apostle Paul: "I can do all things through Christ who gives me strength" (Phil. 4:13). [17]

So there you have it. Development of lay leadership in a local church begins with an assessment of needs, gifts, and call. We base that assessment on a proper and biblical understanding of leadership, both pastoral and lay. Remember, to do this we need to use proper assessment tools. A simple "Privilege and Responsibility" form is essential to recruitment in any congregation. Keep in mind, however, it only surveys interest, not spiritual gifts or call. A thorough assessment represents information from several sources including the potential leader. Interest and experience inventories (like the P & R form) are very helpful; personal interviews provide valuable insights; spiritual gift inventories add a crucial dimension; and discussions in the Christian Education Committee or lay leadership development team put all the pieces together.

Foundational to all of this, however, is a solid program of pulpit and classroom teaching which emphasizes repeatedly the significance of lay involvement in the ministry of the local church.

> For by the grace given me I say to every one of you: Do not think of yourself more highly than you ought, but rather think of yourself with sober judgment, in accordance with the measure of faith God has given you. Just as each of us has one body with many members, and these members do not all have the same function, so in Christ we who are many form one body, and each member belongs to all the others. We have different gifts, according to the grace given us. If a man's gift is prophesying, let him use it in proportion to his faith. If it is serving, let him serve; if it is teaching, let him teach; if it is encouraging, let him encourage; if it is contributing to the needs of others, let him give generously; if it is leadership, let him govern diligently; if it is showing mercy, let him do it cheerfully (Rom. 12:3-8).

## STUDY QUESTIONS

**1.** Review the Menking quote in the section entitled "Needs of the Community." In what ways do you agree or disagree with this approach to pastoral vision?

**2.** Considering the needs of a local church, which of the twelve questions appearing in this chapter would you not use? What other questions should be asked?

**3.** Are you aware of your spiritual gift(s)? Write down what you believe God has gifted you to do and why you feel that is a correct assessment.

**4.** Do you believe God calls people to specific ministries in specific places? Why or why not?

**5.** In what ways can lay people in a local church be made aware of gifts and call?

# ENDNOTES

**1.** Albert Shanker, "A Better Use of Human Resources," *Education Week* (June 18, 1986), p. 20.

**2.** James Garlow, *Partners in Ministry: Laity and Pastors Working Together* (Kansas City: Beacon Hill, 1981), p. 156.

**3.** "Ten Questions Most Often Asked by Church Leaders," *Church Growth Resource News* (Winter 1985), p. 5.

**4.** David E. Mason, *Voluntary Nonprofit Enterprise Management* (New York: Plenum Press, 1984), p. 4.

**5.** Stanley J. Menking, *Helping Laity Help Others* (Philadelphia: Westminster Press, 1984), pp. 23–4.

**6.** R. Michael Harton, "When Does a Church Need a Minister of Education?" *Church Administration* (April 1987), p. 6.

**7.** Marlene Wilson, *How to Mobilize Church Volunteers* (Minneapolis: Augsburg, 1983), p. 22.

**8.** Walter J. Ungerer, *The Barnabas Project* (An unpublished Doctor of Ministries dissertation written at Princeton Theological Seminary, 1983 and available from University Microfilms Intl., Ann Arbor, Mich.), pp. 40–1.

**9.** Much of the material in this section is adapted from my book *Unwrap Your Spiritual Gifts*, published by Victor in 1983. Readers are encouraged to consult that source for additional and more detailed information.

**10.** Les Flynn, *19 Gifts of the Spirit* (Wheaton, Ill.: Victor Books, 1974), p. 201.

**11.** Mark Senter, *The Art of Recruiting Volunteers* (Wheaton, Ill.: Victor Books, 1983), p. 16.

**12.** Jo Ann Miller and Elizabeth Heese, "Discovering Leadership Talent," *Human Development* (Winter 1986), p. 42.

**13.** Menking, pp. 21–2.

**14.** Menking, pp. 48–9.

**15.** Gary Friesen, *Decision-Making and the Will of God* (Portland, Ore.: Multnomah Press, 1981).

**16.** Ted W. Engstrom and Edward R. Dayton, "The Intentional Lay Person," *Christian Leadership Letter* (March 1987), p. 2.

**17.** Ray Syrstad, "What Does the Lord Require?" *Christian Education Today* (Fall 1985), p. 8.

CHAPTER 8

# RECRUITING EFFECTIVE VOLUNTEERS

According to a survey which appeared in *Leadership* journal during 1982, motivating and sustaining active participation of lay members in the church is the most frustrating problem pastors face today. Yet the recruitment and development of lay volunteers remains the key that unlocks the door to church growth. One authoritative source notes, "The more members that become involved in church ministry roles, the easier it is to find the right persons best qualified and gifted for a particular ministry. Unfortunately, history shows that without an intentional priority and effective plan, most churches never reach these realistic possibilities."[1]

At the risk of repetition, let me say again that philosophy of ministry and assessment of needs and resources are both foundational to effective recruitment.

Pastor Rick Stanley has learned this the hard way. He and his deacons have consistently approached every leadership need with negative assumptions—nobody is interested, nobody will volunteer, nobody will stick it out. Their solution to the dilemma was to make the job sound as easy as possible (affording no challenge) and to gladly sign up the first person who nods affirmatively to some public announcement of the leadership dilemma. I agree with John Cionca: "If there is an unpardonable sin in teacher recruiting, it's the old trip-them-in-the-hallway trick, where you thrust a Sunday School quarterly into their hands and you pick them up and point them toward the Junior department."[2]

To be sure, some small churches struggle to find even the bare necessities of program help. But most churches already contain within congregational ranks more than enough potential leaders if gift and call were activated. Let's start by mentioning three things we do *not* practice in effective recruiting.

1. General public announcements. Apart from being futile, such a shotgun approach offers genuine risks since the pellets might hit anybody and produce volunteers unsuitable for the ministry.

2. Last-minute appointments. Understanding the need does not mean recognizing on Wednesday night that a Primary Department class appears to be teacherless for the coming Sunday. As we noted earlier, long-range planning and a personal development strategy should identify needs in the present program and opportunities for new ministry in expanding programs long before the crisis hits.

3. Pressurized appeals. As Rick has learned, such arm-twisting usually belittles the job merely to secure an affirmative answer and get the position filled.

On the positive side, this chapter will teach you how to determine high standards, design an atmosphere of service, and develop effective servants.

## DETERMINE HIGH STANDARDS

Make no mistake about Rick Stanley, he is a fine and godly pastor. His problems are not organismic; they are organizational. His seminary never taught administrative process and he does not know how to work with people in anything other than preaching, classroom, or individual counseling sessions. Developing people in small groups seems as foreign to him as the Ugaritic elective he almost chose his last year in seminary. Sooner or later Rick must learn that when a church considers leadership training, it must first determine standards (1 Tim. 4:11-12). Four areas ought to concern every Christian leader looking for potential volunteer workers either in the local church or in parachurch ministries.

### SPIRITUAL MATURITY

The first area is both the most obvious and the most necessary. We're not talking here about the potential for spiritual maturity *someday*; that would describe everybody in the congregation. Rather, we need to focus on present evidence of spiritual maturity and the quality of spiritual life. A brief reading of the qualifications for elders and deacons in 1 Timothy 3 can bring to the surface the importance of this standard. Kevin Springer warns:

It is entirely possible for people to be highly gifted, but still to be weak or unstable in character. We may be dazzled by such a person—"Now *there* is a leader!"—and not realize how much growth and character would be necessary for the person to be able to offer effective leadership to God's people. For many people it would require an enormous amount of change: for some it is probably not possible. But my experience is that if a person is basically sound in his or her character, and has an openness and a willingness to be used by God, God will add gifts to the person and accomplish great things through him.[3]

What we mean by spiritual maturity may vary from church to church but the standards you develop should clearly be supported by the Word of God. Breakdown in spiritual maturity stands as the single most important damaging factor to leadership in the body of Christ. It leads to rupture between pastor and elders, clergy and laity, professional staff and volunteer staff, and can eventually rip a congregation to shreds.

The Ephesian elders were to be committed to the ministry of raising the sheep, and the centuries have not changed that priority. There is a perceptible restlessness among the sheep today. Battered by the world and bewildered by trends in the church, they long for a deeper and more personal fellowship which mere bigness and busyness cannot provide. Programmed almost to distraction, the sheep are looking anew for pastors who will feed them and tend them in their hours of weakness and need.[4]

## LEADERSHIP SKILLS

While spiritual maturity focuses on life qualities, leadership skills focus on service qualities. Training will develop leadership skills, but there should be some visible evidence of the skill even before training begins. The wise leader pays attention to putting the right people in the right slots. Trained teachers build effective ministry; the more effective any ministry is, the easier it is to recruit new leadership.

But how do you spot people with leadership skills? Springer suggests there are at least three qualities such people will demonstrate. First of all, *the ability to win the respect of others*, the old "E. F. Hutton" signal. Second, *the ability to gain people's trust*. To whom would most members of your congregation turn for help if they had

135

serious personal problems? Whom would they like to have as a prayer partner? Who would be selected to lead meetings effectively? And finally, *the ability to take the initiative* with organized and directed goals. We hear this phrase quite commonly in conjunction with athletics. As we watch a professional basketball game the announcer might say, "Larry Bird has come out this quarter to take charge of the game."[5]

Some years ago the American Association of School Administrators released a criteria sheet to enable local school boards to select competent educational leaders in their communities to serve on the board. Here are some of the items they suggested:

1. Is the candidate reputable as a person and as a public worker and recognized as such by the intelligent leaders of the community?
2. Does s/he have personal courage, exercised with appropriate tact, in facing opposition?
3. Is the candidate likely to avoid fanfare and self-publicity in this post?
4. Does this candidate have the ability to deal democratically and effectively with employees?
5. Is this candidate one who has propensity for keeping his feet on the ground, willing to recognize legitimate precedent, yet also willing to consider appropriate change?

Such a list of standards would have to be adapted for use in the church and many more could be added but it might give you some idea in setting up your own criteria for the selection of lay leaders.
*LEARNING POTENTIAL*
In addition to life qualities and service qualities, we must set standards which deal with intellectual qualities. Some people regularly hold important roles in church ministry, but really do not have the potential for leadership. In the urban area in which I live some 600,000 adults have been declared functionally illiterate. Doubtless many of these folks are very fine people but they are hardly potential Sunday School teachers or leaders. Their learning potential is too low for the necessary training program.

Remember, recruitment is not an end in itself; it merely leads to the next step which is training. And we can cause great grief for the training aspect of the program if we allow a breakdown in the recruitment phase. Some have suggested that every church needs a personnel committee, perhaps a subcommittee working with the board or committee of Christian education. Its duties would be performed on a year-round basis and it would include people who represent a cross section of the church. These "leader-finders" must be informed about what the church is and needs to become, and personable enough to create opportunities for finding and contacting potential volunteers.

Potential leaders tend to be organized people who understand goals and priorities. They make wise use of their leisure time, are able to focus with intensity when necessary, and can handle occasional discouragements. To borrow a phrase from Reuel Howe, they are mature people who are able to work without playing and to play without feeling they ought to be working.

*COOPERATIVE ATTITUDE*

Remember that every new volunteer worker must fit in with the team you already have. Just bringing any person to fill an empty slot could create havoc in an already functioning unit. People with cooperative attitudes know how to relate well to others. An open admissions policy preempts the kind of quality control which enables us to select the right people under the leadership of the Holy Spirit and in line with what God's Word requires.

Your standards can be as high or as low as you set them. Their purpose is to guide the personnel committee or the recruiter(s) who look for the volunteers you need. Remember, somebody must be in charge of this phase of the ministry.

> This is especially important in a volunteer organization, and particularly in the local church, where it is almost a full-time task. There needs to be someone who has an overall understanding of the people within the church, their skills, their needs, an understanding that can be used when the time comes to recruit or to elect someone to a particular role. . . . They have to have a special love of people and some special insights into people in order to help them recognize their God-given potential by fitting into tasks that suit them. Recruiters need to see themselves as enablers of people rather than users. [6]

## DESIGN AN ATMOSPHERE OF SERVICE

We talked about this some in an earlier chapter, but the review may be helpful. Figure 14 reflects the educational cycle with which all students of Christian education will be familiar. I believe it originated with Ralph Tyler and has been adapted through the years in church education books by Lois LeBar, Gene Getz, and myself, among others. Notice that once biblical imperatives and objectives are set, the focus immediately shifts to current needs and then heads on around the cycle with each item appearing in order, assuming that the previous items have been set.

Studying the cycle in a vacuum is not as helpful as seeing it laid

FIGURE 14

# EDUCATIONAL CYCLE

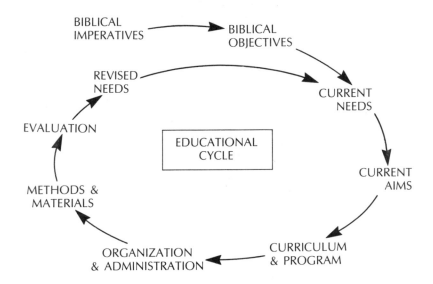

beside your programs because the atmosphere of service is two-dimensional. We must keep in mind both the nomothetic dimension (organizational roles) and the idiographic dimension (personal needs). Paul J. Loth reminds us:

> Often churches have been guilty of viewing lay ministry only from the "employer viewpoint." We recruit volunteers as a means of accomplishing the work of the church or of a particular program. On the contrary, however, the volunteer activity must also accomplish the personal goals of the volunteer. There are two purposes for volunteer church work—one is to develop the church program and the other is to develop the

individual. People who aren't growing as they serve stagnate early and become candidates for complaining rather than contributing.[7]

Loth goes on to list seven "attitude competencies" which must be a part of the personal and professional profile of the recruiter(s).

1. Vision for a potential volunteer serving in the church.
2. Belief that people are more important than positions or programs.
3. Willingness to work with volunteers to see them reach full potential.
4. Love for the volunteers.
5. Belief in the importance of the church's ministry.
6. Desire to help volunteers develop.
7. Belief in the abilities of the volunteers.

*ELEVATE MINISTRY INVOLVEMENT*

Assuming we have recognized spiritual gifts, emphasized the significance of call, and taken into consideration experience and personal interests, we now stand at the crucial first public step elevating the opportunity for ministry. Churches are doing a number of good things in this area—teacher appreciation banquets, distribution of ministry certificates, appropriate recognition for teachers and leaders who take advantage of conventions, seminars, and training programs—but elevating ministry involvement is a constant task for the pastor and all other leadership staff. This is not a new idea; some of us have been saying it for decades. Back in the '60s Scripture Press Foundation released a monograph by Dr. Roy Zuck stressing precisely this point.

Keep the standards high. One Christian educator reported that in Sunday School departments where the enthusiasm is high and Bible teaching is above average, two factors have almost invariably been present: (a) a high degree of spiritual reality and (b) high standards of workmanship.

Magnify the position to your prospect in words something like this: "The Board of Christian Education (or Sunday School Cabinet) has prayed about people to serve in our Sunday School and has chosen your name as one whom they feel is qualified for, and may be interested in, teaching our class of junior boys (or other position). We would like for you to prayerfully consider it."[8]

Traveling around the world in Christian education ministry I meet hundreds of Sunday School teachers every year. When asking them what ministries they carry out in their local churches I commonly hear the response, "I'm just a Sunday School teacher." The implication suggests that the teacher feels less than a significant importance about his or her ministry. Not a pastor, not an elder, not a deacon, not a committee chairman—*just* a Sunday School teacher. If we really elevate ministry involvement we can eliminate this negative image of ministry.

## EXPLAIN MINISTRY INVOLVEMENT

The concept of job description is crucial. Many don't like the term because they feel it connotes a secular position rather than ministry. But we use the word "work" commonly and the Bible even applies it to our service for the Lord (Col. 3:23). Treating volunteers like staff provides the key to all good volunteer programs.

It begins with someone having thought through the question and having written a position description. The position description should describe what the job entails and what qualifications are needed to do it. Having a position description is the first indicator that the organization expects a high level of commitment from its volunteers and that it intends to choose them carefully with respect.[9]

Worker orientation offers a corollary to an effective position description. Orientation is a part of training, but we want to view it here as preliminary to the formal training process. College educators know that the way a freshman gets started in the first two months of his college years will determine the success not only of his first full year but his entire time at college. So it is in local church ministry. Finding effective people is only the first step; launching them into ministry is just as important. As we stress spiritual opportunities and explain ministry responsibilities, we want to thoroughly detail what we expect. Many later failures can be traced back to inadequate orientation.

## EVALUATE MINISTRY INVOLVEMENT

We're not ready to examine supervision and evaluation, but remember the importance of announcing to all volunteers right up front that their ministry will be evaluated. Actually, evaluation starts right at the beginning as we ascertain whether a potential worker meets the *standards* which have been set. Then we measure his or her *progress* in the orientation and training program. Finally, we evaluate the actual *ministry*. Sometimes we might want to try a probationary period, such as, a substitute teaching role for three or six months. On other occasions an internship could be used for early evaluation purposes. The secret lies in communicating the idea that evaluation is neither negative nor punitive—it offers a service to the volunteer to help him improve in ministry.

## EXPECT MINISTRY INVOLVEMENT

Remember Rick Stanley whom we met at the beginning of the chapter? We've already discovered that he does not expect people to respond affirmatively to requests for ministry involvement. Oh, sure, we could excuse him for being a bit gun-shy after all the turn-downs he's experienced in nine years of ministry. On the other hand, he has brought the problem on himself by asking in inadequate and improper ways. In a very helpful book, Douglas Johnson talks about developing good relations with volunteers by remembering the five "nots" in working with them.

1. Volunteers are not members of the staff.
2. Volunteers are not full-time workers.
3. Volunteers cannot be taken for granted.
4. Volunteers are not paid.
5. Volunteers are not bound to a job in the church for long periods of time. [10]

To his five "nots" Johnson adds three "needs." Volunteers need to hear thanks; volunteers need recognition; volunteers need to be treated courteously.

Stanley's predicament serves up a rehash of the old chicken-and-the-egg problem. Does his failure to obtain involvement bring about his lack of expectancy or does his lack of expectancy create negative response? Probably a little bit of both. Danny Gales puts it succinctly: "Building an achievement-oriented atmosphere begins by understanding people and placing a high value on them. We must credit everyone with more potential than 'limited intelligence and unlimited time.' "[11]

## DEVELOP EFFECTIVE SERVANTS

Since Pastor Rick has never held a managerial role in business or industry, he is not familiar with the concept of quality control. He tends to spiritualize (almost mysticize) the process of recruiting

workers while at the same time practicing the most pedantic processes for filling the many and frequently open ministries in his
church. In order to develop effective servants he must realign his
understanding of standards and retune the whole atmosphere of
ministry which he has created.

In addition he needs to take definitive steps to improve the recruitment process which starts with a better focus on potential
volunteer candidates. After all, if his church stands anywhere near
average it needs a constant flow of new personnel. We lose nearly
20 percent annually through general population mobility and require
at least another 10 percent for growth and other flexible factors.
That totals at least 30 percent new personnel every year just to
keep up with reasonable maintenance and growth patterns of the
average church.

## MATCH PERSONS AND POSITIONS

Assuming we've identified gifts, interests, call, and needs, we are
at the point of putting together ministry opportunities with ministering people. At times that may require protecting people from themselves, those ever-eager souls who will take on yet another ministry for whatever good or questionable motivation. Choun sees this
as the function of the "Screening Committee" which could be identical with the Personnel Committee or represent a portion of the
Christian Education Committee.

> Another committee function is to protect those workers who
> have demonstrated their usefulness and been asked to assume
> too many responsibilities. It may take just one more job to
> send an already overloaded superintendent/treasurer/secre-
> tary/janitor to that nice church down the street. [12]

Mark Senter compares this matching of persons and positions
with the introduction of two friends of the opposite sex.

> The introduction process is as delicate as that of introducing
> your daughter to your best friend's nephew who has just re-
> turned from his second year in college. You want to create the
> opportunity for a relationship to develop without pushing so
> hard as to destroy the possibility.
> It's almost as if the pastor of Christian education is merely a
> spokesman for God, a provider of information, and a resource
> for people who desire spiritual development. [13]

Obviously, not every church has a pastor of Christian education, so that deployment of servants may fall to the only pastor or to the chairman of the Christian Education Committee.

## FOLLOW PROVEN PROCEDURES

Recruitment continues all year, aiming to keep a ready reservoir of servants in order to protect the stability of the church's ministries. Recruitment must be coordinated. One large church with several pastors finds itself in constant turmoil because the pastors vie with one another, recruiting people for their various ministries. That congregation needs a central clearinghouse, which may be the pastoral staff meetings or some other group. In the smaller church, the Christian Education Committee could very well serve as the coordinating body for worker recruitment.

One writer describes a "ministry bank" in which the recruitment team invests information which has been gathered from new members.

The bank is actually a large card file which we keep in the church office. For each category listed on the Personnel Commitment Form, we have set up a major section in the file. Each card in the file is printed with a place for the individual's name, phone number, and all the specific areas of service to be filled in. [14]

Proven procedures take in virtually everything we've said so far—determining the standards; elevating the ministry; explaining ministry involvement; evaluation; attitudes of expectancy; matching people and positions; writing careful job descriptions; preparing and using a prospect list.

Let's add a few more practical guidelines before we discuss how to approach the potential volunteer.

1. Start early—enlistment should take place at least three months before the person actually begins serving in order to allow time for orientation and training.

2. Make all contacts face-to-face if possible. Sometimes a phone call may be necessary, but direct conversation is much better.

3. Have your information in hand. Know the experience, gifts, and interests of the potential volunteer so you can genuinely affirm the committee's selection in light of the best information available.

4. Anticipate excuses.

5. Assure him of your help and prayer.

Figure 15 shows a table of double expectations I used at a church in Illinois. On the left the Christian Education Committee tells the volunteer what is expected of him while on the right it details what the workers in the church's educational program may expect from the committee.

FIGURE 15

# DOUBLE EXPECTATIONS

| What We Expect of YOU | What You May Expect of US |
|---|---|
| 1. Personal spiritual living | 1. Personal spiritual living |
| 2. Faithfulness in attendance and service | 2. Support in prayer, equipment, and counsel |
| 3. Positive attitudes toward colleagues, agency, and church | 3. Serious commitment to committee planning and decision-making |
| 4. Regular attendance at monthly staff meetings | 4. Profitable monthly staff meetings |
| 5. Prayer | 5. Communication |

## SPECIFY PERSONS, TASKS, AND TIME

For years my students have heard me parrot the central axiom of recruitment: *Ask specific people for a specific ministry for a specific length of time.* That one-liner should be obvious by now in the discussions of this chapter.

**1.** *Specific people.* No general announcements or universal invitations. We are approaching people who have been prayerfully selected by the appropriate committee or recruitment team.

**2.** *Specific ministry.* We don't ask these people to serve "in general" but attempt to match our understanding of their spiritual gifts, interests, and experience with the various needs in the church. The specific opportunity we wish to discuss is the one that seems to best fit all these important variables.

**3.** *Specific time.* Serving Christ in the church is not a life sentence in one unchanging post. I recommend that you set a one-year boundary (perhaps the curriculum year from September 1 to August 31) and recruit volunteers for that specific time frame.

Of course this does not mean that we expect a complete turnover on an annual basis. It does mean, however, that we don't want people accepting a position in August and then resigning it in November just because they tire of the preparation and study. The time factor must be emphasized; people will not understand one-year ministry appointments unless you clearly communicate that concept.

When a vacancy appears sometime during the ministry year, the appointment should be made just until the end of the year, at which time all workers are evaluated and reappointed or assigned elsewhere.

## DETAIL THE RESPONSIBILITIES AND DUTIES

In a helpful brochure designed for camp directors, CCI Executive Director John Pearson warns:

> The greatest sin in volunteerism is in not adequately defining the task to be completed. Even simple requests will be performed better if the task is written down. Why? A written objective is usually much clearer and easier to understand than a verbal request. Before approaching a volunteer, the following elements of the job should be determined: the exact job, the timetable, the final results desired, and the working relationships. [15]

There is some overlap here with our earlier discussions about explaining ministry involvement. Perhaps the very nature of this crucial dimension of recruitment requires double handling. The work of the chairman of the Christian Education Committee or the recruitment team includes contacting potential leaders. The contact person needs to be able to talk intelligently about each specific ministry, the tasks that the volunteer will be asked to perform, and specifically when the ministry will begin. Obviously this process must be bathed in prayer and we never want to rush an answer on the part of the recruit.

One more dimension requires our attention. College recruiters refer to it as "student retention," holding onto the people you already have. College student recruitment is big-time business in our day and a massive amount of research has gone into the best techniques to get the job done. Every recruiter will tell you that retention is both easier and less expensive than recruitment.

That means we need to learn to plug up the leaks in the present leadership program which cause both present and potential volunteers to become discouraged. Why do lay leaders leave the ministry?

1. Because willing people become overworked and burned out.

2. Because volunteers don't receive much-needed help.

3. Because lay people have personal and spiritual needs of their own which aren't being met in the framework of their ministries.

4. Because we do not adequately show appreciation.

5. Because they have not been provided proper equipment and materials.

6. Because they have not been trained adequately for the ministries they have been asked to carry out.

7. Because friction has developed between or among workers in a given ministry area.

8. Because they have lost interest, enthusiasm, and commitment for the ministry.

9. Because supervision is inadequate or perhaps even abrasive.

10. Because evaluation has not been carried out or results have not been identified as a positive thrust for ministry improvement.

Every college recruiter knows recruiting is everybody's job—people currently involved in ministry need to be finding new volunteers for ministry. Teachers look for helpers, departmental superintendents look for teachers, etc.

Keep the process dignified and spiritual. Trust God to provide the workers you need. In detailing the process of recruitment we may use terms like "job," "position," and "work," but we must always emphasize the spiritual and biblical dimensions of ministry.

Remember, *people rarely perform above the level at which they were recruited.* If we play down the importance of the ministry just to get them to say yes, we must expect a minimal performance. We'll talk more about motivation, but remember in recruitment to appeal not so much to duty and responsibility as to opportunity and benefit. Mutual ministry serves both the church and the volunteer whose family, parenting skills, relationships with other people, and general spiritual life should be enhanced by his involvement in ministry.

## STUDY QUESTIONS

1. List one example of organismic and another of organizational problems in the church.

**2.** Review the criteria list prepared by the American Association of School Administrators. How would this have to be changed for use in the church?

**3.** Review the educational cycle and then take one program of a church with which you are familiar and identify the various phases of it in relationship to each step on the cycle.

**4.** Think about the church you now attend in light of the statement "The average church needs at least 30 percent new personnel every year just to keep up with reasonable maintenance and growth patterns." Do you agree with the statement? What plans do you have for finding those 30 percent?

**5.** Think of the ways your church recruits people in the light of the information in this chapter. If you were grading its performance on an A to F scale, what letter would you choose?

# ENDNOTES

1. "Motivating and Sustaining Active Participation of Lay Members in the Church," *Church Growth Resource News* (Winter 1985), p. 4.

2. John Cionca, "C.E. Doesn't Run on Auto Pilot," *Leadership* (Fall 1984), p. 62.

3. Kevin Springer, "Diamonds in the Rough," *Pastoral Renewal* (January 1986), p. 97.

4. Donald L. Roberts, *The Perfect Church* (Harrisburg, Pa.: Christian Publications, 1979), p. 59.

5. Springer, pp. 97–8.

6. Ted W. Engstrom and Edward R. Dayton, "Recruiting," *Christian Leadership Letter* (October 1979), p. 2.

7. Paul J. Loth, "How to Involve Volunteers in Church Ministry," *Christian Education Today* (Fall 1985), p. 9.

8. Roy B. Zuck, "The Superintendent and Teacher Enlistment," *Christian Education Monographs #3* (Glen Ellyn, Ill.: Scripture Press Foundation, 1968), p. 3.

9. Engstrom and Dayton, "Volunteers—Bane or Blessing?" *Christian Leadership Letter* (May 1986), p. 2.

10. Douglas W. Johnson, *The Care and Feeding of Volunteers* (Nashville: Abingdon, 1978), pp. 22–5.

**11.** Danny Gales, "Disarming Tensions between Paid Staff and Volunteers," *Preacher's Magazine* (March-April-May 1985), p. 25.

**12.** Robert J. Choun, "Seven Steps to Securing Servants," *Christian Education Today* (Fall 1985), p. 11.

**13.** Mark Senter, *The Art of Recruiting Volunteers* (Wheaton, Ill.: Victor Books, 1983), p. 19.

**14.** Arthur J. Helin, "A Program for Recruiting and Involving Laymen and Laywomen for Ministry in Apostle United Presbyterian Church, West Allis, WI" (A Doctor of Ministries project written at Trinity Evangelical Divinity School, 1984), p. 48.

**15.** John Pearson, "How to Recruit and Encourage Volunteers" (Christian Camping International Focus Series #8), p. 1.

# CHAPTER 9

# CHANGING PEOPLE AND THINGS

According to Alvin Toffler, future shock is the shattering stress and disorientation that we induce in people by subjecting them to too much change in too short a time. In 1948, for example, 50 percent of the work force in the United States was engaged in making things. Thirty years later less than 25 percent was employed in production-type activity. In 1790, 85 percent of the United States population was engaged in farming, but by 1979 only 3 percent; since then their ranks have been constantly threatened. In 1880 the United States shut down the U.S. Patent Office because, after all, what else could possibly be invented? Yet between 1965 and 1980, 1 million new patents were issued (*Future Shock* [New York: Random House, 1970]).

Toffler's theories, written more than a decade ago, seem to have been prophetic. The rapidity of change actually makes people sick. They no longer feel certain of anything—job, spouse, beliefs, morality—everything seems to be changing all the time. A pervasive uncertainty hangs like London fog over everything in the modern world.

There was a time when change was welcomed, particularly during the Industrial Revolution. Alfred Lord Tennyson once wrote, "Let the great world spin forever down the ringing grooves of change." Somehow since World War II, perhaps even just in the last twenty-five years, social change has become something of a tidal wave threatening to smash everything in its path. Suddenly we're surrounded by revolutions, and everybody of every color, age, or belief wants something changed.

Yet change is a wholesome and biblical concept (Rom. 8:28-30). Growth causes change and Christians should be constantly growing. Certainly salvation causes change, dramatic rebirth in which "all things become new." So to some extent at least, Christians promote change while Christian leaders initiate and nurture it. This chapter assumes that proper change is in line with biblical standards, wholesome and useful for the development of the body, and understood by those who serve together in the church.

This last criterion provides the problem and offers occasion for this chapter in a study on church leadership. Somebody has said that in the process of change there are the leaders, the followers, and the brakers. And the leaders are not necessarily those in titled positions, nor necessarily those who talk continuously about change. Let's begin by reviewing some of the basic principles of change.

1. Change nothing major the first year because you're just learning how things work and attempting to adapt to existing structure. Frankly, you don't know enough about why things work the way they do in order to make major changes during the first year.

2. Changing people is more important than changing things because if you only change things the people will change them back again as soon as you are gone.

3. Change begins at the point of greatest control (e.g., for a pastor that might be the Sunday sermons or the order of service).

4. Change is facilitated as more people participate in its planning.

5. Change relates to the maturity of the group—that is, immature people tend to fight change (the Linus-blanket syndrome), and mature people who have had varying experiences (and apparently lived through them) seem more likely to accept new experiences.

6. Change begins at the point of the most predictable results because you want to know what will happen when you begin changing structures in the organization.

7. Change requires that we explain to people why and how, that we communicate effectively about change.

8. Change relates negatively or positively to the credibility of the leader—the more they believe in you, the more tolerant they will be with changes you propose.

9. Change must move forward by small steps. Even if the change itself looms large (the transfer from Sunday evening services at the church to house churches or mini-flocks), the process

can be spread out and the steps taken in such a way that it appears less threatening.

10. Change in a Christian organization must be bathed in prayer and carried out in harmony. Programs and ideas belong to the people, not just the pastor; *don't move into a new situation and radicalize everything you find there, remaking it into your own image and then asking people to rejoice over it.*

## STAGES IN IMPLEMENTING CHANGE

Clay has been the Christian Education Director at First Church for only six months. One of his first tasks was to evaluate the children's ministry and assess what changes needed to be made. As he studied the situation he saw that the auditorium was overcrowded frequently enough to initiate serious discussions about considering two services on Sunday morning. Yet approximately one third of the audience in the morning service consisted of preschoolers and elementary-age children. It didn't take Clay long to see the need for children's church.

But where to begin? At First Church there was only one place to begin—with the pastor. He and some of the veteran saints needed convincing that children can actually learn to worship better on their own levels and in their own services if that phase of education is handled properly. Clay was able to point out some very significant reasons why a children's church program would benefit the children as well as the adults. He suggested First Church start with one Sunday a month and slowly move into a full-time, full-scale children's church program.

*PLANNING STAGE*

The planning stage, which we have already noted, should involve a maximal number of people and consists of four steps.

Of course it's not quite as neatly packaged as the diagram indicates, but we identify *needed change* by *determining* where we stand now and how we have been unsuccessful in meeting previous goals and objectives. Let's go back to the idea of discontent.

Suppose at an annual report (which is an evaluation of sorts) we discover the attendance for a given year had dropped by 10 percent. Obviously if we'd been watching carefully through the year we'd have noticed this much sooner, but for purposes of illustration let us say it is first announced to the congregation at the annual meeting. Needed change points toward attendance increase and the *direction* is clearly upward. Such a decision cannot come only from

FIGURE 16

# IMPLEMENTING CHANGE—STAGE 1

Determine needed change

Decide on direction

Design implementation

Declare plans and process

the pastor or the pastoral staff. The end result might be a goal to increase attendance 15 percent by next year to make up for the loss and include a gain of an additional 5 percent.

The third step, *design*, also results from long-range planning. In this simple illustration our goals and realization procedures might include more door-to-door evangelism, follow-up on people who have left to find out why we lost 10 percent, home Bible studies, programs on friendship evangelism, or a host of other ideas which have been successful in recent years. The particular design is not important, but the group itself must agree on the best way to approach the problem.

Finally the *declaration* step leads us into the second stage and also presents us with the first major problem because we have now "gone public" with what we plan to do. As soon as we declare plans and processes we set up targets for resisters. Their negative subjectivity can now focus more clearly on specifics.

*ANNOUNCEMENT STAGE*

The announcement stage, launched by the fourth step of the planning stage, is a very significant development in the whole change process. Remember the point earlier about communicating to people? How we do that will to a large degree determine how much negative feedback and resistance we'll stir up. Again, it has four steps.

Unlike the planning stage, the announcement stage has no steps which neatly flow one from the other. Order exists, but the time factor of the announcement rarely permits a "cushion" common to the planning stage. To stay with our sample illustration about

FIGURE 17

# IMPLEMENTING CHANGE—STAGE 2

1. Change will occur
2. What will change
3. How it will change
4. Reports of progress

attendance shrinkage, the day we announce change will occur we have raised the what and how questions. So we explain a program to attract people to our church, present the Gospel through detailed follow-up with the visitors, three new home Bible classes beginning in January, and an optional door-to-door evangelism program scheduled during the Bible study on Wednesday evening.

Such information covers the first three steps in the announcement stage—something will change, what will change, and how it will change. They are virtually impossible to separate, especially in a simple illustration like this one. As in planning change, the fourth step in announcing it launches us into yet another stage.

It has to do with how we report progress after we start the change process. In reality, the resisters mounted their attack back at step one of stage two when they found out that change would occur. Let's look at the two stages together to see how different people resist different phases or aspects of the change process.

Study this last section carefully because it contains the key many people miss in dealing with resistance to change. We tend to assume that people always resist change out of habit, but that's not true. Some people *do resist any change* just because they want things to stay as they are; they fall into the step-one resistance stage group. Do these people like the 10 percent attendance decrease over the past year? Hardly; but none of the proposed plans pleases them. They may feel, for example, the problem lies with the preacher and that they need to get rid of him not add new programs or efforts to attract more people.

That comes very close to the second step which describes people who *resist the way* leadership has approached the problem. They openly admit that the decrease in attendance must be stopped. Something must be done, but *not* home Bible classes, and certainly *not* more careful follow-up of visitors because we tried that five years ago and several people got angry when we tried to visit in their homes.

FIGURE 18

# IMPLEMENTING CHANGE—STAGE 3

Change will occur ——►Resistance to all change
(Resistance stage)

What will change ——►Resistance to the design

How it will change —►Resistance to the implementation

Reports of progress ——►Resistance to the process/progress

Then there are folks who really don't quarrel with the fact of change or the design of change but *resist the implementation.* They simply don't like the way we're putting the decision into action. Have a door-to-door visitation program if you must, they say, but certainly not during the Bible study on Wednesday evening! Please notice that resisting implementation is very different than resisting all change and, until we sort out what people really feel, we tend to lump all the resisters together, thereby creating more problems than we solve.

Finally, there are folks who stand with you all the way in the change, the design, and the implementation, but they join the resistance movement because they simply feel uninformed. These good people want to know what's going on; they want to be a part of the ministry. They sense the leadership has taken on an "oval office" look, carrying out clandestine actions which affect their lives (implemented with their money) and yet not letting them in on what's going on. *If what they say is true, they are right and the leaders are wrong; we have brought resistance on ourselves.*

Before we leave the stages in implementing change, let's review some of the reasons for resistance, looked at from just a little different perspective. Roadblocks to change include such things as fear of disorganization, vested interests, insecurity of personality or position, and the threatening of traditional values or standards. Think of how many congregations have struggled and perhaps even split over a change from the use of the *King James Version* to the *New American Standard Bible* or the *New International Version.* With many, the issue at stake has nothing to do with quality of translation, authority of the text, or the doctrine of inerrancy—it is purely a matter of tradition—what I like and what makes me feel comfortable.

Remember too that people rarely change from motivations of pain or guilt though we commonly use these tactics. Guilt brings anger and resistance—not change. Pain brings tenacious determination which sets people on a radical search for remedy, not harmony and agreement.

## COMPLEXITIES OF ATTITUDINAL CHANGE

Let's go back to that point about changing things, not people. Obviously it's easier to change things than people but the latter is much more necessary. How do we go about doing that? How do we get somebody who seems to fight everything different in the church to become a team member and colleague who helps bring about necessary and biblical shifts in the congregation? "This, in a capsule, is how change works"—writes Bruce Powers, "awareness of and efforts to solve problems so that tension is kept at a minimum."

Now, obviously, the solution of one problem does not indicate a new pattern of behavior. But it does provide information that will affect subsequent actions. The point is that a change agent must understand and use these natural principles that are always operating. Rather than contriving ways of leading people to change, he should build on the innate need of man to solve his problems. [1]

Though not every Christian leader can be expected to be a psychologist, we can all follow certain basic axioms when dealing with our roles as change agents. One states that *people do things that make sense to them.* Resistance to the starting of three home Bible classes may seem irrational to us but not to the resister. In his own mind, he has rationalized some reason why the church should not engage in this particular kind of ministry. It does no good to write him off as a kook or complain that some people always resist change. We need to find out how he thinks and why that leads to resistance.

A second presupposition of human behavior suggests that *resistance cannot be viewed as an attitude in isolation, but a part of the total environment.* Where does he stand in relationship to everything that's going on in the church? He might not resist all Bible classes. Maybe he thinks the pastor has introduced them as a way to get out of giving Sunday morning invitations. Don't trample minority resistance in the rush to institute a new plan. However "wrong" the resister may be, he still belongs to the body of Christ and we have the responsibility to minister to the whole body. Remember the words of Hebrews 12:12-13, "Therefore, strengthen your feeble arms and weak knees. Make level paths for your feet, so that the lame may not be disabled, but rather healed."

All of this assumes the leader is right and enjoys the support of the group. But picture the minority resister, looking foolish and irrational in his posture of traditionalism. He just might be the stable voice on any given issue. Unless we talk to that person (and listen) we will never know.

## VALUES AND THE PSYCHOLOGY OF CHANGE

Whenever I teach or write about change, I'm compelled to remember a gentleman in one of the churches I pastored. Genuinely committed to Christ and the ministry of His church, this brother clung rigidly to what he saw as the way things ought to be because, in his view, they had always been that way. Of course they had not; subtle changes had occurred all through his adult life, but at the time I worked with him, he had planted his feet and determined to resist any further "falling away."

As a change agent in that setting, it was necessary for me to "thaw the current situation," to borrow a phrase from Powers. My task with him focused on a vision of what God wanted to do in that congregation which would lift his eyes beyond the here and now to the then and there. He needed to see that the current situation lacked potential benefits for the congregation and we should all, therefore, be at least mildly discontented with where we were. I claim no particular success in this specific story but the process represented a basic axiom.

One more time. *People only welcome change when they are discontented with the status quo.* Yet institutional habits generally represent values and standards built up over a long period of time. As we learned above, the way we introduce change is every bit as important as the change itself, it may be the determining factor in whether the change will succeed. Leaders who emerge as effective change agents understand how people respond, and that requires comprehending how crucial their current values seem to them. Familiar patterns will be interrupted; people who held authority may lose it; what seemed like a reasonably stable situation (the sermon *always* following the choir anthem) all of a sudden appears up for grabs. A sense of loss results, bringing with it a willingness to fight for what was lost, perhaps trying to recapture the old ways.

Don't relate all this to some major doctrinal rift; I have deliberately chosen simple, common church issues like changes in programming, order of service, or Bible versions. These little matters create major schisms in congregations, not because they are themselves big issues; they are not. These issues become big because we mishandle the process of change when we fail to correctly assess presuppositions of human behavior and the kinds of psychological values people hold in their lives. *More often than not the process of the leader rather than the resistance of the traditionalist is at fault.*

Before we leave this section let's review some things psychologists have discovered about how people are motivated.

1. Different people are motivated by different things.
2. One motivation that seems important to most people is the feeling that they are doing something worthwhile.
3. The more people understand the value of what they do, the more motivated they become to do well.
4. People tend to be consistent in their level of motivation.
5. People tend to perform at about the same level as others who work close to them.[2]

## FACILITATING ATTITUDINAL CHANGE

Once we understand why folks fight for certain things and not others, how do we go about actually changing people rather than changing things? Essentially, attitudinal change is facilitated in six ways that are related but different parts of the leader's task. And all link tightly to the material we shall study in chapter 15, "Working with People in Groups."

**1.** *Attitudinal change may be facilitated by interaction.* People change as they talk with each other, usually in the group related to a given change. For example, members of a church board can change their attitudes on a given issue as they thoroughly discuss all the pros and cons. Interaction does not guarantee change, but the absence of interaction may very well guarantee stonewalling on a certain position.

**2.** *Attitudinal change may be facilitated by events outside the group.* A church board, struggling, perhaps even quarreling over certain issues, may find itself drawn together by a major crisis in the community. Perhaps an automobile accident involved several teenagers in the local high school. Or maybe a fire gutted the home of one of the parishioners. Neither of these events has the slightest bearing on the agenda items being discussed by the board, but it can change the whole environment in which that discussion takes place.

**3.** *Attitudinal change may be facilitated by external authority.* Sometimes a group has no choice on change. A denominational official or perhaps even a decision by the zoning board or other civic body forces a whole reorientation on the part of a planning group. They didn't anticipate it, they didn't want it, but now they must work with the way things are, not the way they would like them to be. Immature leaders grumble and complain about such situations; mature leaders accept them and move on from there.

**4.** *Attitudinal change may be facilitated by interpersonal contact.* This is different from the interaction within the group. We're talking here about casual, even social contact on the part of group members. As people get to know one another outside the frame of reference in which change issues are embraced, they feel differently toward each other in the formal situation. To put it another way, change in informal social structures leads to change in formal business structures. Think about students getting to know a college or seminary professor outside of class. Their attitudes toward what he says in class may be greatly altered after spending an evening at his home chatting by a fireside or playing table games.

**5.** *Attitudinal change may be facilitated by the increase of similarity.* One argument for retaining board and committee members in positions for longer periods of time is that they learn to work together. Constantly changing board membership has the value of bringing in new life, new blood, and new ideas, but it does promote instability and does not allow people to feel comfortable working with one another. Like a husband and wife who have lived together for thirty years, board members who have served side by side through crisis and calm, through the coming and going of pastors, through building programs and missions budgets, tend to learn how to work with one another even though their personalities may be vastly different. We would hope such behavior evidences the Spirit of God in their lives helping them to grow in grace.

**6.** *Finally, attitudinal change may be facilitated by crisis in the group.* In item 2 we focused on something that happened totally apart from group activity. Here the event is internal—perhaps an illness of a group member or a pending divorce. Formerly unpliable and even hostile attitudes change as people begin to see one another as human beings, not just members of the board. I believe God sends such crises at times to loosen up congregations and force people to carry out His work in ways they might never choose in their own stubborn carnality. I could multiply illustrations at this point, but then you can plug in your own as well.

# TECHNIQUES FOR MANAGING CHANGE

Since the process of change is a normal function of administration, change can be managed. Indeed, if it cannot, our entire discussion in this chapter crumbles in futility. Even twenty years ago management experts were talking about "techniques" related to the managing of change and though the models have become more sophisticated in the two intervening decades, the principles remain somewhat the same.

## CREATE AN EFFECTIVE GROUP

So wrote Thomas Wickes in 1967 while emphasizing the interactional process we talked about earlier in the chapter. He says "association" provides the first link in a five-link chain which also includes involvement, relationship, commitment, and action.

> *Association* implies more than just working at an individual position—and more than just the usual interaction with other people on the job. It implies periodic contacts with the boss and the others who work in the same unit. It suggests a pattern of association, such that when the members of the group meet with each other they are exposed to each other's ideas and interactive styles.[3]

Remember what we said earlier about the maturity of the group and how it relates to change? Maturity comes about through experience, and as you already know, experience can only be gained by experiencing it. Just as we have seen in our discussion on planning, some people do not work well in a change management group. Growth and maturity in leadership coupled with the replacement of certain divisive members can pull together the kind of management team that will become "an effective group."

## CULTIVATE INTERACTION AND DIALOGUE

Yes, this too sounds like an echo. Remember my suggestion earlier that we create our own problems in change? Genuine involvement of people means genuine two-way discussion. But leaders serve as more than just reporters; they facilitate dialogue. People need opportunities to ask questions, to discuss implications of the change in their lives and families, and to express disagreement if necessary. Dialogue may not result in total unanimity but it will at least guarantee a feeling of "having been heard" on the part of all of those who genuinely participate.

Throughout the dialogue we must ask the right kind of questions. For example,

"What present problem makes this change necessary?"

"What are our motives for this change?"

"Why do some people seem to strongly favor the change while others seem to resist?"

"Have we established a workable and reasonable time frame?"

"Have we allowed everyone (who wishes to do so) to speak to the issues involved?"

## COMMUNICATE A SPIRIT OF UNDERSTANDING AND HARMONY

*If we really understand why people resist change* (see the first section of the chapter), *we can interpret the resistance and deal with it logically while at the same time behaving like children of God and walking in peace and harmony rather than confusion and bitterness.* People cope with stress all the time in the church, and change introduces more. As leaders we should minimize stress whenever possible.

Of course all of this must be related to our short- and long-range goals and we need to constantly communicate the whys. As British General Montgomery once put it, "Let the troops know what you know and they'll follow."

Here's one thing we know about change; people tend to *underestimate* their capacity for handling it. Heavy publicity about the crushing horrors of future shock has made all change look negative. Followers tend to see the pain involved with change; leaders provide the vision which helps them look above the pain to the potential.

Throughout the process the biblical dimensions of unity and harmony must be kept at the forefront of our collective attitude: "Do everything without complaining or arguing, so that you may become blameless and pure, children of God without fault in a crooked and depraved generation, in which you shine like stars in the universe" (Phil. 2:14-15).

Does the Bible offer a change model in which real people had to confront a major issue of change and handled it in an exemplary manner? Doubtless many could be identified throughout the Book of

Acts but I think particularly of the 15th chapter where first-century believers faced the crucial question, "What does a Gentile have to do to be saved?" The decision had already been made to proclaim the Gospel to the Gentiles (11:15-18). But now some had raised the issues of circumcision and law-keeping since many Gentiles trusted Christ during what we now call the first missionary journey. Notice several things about the passage.

1. Regardless of their viewpoints, all parties were invited to speak freely (15:4-5, 7, 12).

2. They stuck to the biblical issues rather than getting side-tracked in emotional traps strewn all around this particular battle-ground (vv. 7-10, 12).

3. James tried to create a cohesive group by seeking consensus and reviewing the issues in detail (vv. 13-21).

4. The decision, though viewed in the late twentieth century as somewhat stiff and uncompromising, was, in the context of the first-century church, a strong emphasis on grace (vv. 19-21).

5. The Jerusalem church protected its integrity throughout the process, particularly in reporting the results of the conference to the Gentile brethren. Had the message been sent with Paul and Barnabas alone, they could have been accused of slanting the interpretation or even persuading the council. The addition of Judas and Silas protected the purity of the report (vv. 22-29).

6. The process resulted in acceptance on the part of the Antioch church, acceptance on the part of the majority of the Jerusalem church, and continued growth of the missionary movement (vv. 30-41).

To be sure, we could not argue that James and the leaders of the Jerusalem church went through a planning stage, an announcement stage, and a resistance stage. Their delicate and sensitive handling of the major change issue, however, does demonstrate an understanding of human behavior, a grasp of the stress and trauma of change, and a willingness to focus on changing the attitudes of people rather than just the bylaws of the organization.

## STUDY QUESTIONS

1. Study the ten principles of change (pp. 150–151). Rate them on the following agreement scale, then be ready to explain your disagreements. (Circle your choices.)

| 1. | Strongly Agree | Agree | Neutral | Disagree | Strongly Disagree |
|---|---|---|---|---|---|
| 2. | Strongly Agree | Agree | Neutral | Disagree | Strongly Disagree |
| 3. | Strongly Agree | Agree | Neutral | Disagree | Strongly Disagree |
| 4. | Strongly Agree | Agree | Neutral | Disagree | Strongly Disagree |
| 5. | Strongly Agree | Agree | Neutral | Disagree | Strongly Disagree |
| 6. | Strongly Agree | Agree | Neutral | Disagree | Strongly Disagree |
| 7. | Strongly Agree | Agree | Neutral | Disagree | Strongly Disagree |
| 8. | Strongly Agree | Agree | Neutral | Disagree | Strongly Disagree |
| 9. | Strongly Agree | Agree | Neutral | Disagree | Strongly Disagree |
| 10. | Strongly Agree | Agree | Neutral | Disagree | Strongly Disagree |

**2.** Describe a change you would like to see occur in your church. Now describe how people's attitudes will have to change to make it possible. Use the six-part attitudinal change list which appears in this chapter.

**3.** Evaluate the Powers quote on page 155. Rephrase it, rewrite it, argue with it, explain it.

**4.** Study Acts 15 in the light of the change process. Name some *additional* helpful lessons you think will work in your church.

# ENDNOTES

**1.** Bruce Powers, *Christian Leadership* (Nashville: Broadman Press, 1979), p. 41.

**2.** David Campbell, *If You Don't Know Where You're Going You'll Probably End Up Somewhere Else* (Allen, Texas: Argus Communications, 1974), pp. 71–3.

**3.** Thomas A. Wickes, "Techniques for Managing Change," *Automation* (May 1967), p. 37.

CHAPTER 10

# MOTIVATING WITHOUT MANIPULATING

There he stands—your new recruit. He has been carefully selected, enlisted, oriented, trained, placed, and already involved in the decision-making process. Now it becomes necessary to anchor him in a leadership role for a long period of time. To be sure, that can be done through manipulation, a process we commonly use with children and often carry over into working with adults. Interestingly, the three fearful emotional states used to manipulate children—ignorance, anxiety, and guilt—are the same ones used in leadership with adults and passed off as motivation. Wives and husbands do it all the time, like when somebody must jump in the station wagon and go out to football practice to pick up Jimmy, usually less than an hour after they both have just gotten home from a hard day's work.

We need to be a bit careful here because the question of manipulation hinges very closely on the question of loyalty, to which we must return later in this chapter. For example, we could give simple lessons on how not to be manipulated—judge your own behaviors, offer your own reasons to justify your behavior, change your mind if you wish to, admit it when you don't understand, or perhaps even don't care about an issue—but such behavior, while alleviating manipulation, could lead to a hopeless selfishness, hardly the goal of godly motivation for Christian service.

On the other hand we don't want to rehash Herzberg and mutter over Maslow in this chapter. Gary Gray, however, provides an interesting twist to the Maslow model which accounts for why motivation seems to be such a constant problem. He points out that achieving esteem and self-actualization must be done over and over again throughout the years of one's life. He shows at least four

163

points at which the struggle to work one's way up through the various kinds of motivational need patterns occurs at least four times in the life of almost everyone (Fig. 19).[1]

This could be enlarged to take into account the current demographics which show that people change careers three times and jobs seven times during their adult lifetimes. Or, relating to different kinds of ministry in the church (I may be stretching the model a bit), the principle of Maslow's theory still fits. Consider the importance of motivation in each of the areas shown in Figure 20[2] and how many years might be encompassed in this kind of ministry motif.

So that's what our chapter is about. How to keep people motivated without manipulating them or, for that matter, allowing them to manipulate us.

## UNDERSTANDING THE DYNAMIC OF MOTIVATION

We have been so blinded by Madison Avenue hype that we can carry its techniques into the church and never even notice the

### FIGURE 19

# GRAY'S MOTIVATIONAL PATTERNS
## Subcultures

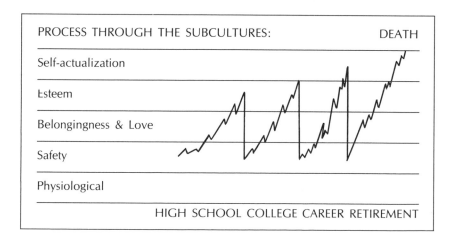

PROCESS THROUGH THE SUBCULTURES:     DEATH

Self-actualization

Esteem

Belongingness & Love

Safety

Physiological

HIGH SCHOOL COLLEGE CAREER RETIREMENT

grievous sins we have committed in so doing. In fact, commercial hype is such a part of our culture it can even parody itself for a laugh. Joe Isuzu assures us with what can only be described as a sneer, "You have my word on it."

We have treated motivation as an understanding of the way we *make* people do things or perhaps make them *want* to do things that we clearly understand they ought to do. Most of us would prefer to be light-handed rather than heavy-handed, but the carrot-or-the-stick mentality prevails—offer them a reward or threaten punishment; that'll get 'em.

## WHY DO PEOPLE DO THINGS?

Or more properly ask some pastors, why *don't* they do things? A host of reasons could be given but let's focus on just three. First of all, the lay leader may be *unclear about his role* in the church. He is really not sure what is expected of him and how he fits into the larger scheme of things. Secondly, he may be suffering from a *feeling of inadequacy*; competent in business, he feels untaught and

FIGURE 20

# GRAY'S MOTIVATIONAL PATTERNS
## Ministries

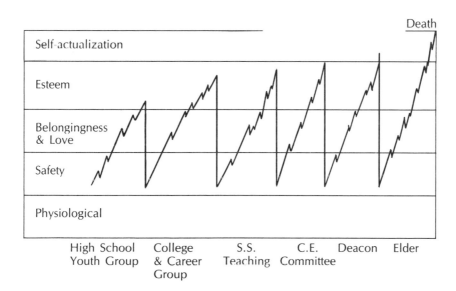

inadequate to carry out the kinds of things which go on in the church. Finally, it's possible that we have *never really challenged* him. Our effort at recruitment (see chap. 8) may have centered on problems and predicaments rather than exciting potential.

So he ends up fitting somewhere on Figure 21, often just about where the arrow points.[3] Certainly we are sometimes guilty of moving lower on the scale, appealing to arm-twisting motives of duress and (God help us) even threat. But we can also move higher on the scale to the self-actualization levels taught us by Maslow and Herzberg. But essentially, we evangelicals plod along near the median level, content if we can just "get folks to do their duty."

FIGURE 21

# WHY DO PEOPLE DO THINGS?

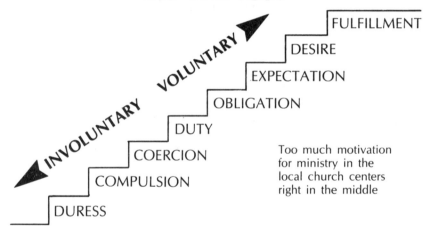

FULFILLMENT
DESIRE
EXPECTATION
OBLIGATION
DUTY
COERCION
COMPULSION
DURESS

VOLUNTARY

INVOLUNTARY

Too much motivation for ministry in the local church centers right in the middle

*WHERE DO MOST MOTIVATIONAL ATTEMPTS CENTER?* The answer to that depends on whether you're talking about the motivator or the motivatee. But then again, maybe it doesn't. Seemingly we evangelicals have settled for a general allegiance to duty which renders much service to Jesus Christ nothing more nor less than a neurotic compulsion—"I do it because I have to." Since we know people will operate from that basis, we approach them on that basis. It's not effective; but at least it's simple and we all understand each other.

How different the words of Jesus when approaching Peter and

Andrew by the Sea of Galilee—"Come follow Me and I will make you fishers of men." Not "I will make you the best fishermen in this area" or "I will help you catch more fish than you've ever caught before." The Master couched the invitation in an entirely different dimension. The challenges to the missionary team throughout Acts, the exhortation of young churches in the epistles, and the general expectancy the Lord has for all His people should raise our sights above that general compulsion to duty.

No longer do we face the question of overload; no longer are we asked to take a position no one else wants or one which does not require any ability; no longer must we face a life sentence; no longer need we grope about for objectives and methodology. All are inherent in the clarity of the Master's call. Rather than superimposing something *on* the disciples Christ releases something *within* them (more on this later).

We've been talking a lot about Herzberg and Maslow (and we could add Hughes and MacGregor to round out the team). More recently two other researchers, David McClelland and John Atkinson, have isolated three distinct motives which affect people's work-related behavior—the need for achievement, the need for power, and the need for affiliation.[4]

Marlene Wilson diagrams this in the form of a "reservoir motivation" and argues that "everyone has all three valves or motives, but the valves vary as to size and how much they are used from one person to another" (Fig. 22).[5] Again Wilson says, "A weak motive is a tight or sticky valve that allows only a tiny bit of energy through— almost like it's a rusted ship."[6]

McClelland and Atkinson argue that the presence and strength of these vows (motives) can actually be tested through what is called a *thematic apperception test* (TAT). We have no time to describe that in detail here and the reader is referred to Wilson's summary in the source cited at the end of this chapter.

To be sure, McClelland and Atkinson haven't talked about spiritual gifts and the call of God. But when we fit together everything we have learned so far in this book we can see how this new piece of the puzzle helps us understand why people choose to do some things and not others, and why some people choose to do many things and others next to nothing.

## WHAT KEEPS PEOPLE FROM VOLUNTEERING?

We have already answered this question in a number of different ways, but let's attack the elephant from yet another side. There are some common "blockades" to effective motivation. Some people simply feel bad about themselves and their own abilities; they have what we would call a low self-concept.

FIGURE 22

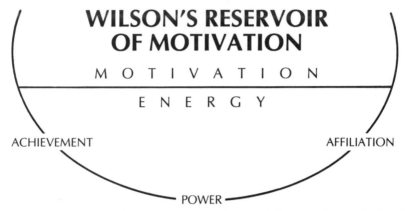

WILSON'S RESERVOIR
OF MOTIVATION

M O T I V A T I O N

E N E R G Y

ACHIEVEMENT

AFFILIATION

POWER

Others seem hesitant because of past failure—they tried volunteering and it didn't work. Perhaps they had difficult experiences; maybe they were criticized by others; or they may have felt some personal or financial loss as a result of their willingness to serve. The incident itself contains no importance; the fact is sufficient.

Often we encounter the matter of complacency. Call it lack of commitment if you wish, but complacent people simply do not see that they have a responsibility to be involved in the ministry of the church. Such people feel the organization has not been meeting their own needs, so why should they respond in a positive way. People are motivated by the things they like to do, by the things they feel are successful, and by things which obviously help other people. We need to accentuate these positives.

Keep in mind too that some folks, raised with negative habit patterns as children, have developed low achievement drives and will be more difficult to motivate than others. People may be created equal, but in this strange and changing society they don't stay that way long.

Let's go back to Wilson one more time for a list of the principle reasons that people volunteer in church settings.

They want to be needed.
They want to help others and make a difference.

They want to learn new skills and use skills they already have.
They want to belong to a caring community and feel accepted
as members.
They want self-esteem and affirmation.
They want to grow in their faith and share their God-given
gifts.
They want to keep from being lonely.
They want to support a cause they believe in.[7]

# CHANGING THEORY TO PRACTICE – PRINCIPLES OF MOTIVATION

I struggled with whether this portion of the chapter should precede the last, but perhaps it's better to raise the questions first
and then come back with some answers. When one begins to list
principles there is hardly a magic number. There may be ten
principles of motivation, or perhaps fifteen. Maybe they can be
stated in three or four which form an attractive acronym. I have
settled on five derived from years of research and experience in
working with local church volunteers.

*MOTIVATION DEPENDS ON MUTUALLY ACCEPTED GOALS*
Readers who also spend much time in the kitchen will think this
principle sounds like the familiar "white sauce." It may not do
much by itself, but it blends into everything. Once the authority of
Scripture has been affirmed and its imperatives claimed, educators
constantly emphasize two things—*needs and objectives.*

In this situation we use the term "goals" as synonymous with
objectives, though the word is not always used that way. *People
tend to be motivated toward ministry opportunities when they perceive
that their goals in ministry are equivalent to or at least closely approximate the goals of the organization.* If we wanted to get theoretical
and scientific about this we'd look into Andrew Halpin's research
and talk about the theory of transactionalism, but that's not our
purpose at this point.[8] People may not automatically see this parallel and it becomes the leader's task to show how serving Christ is
normal and healthy.

*MOTIVATION IS UNLEASHED, NOT SUPERIMPOSED*
Here again I'm repeating myself but with deliberate intent. Motivation, like creativity, already resides in the person, and the leader
(teacher) finds the right way to unlock it. Cashin helpfully relates
this view to college students. Coming at it from a negative point of
view he suggests that,

Those who are not motivated to learn resist new information, tend to make snap decisions, use categorical reasoning (good or bad) rather than an evaluation continuum, and freeze their judgment even when new information suggests the wisdom of revising it. These findings have implications to those of us who teach. Since motivation and commitment are personal matters with each student, we as teachers should do what we can to eliminate the barriers that block them.[9]

After pummeling the subject for four pages Cashin really doesn't come up with anything we don't already know: motivation is a significant variable in learning; most students are innately curious; these positive assets can be used by the wise teacher; and motivation primarily occurs in a certain kind of atmosphere which stimulates discovery of learning.

Once again we see that the administrator is essentially a teacher in disguise, one who assists subordinates and volunteers to learn better ways of doing things.

## MOTIVATION BUILDS ON THE BASIS OF NEED FULFILLMENT

The Gray chart offered earlier in the chapter identifies this precise point and builds (as does most need-fulfillment theory) on the research of Abraham Maslow. Since I have promised not to plunge into Maslow again in this work I will keep that promise. But I should note that, apart from highly specific theological analysis, Maslow's approach to human motivation can generally be regarded as theoretically sound. My main quarrel is that he deals a bit too much with "here and now" behavior without relating issues of motivation and valuing to "then and there" experiences of the person. Furthermore, the Christian has to add dimensions of supernatural control and Holy Spirit motivation which are unaccounted for in the Maslow scheme.

## MOTIVATION TENDS TO FOLLOW POSITIVE MINISTRY SATISFACTION

When a leader expresses concern over someone's motivation he is more than likely trying to create a need to work than attempting to satisfy a need of the worker. Since behavior is influenced by its consequences, leaders can do several things to realize the optimal effect of this relationship.

1. Train in such a way that the behavior experienced on the job will reinforce the training.

2. Design ministry opportunities so that rewards will be built in at periodic points.

3. Select reinforcers that are indeed reinforcing to this particular worker (e.g., more money might not be a reinforcer to a $500,000 chief executive officer).

Nevertheless, apart from banquets, plaques, applause, and public recognition, ministry itself must provide the ultimate reward. Paul's point about serving cheerfully for a reward and grudgingly without (but nevertheless serving) focuses the concept of Christian motivation. We don't want to miss all the good points that we can integrate from secular studies in managerial science, but we never want to cave in to those techniques which border on manipulation.

And let's not forget what some have called "negative reinforcement." One of the less attractive responsibilities of leadership is rebuke, and the flip side of recognition is reprimand. Engstrom and Dayton offer some guidelines from the standard Marine Corps military handbook which relate to this business of reprimand.

> Public praise and private reprimand: the basic rule is praise in public and reprimand in private.
>
> Public reprimand, no matter how much deserved, wounds the person's pride and often embarrasses staff members around the person who is publicly reprimanded. Anything that destroys a staff person's healthy pride not only engenders resentment, but also destroys the self-confidence which he or she needs for corrective action.
>
> Never give a person a dollar's worth of blame without a dime's worth of praise.
>
> Avoid collective reprimands. This also applies to collective punishments. Nothing so rightly infuriates an innocent staff person as to be unfairly included in a collective "blast" or punishment.
>
> Never make a promise or threat which you are not capable of fulfilling or which you do not intend to fulfill.
>
> Like reward, the effectiveness of the proof is in direct proportion to its immediacy.[10]

## MOTIVATION RELATES DYNAMICALLY TO LEADERSHIP STYLE

We've said this before? Sorry, just seemed important to emphasize it again here. Gary C. Newton, a professor at Taylor University, has done some interesting research on volunteers in the Wesleyan denomination, particularly in Midwestern churches. He set out to identify characteristics, behaviors, and skills of persons who had been selected by volunteers as significant in their continued motivation. In other words, how do we locate the kind of leaders who motivate people? More to the point, how do we become the kind of leaders who motivate people?

Newton's research responses help answer that question, and he sums up his conclusions in the following paragraph:

> Leaders would support volunteers by encouraging them, affirming them, praying for them, and showing them appreciation. Although their general personality characteristics might differ they would tend to be friendly and open with others. They would have good communication skills, being able to listen well and share on a personal level. As people with integrity they would win people's respect because of their commitment to live what they profess to believe in. Their sensitivity to God would be evident to those around them.[11]

## RELATING LOYALTY TO MOTIVATION

How much of what people do in service for Christ through the church relates to their positive feelings (loyalty) toward their leaders? How does mutual loyalty speak to questions of motivation?

The traditional view of direction and control argues that the average person has an inherent dislike of work and will avoid it if he can (Douglas McGregor). More recent research, however, suggests that management has generally adopted more humanitarian values and has striven to give equitable and more generous treatment to employees. Unfortunately, the underlying presupposition hasn't changed!

What do we believe about people? Well, you say, we believe they are sinners, fallen in Adam, and capable of the worst possible kinds of sin. True. That accounts for the horrors we see all around us in the world. But they are also capable of regeneration, being reborn to the image of God in which they were originally created and, therefore, potentially using ministries to serve the risen Christ.

When Peter wrote to the elders in the early church he dealt with the question of motivation.

Be shepherds of God's flock that is under your care, serving as overseers—not because you must, but because you are willing, as God wants you to be; not greedy for money, but eager to serve; not lording it over those entrusted to you, but being examples to the flock (1 Peter 5:2-3).

Notice there are several "not/but" sections to our passage. People should not serve under pressure (guilt) but with *pleasure* by being available. People should not serve for profit (gain) but rather for *progress* of the body, to be positively anxious for its advancement and enhancement; people should not serve for prestige (glory) but rather through distinctive *portrayals* of the ministry of Christ, to be active in ministry as He was active in ministry.[12]

Crucial to our use of this passage is awareness that Peter wrote it to elders! If the elders serve from proper motives, their biblical loyalty to the Saviour will trickle down throughout the various levels of the ministry. Forget traditional loyalty characterized by blind obedience. Forget contemporary loyalty characterized by organizational ownership. Focus on biblical loyalty which strives to carry out every task to the glory of Christ.

## STUDY QUESTIONS

**1.** Review the reasons why people *don't* do things. What other reasons could be added to the list?

**2.** Review the Wilson diagram; how can this be applied in your church?

**3.** State why goals are important in the process of motivation.

**4.** What do we mean when saying, "Motivation is unleashed, not superimposed"?

**5.** If traditional loyalty was marked by blind obedience, what characterizes contemporary loyalty?

## ENDNOTES

1. Gary M. Gray, "Wisdom, Stature, God and Man," *Church Management—The Clergy Journal* (February 1987), pp. 32–3.
2. Gary M. Gray, "Wisdom, Stature, God and Man," *Church*

*Management—The Clergy Journal* (February 1987), pp. 32–3.

**3.** I attribute this chart to Dr. Ed Hayes who used it in his classroom ministry at the Conservative Baptist Theological Seminary.

**4.** Published in George H. Litwin and Robert A. Steiger, Jr., *Motivation and Organizational Climate*, 1968.

**5.** Marlene Wilson, *How to Mobilize Church Volunteers* (Minneapolis: Marlene Wilson, 1983), p. 29.

**6.** Wilson, p. 30.

**7.** Wilson, p. 87.

**8.** Kenneth O. Gangel, *Building Leaders for Church Education* (Chicago: Moody Press, 1981), pp. 372–76.

**9.** William A. Cashin, "Motivating Students," *Idea Paper No. 1* (Lawrence, Kan.: Division of Continuing Education, August 1979), p. 2.

**10.** Ted W. Engstrom and Edward R. Dayton, "Recognition and Reprimands," *Christian Leadership Letter* (May 1987).

**11.** Gary C. Newton, "The Motivation of the Saints and the Interpersonal Competencies of Their Leaders" (Independent research carried out at Taylor University, Upland, Indiana, 1986), p. 7.

**12.** I owe the interesting alliterative arrangement to my friend and colleague, Professor Ron Blue.

# CHAPTER 11

# DELEGATING YOUR WAY
# TO SURVIVAL

In their effective book *Managing Your Time*, Engstrom and McKenzie claim that delegation may be the most important single skill of an executive. It has to do with assigning a part of your job to someone else, entrusting responsibility and authority as well as tasks to other people who share the ministry with you.

Sometimes servant leadership seems to require doing everything that needs to be done around the church or parachurch ministry to show that one has a humble spirit of service (and to make sure that things get done on time and well). Some people even describe delegation as "doing all you can and giving away whatever work remains." Actually the reverse is true. *Delegation means getting rid of everything you can and doing only what remains.* Remember the activity analysis chart? The third line identified column 1 items as those things which "must be done by me"—everything else can be delegated.

## PRINCIPLES OF DELEGATION

No facet of managerial behavior stands more clearly attested in God's Word than delegating. Shortly after the Exodus in 1446 B.C., Moses bogged down in the desert with leadership problems. In order to destroy the Egyptian army the Israelites marched north-east toward Sinai, accompanied by Jehovah's provision. Exodus 17 records the victory against the Amalekites at Rephidim.

The real problem, it appears, was internal. It is possible that Moses practiced an ancient form of "corporate bigamy," trying to run everything at the office while his wife and children stayed with her parents. Moses' father-in-law, Jethro (also called Reuel), brought the family back to Moses again and there this outside observer offered insight on how to solve the leadership problems of the nomadic Israelites. Though the passage is extensive, it may be useful to reproduce it here for review.

> The next day Moses took his seat to serve as judge for the people, and they stood around him from morning till evening. When his father-in-law saw all that Moses was doing for the people, he said, "What is this you are doing for the people? Why do you alone sit as judge, while all these people stand around you from morning till evening?"
>
> Moses answered him, "Because the people come to me to seek God's will. Whenever they have a dispute, it is brought to me, and I decide between the parties and inform them of God's decrees and laws."
>
> Moses' father-in-law replied, "What you are doing is not good. You and these people who come to you will only wear yourselves out. The work is too heavy for you; you cannot handle it alone. Listen now to me and I will give you some advice, and may God be with you. You must be the people's representative before God and bring their disputes to Him. Teach them the decrees and laws, and show them the way to live and the duties they are to perform. But select capable men from all the people—men who fear God, trustworthy men who hate dishonest gain—and appoint them as officials over thousands, hundreds, fifties and tens. Have them serve as judges for the people at all times, but have them bring every difficult case to you; the simple cases they can decide themselves. That will make your load lighter, because they will share it with you. If you do this and God so commands, you will be able to stand the strain, and all these people will go home satisfied."
>
> Moses listened to his father-in-law and did everything he said. He chose capable men from all Israel and made them leaders of the people, officials over thousands, hundreds, fifties and tens. They served as judges for the people at all times. The difficult cases they brought to Moses, but the simple ones they decided themselves (Ex. 18:13-26).

Several key principles of delegation surface in this passage;

let's look at them in the order they appear.

1. Delegation does not come naturally to a leader. Moses was skilled in all the learning of the Egyptians, trained for politics and war, instructed in philosophy and geology. Yet supervising this massive movement of people through the desert seemed beyond his managerial competence. Despite his learning, he never reached the logical conclusion that he needed assistance in leading God's people (v. 13).

Delegation does not come naturally to a leader, even a good one, because *the reasons for not delegating are emotional and not rational.* Leaders do not sit down and logically arrive at the conclusion they should not delegate. They fail to delegate because they don't know how, or because they fear people will be unwilling to work hard. Perhaps they suspect someone will do the job better than they, or not do the job as well. All these reasons and more have their basis in some emotional reaction rather than carefully planned action. They result in two problems: individual frustration for the leader and the failure to develop new leaders.

2. Delegation is essential for survival (v. 18). In all the history of management science on the subject of delegation there appears no more poignant phrase than verse 18. "The work is too heavy for you; you cannot handle it alone." We hear a great deal today about stress and the workaholic tendencies of many Christian leaders. The quickest way to insure both stress and workaholism is to fail at delegation.

3. Delegation does not reduce the leader's accountability (v. 19). Let's make a distinction here between "responsibility" and "accountability." The former goes with the task and authority given to the subordinate so he can carry out whatever work he is expected to achieve. The latter stays with the delegator and punctuates his responsibility for the quality of the subordinate's performance. Moses answered to God; college presidents answer to their boards; pastors answer to elders or deacons; Sunday School superintendents answer to the Christian Education Committee or Sunday School board—every leader must account to someone or some group for the function of his subordinates.

But all the above depict upward accountability. There is also downward accountability; i.e., accountability to the people whom you serve as leader. One of the dangers in currently popular "elder rule" may lead to a breaking away from the trenches of real people.

4. Delegation should be practiced with qualified people. Notice

again verse 21 in which Moses is urged to "select capable men . . . men who fear God, trustworthy men who hate dishonest gain." Qualifications for different tasks will demand different capabilities in the people we lead. *Wise leaders select the right people for the right tasks, thereby minimizing failure and creating an in-service training program in the process.*

Building a leadership team takes time. Some Christian leaders speak the truth when they say they have no one to whom important tasks can be delegated. We expect such a predicament in a small or new organization for the first year or so, but if it continues beyond that, the leader and not the subordinates must bear the blame. George Williams says it plainly:

> Why do so many "parish managers" want to keep running the whole show? Probably because no matter how high one advances, it is hard to let go of previously performed duties, especially if one excelled at them. It is especially difficult to turn such functions over to someone less adept. In some instances, a part of such duties may be retained, but delegation generally is called for if managing is to take precedence.[1]

Often there's the question of determining the risk factor. A low failure/risk item can be given to a person whose competence we doubt. The result might be a surprising demonstration of faithful service and a greater degree of confidence next time. Mainline, decision-making goals, however, must be delegated to people who are competent to handle the responsibilities we hand them.

5. Delegation results in a harmonious organization (v. 23). The passage ends in a spirit and tone considerably more mellow than the way it began. That reminds us of another lesson in delegation Moses learned at Taberah (Num. 11). The Scripture tells us that "the rabble with them began to crave other food, and again the Israelites started wailing" (v. 4). As the horror of the scene builds, verse 10 presents the dilemma of leadership: "Moses heard the people of every family wailing, each at the entrance to his tent." Few pastors and Christian leaders have not experienced similar trauma, though admittedly, the collective wailing of 2 1/2 million Jews in the desert must have been an awesome sound.

As usual, Jehovah had a solution for His servant: "Bring me 70 of Israel's elders who are known to you as leaders and officials among the people. Have them come to the tent of meeting, that they may stand there with you. I will come down and speak with you there, and I will take of the Spirit that is on you and put the Spirit on them. They will help you carry the burden of the people so that you will not have to carry it alone" (vv. 16-17).

One could argue that the Christian organization should be harmonious even if its leaders do not delegate well. The common sense of purpose in a Christian organization tends to make many of its people believe they know what's best and, therefore, don't need you to tell them. Such a problem stems not from delegation itself, but from leadership style and the way you treat subordinates.

# PURPOSES OF DELEGATION

The title of our chapter was not lightly conceived—this managerial function is indeed the "key to survival." All things considered, the delegating leader accounts for a significant amount of the achievement level in any organization.

## SURVIVAL IN THE MINISTRY

Effective leaders try to make sure people serve where they belong. Peter Drucker likes to say there are no poor employees, only poor bosses, because staffing decisions center on emphasizing strengths. If we don't know where people are strong, we can't put them in positions which utilize and emphasize their strengths.

Imagine a professional football coach playing a 180-pound nose guard or inverting the positions of quarterback and center. *Survival requires building a team and making that team interdependent.* A good leader understands who depends on him and whom he depends on in the day-to-day conflicts of ministry. The organizational chart provides a skeleton, necessary to hold up the body but hardly a channel for nourishment.

## REDUCTION OF STRESS IN LEADERSHIP

Recent research shows various kinds of stress in the ministry, and that stress or "stressors," as they are now called, tend to differ among senior pastors with staff, senior pastors with no staff, and associates, such as, youth directors or ministers of education. Yet all lists include such things as fear of failure, frustration, inadequacy, anxiety, proliferation of activities, no time for study, and spiritual dryness.

Psychologists and others who have worked with stressors in leadership tell us that stress management is available to any leader who really wants to do it and propose such things as:

1. avoiding stressful situations

2. working toward a realistic self-concept
3. forgiving yourself for deficiencies
4. learning techniques of relaxation
5. developing a capacity for spontaneity
6. building strong, positive friendships.

They all sound great and are all probably impossible unless work the leader knows must be done can be parceled out to others. Sound like more survival talk? That depends on whether we measure survival in terms of one's ability to continue with the organization or to maintain good spiritual, physical, and psychological health. Stress attacks these latter areas, and delegation alleviates the tension.

## TRAINING OTHERS FOR SERVICE

Young Christian leaders find themselves in a "Catch-22" situation. On the one hand, they desperately need positions which offer experience. Yet those very positions often seem to be available only to those who already have experience! The effective leader solves this problem by training staff in-house—both paid staff and volunteers.

Workers tend to be ineffective because they lack confidence in themselves, a posture which often results from the lack of confidence shown by leadership. Is the worker in the wrong position? Who put him there? He doesn't like the job and serves from a position of unhappiness and frustration. Who leaves him there? Is he ill trained, frustrated, and ready to quit? Who failed to train him? Delegation tends to be seen as something which benefits the leader and, of course, it does. But it also benefits every worker to whom important, challenging tasks are given, enabling growth and development in leadership skills.

## PERPETUATION OF THE ADMINISTRATIVE TEAM

The effective leader functions as himself. He doesn't need to hide under some kind of mask; he doesn't try to be someone else; he assumes that God can use him with the gifts and training that he has. But such a reality assessment also takes into consideration his weaknesses and the gaps in his own training and experience. Pulling around him an administrative team to whom he delegates massive amounts of responsibility for the ongoing of the church, school, or other ministry, he strengthens and perpetuates that biblical team concept of ministry.

Note how often we see that exemplified in the work of the Apostle Paul. He constantly sent Timothy here or Titus there, expected Luke to arrive with this or that, or dispatched funds to one of the churches through another associate. Members of the missionary team were recruited, trained, and then effectively used in the broadest possible way. Paul may have been trained in rabbinical studies but his approach to delegation is textbook administrative process.

# PRACTICE OF DELEGATION

A study done earlier in this decade noted that at least 10 percent of all pastors are attempting to become "spiritual supermen" and another 25–30 percent just struggle to stay afloat until retirement. Family time, vacation time, and prayertime are all devoured by compulsion to ministry. Why? My experience suggests that many pastors don't delegate simply because they don't know how. They don't even know how to begin much less carry through with control, supervision, and evaluation. How about you? Consider these four essential steps.

## EXHIBIT CONFIDENCE

Notice how we're making progress in a logical way. Once we agree on the importance of delegation and select qualified people, then we can parcel out responsibility with an expectation that it will be done well.

Not an uncommon attitude for Christian leaders, though it is often unexpressed. But it is hardly a positive note on which to proceed with effective delegation. If you don't believe people are going to succeed, and you convey that impression, you've greatly lessened the likelihood of that success. Exhibiting confidence is more than just saying, "Jack, I'm sure you can handle this for us." It's the *kind of task* we give him, the *way we assign it*, and the *quality of reinforcement* the worker receives all along the way.

## DEFINE EXPECTATIONS

Not procedures, just expectations. Once again, the necessary detail will differ in varying situations. A secretary working with the same boss over a period of years can almost second-guess what he wants when he says, "Please take care of this." A new youth director, still trying to gain self-confidence and job control in his new ministry, needs much more detailed instruction as to what his pastor expects of him in a given delegated task. It may even be important to tell someone *why* you have selected him or her. That kind of information could be useful both in defining expectations and demonstrating confidence.

Common pitfalls in delegation include ill-prepared objectives (what do you want the worker to achieve?), inadequate job descriptions (what tasks fall within those areas of responsibility?), inter-ference (has there been a violation of line staff relations?), and failure to follow up the initial delegation (how should we be check-ing up on the process?). The latter is so important it probably accounts for the majority of failures in delegation, so let's devote our last two steps to that key problem.

## PROVIDE RESOURCES

What will it take for the worker to actually achieve what you want done? Time? A certain commitment of budget? Access to informa-tion or areas not normally open to him or her? The delegator needs to determine the answers to these questions in advance in order to cut down on the frustration level at both ends.

A college dean assigns a new teacher a course he has never taught before. Great challenge and genuine excitement — unless he discovers he must work in a vacuum. If, for example, that course has been taught previously in that institution by other faculty, there ought to be a departmental file containing all kinds of syllabus materials, bibliographies, and other information, the wise dean or department chairman delegating the course to the new professor hands him all the information in the files with the clear assurance that he need not follow what any previous teacher has done before.

## ESTABLISH CONTROL

Let's assume that a certain delegated task goes on over a period of nine months. Perhaps that youth director has been assigned by his pastor to plan some kind of social event for the teenagers in the church. If the event will occur in September and the assignment was made in January, the pastor must work out various times to meet with the youth director for progress reports and information updates on the planning project. Effective leaders anticipate prob-lem areas, trouble points in a project. Are there certain points at which the delegatee might stumble? Make him aware of them in advance. This involves an adequate reporting system (which can be done orally at the meetings mentioned just above), best done in writing.

If the youth director hands the pastor a monthly written report, some segment of that report from January to September (from the point of delegation to the point of event) should provide explana-tion of his progress. Such a reporting system enables the leader to make corrections as the project unfolds, to assist and nurture his subordinates, and to look back at where things have gone wrong when it's time to evaluate both project and process.

Failure to delegate leads to workaholism, a syndrome of problems related to success addiction. *Workaholism is performance-dependency often brought about by exaggerated views of the leader's importance and indispensability.* Frank Robbins, vice president and chief executive officer for the Wycliffe Bible Translators from 1976–1984, described his process of delegation in the *Evangelical Missions Quarterly.* He tells how he gathered around him a staff of four to whom he gave over everything but his top priority matter (people supervision) "to the area directors and vice-presidents, to the board, the half-dozen other boards I served on, and to certain meetings of mission leaders." Robbins testifies:

> I was thus free to put my energies to relating with a solid base, and to the creative items I felt should have my priority. My experience suggests the executive does not have to be harried; the pile does not have to be impossible. How it can be avoided is individual to each person's situation, but the principles are simple and familiar—identify the job, staff for it, determine priorities, and delegate.[2]

Suppose you don't know whether you're delegating effectively or not. Here's a list of ten questions to ascertain that very important answer. Notice you are not asked to assess yourself with an "A" or a "10" but simply whether you're *satisfied* or *not satisfied* with current levels of operation.

|  | **Satisfied** | **Not Satisfied** |
|---|---|---|
| **1.** Have I been successful in retaining effective staff? |  |  |
| **2.** Am I exploring and discovering the gifts and talents of my staff? |  |  |
| **3.** Am I effectively using both professional and lay leadership resources? |  |  |
| **4.** Are people demonstrating spiritual and professional growth under my leadership? |  |  |

5. Am I finding time to get daily relaxation?

6. Do I take the time to sit and think creatively?

7. Am I able to leave my leadership role for periods of time with assurance that the work will go on well?

8. Do my subordinates delegate effectively?

9. Am I discovering new leaders in the organization?

10. Am I increasingly comfortable with the adequacy of my own personal goal achievement and the goal achievement of the organization?

# STUDY QUESTIONS

**1.** Failure to delegate is identified as an emotional problem. Name some reasons why your delegation may have been less than effective.

**2.** In a short, simple paragraph explain how proper delegation alleviates leadership stress.

**3.** Can you remember having been delegated a task *without* confidence? How did that create problems for you? What steps do you take as a leader to avoid doing that to others?

**4.** Find and review the "common pitfalls" in delegation. Select a sample task and respond to the four accompanying questions. Remember steps 3 and 4 both deal with the fourth question.

**5.** Evaluate your own delegation by answering the ten questions at the end of the chapter.

# ENDNOTES

**1.** George M. Williams, "Don't Hesitate—Delegate!", *Today's Parish* (Nov./Dec. 1983), p. 15.

**2.** Frank Robbins, "Here's Help for the Harried Executive," *Evangelical Missions Quarterly* (October 1984), p. 422.

# MAKING GOOD TEAM DECISIONS

"I propose that either we elders be more involved in the leadership and decision-making of this church," stated Earl Anderson, "or else we just assume the name 'Counselors' and let this church continue to be run entirely by 'momma' and 'papa' as it has since the beginning."

The statement hung in the air of the May 21 meeting. The five elders, pastor, and associate pastor gathered for their regular weekly meeting and time of prayer, when elder Earl suddenly came forth with the proposal. Pressures had been increasing for some time, and Mark Stevens, the associate pastor, wondered if he should enter the discussion and speak out on what he knew.[1]

So begins a fascinating case study entitled "Split Devotion" prepared by Gloryanna Hees at Fuller Theological Seminary in 1976. We'll not study the case further but those two opening paragraphs unlock the door for a major study of church process; namely the question, "Who's in charge here?" observed by analysis of how decisions are made. Ineffective decison-making results from such things as lack of clear-cut objectives, insecurity of position or authority, lack of information, and fear of change.

Contrary to what the reader might expect, however, it will not be our purpose to show how those problems can be alleviated but rather to turn our focus almost exclusively to team or group decision-making, a process given far too little attention in management literature through recent years. What we shall study is often called the "Noetic process" of decision-making, a conscious voluntary group effort centering on interaction and including broad viewpoints geared to developing new perceptions. The central theme of the chapter will argue that the best decisions are made by quality leadership teams and not by individual executives, though admittedly, this flies in the face of the reigning traditional wisdom in management science.

# INGREDIENTS OF EFFECTIVE TEAM DECISION-MAKING

Assuming the leadership team has been pulled together and each member knows his responsibilities, it still takes awhile for that team to become a solid decision-making body, completely contributory to the issues at hand and mutually responsible for the outcome of the organization. We are reminded again of the impact of followers on leaders, particularly the now famous "West Point Thesis" which argues "that leadership may be chiefly an achievement of followers—that able leaders may emerge only from the ranks of the able followers." Litzinger and Schaefer argue that group decision-making rests squarely on a proper understanding of management by objectives.

> In MBO, leadership is a shared effort in which all, leader and follower alike, not only struggle for goals, but also set them. A central purpose of MBO is to substitute for the supervisor's role of judge that of "helper." This connects the "followership of the leader" with the "leadership of the follower." MBO receives "good grades" in the school of Hegel.
>
> The paradoxes of Hegel's thought may be less unsettling when we recall how the Pope of the Catholic Church designates his own leadership; he is "the servant of the servants of God." Where leader and follower alike are held in obedience to defined doctrine, neither may act on his own autonomous will alone. Leadership endures so long as it assumes a posture of humility and a spirit of followership.[2]

What ingredients make such team decision-making possible?
*CLARITY, ACCURACY, AND TIMELINESS OF INFORMATION*
A leader is only as good as the information with which he works and in a computer age, that information ought to be better and better. A college president faces a quarterly board meeting and he depends on the financial accounts given him by the treasurer and/or institu-

tional comptroller, the faculty data provided by the dean, the student issues outlined by the director of student services, and so on. It appears less crucial in a staff with fewer professionals, but in actuality it is not. The only thing that changes is that a pastor receives his information from unpaid, volunteer, possibly untrained staff members who may be extremely efficient or may be carrying out their ministries by guesswork.

If you want to be an effective leader in any organization, at any level, with any kind of staff, you must design channels for obtaining and, insofar as possible, guaranteeing the clarity, accuracy, and timeliness of the information necessary to make decisions. And since it is impossible to get it all yourself, you will be forced to develop others who can assist you in information gathering.

## USE OF APPROPRIATE PARADIGMS

The traditional wisdom in managerial decision-making virtually reduces every decision to a problem. The appropriate and popular paradigm, therefore, is the problem-solving model generally found in seven steps. Its form varies but Warren Anderson's use is as common as any (Fig. 23).[3] One can immediately see the values of this kind of paradigm. It enables us to orient to the situation, identify key facts and issues, sort out causes and options, and monitor the decision for effectivenenss.

This is only one paradigm, of course, and it may not even be the best; but it represents the paradigmic approach to decision-making which rests securely on linear thinking and human logic. Group decision-making on the other hand has a much greater latitude for intuitiveness, the role of the Holy Spirit in the various members, and the pulling together of pieces in what might be called vertical as well as lateral thinking.

## MAXIMAL PARTICIPATION

*People will be involved in assisting and working with an organization to the extent that they feel a sense of ownership or responsibility for the outcome.* Just like Earl Anderson at the beginning of our chapter— let's either get with it or stop pretending that we really have any distinct leadership role here. As in long-range planning or the process of change, so in decision-making we want to bring in the maximal number of people at least for advisory purposes as early as possible. Of course I am not suggesting that an effective decision-making team is anything like an entire congregation in size. Remember—we discuss leadership style in these pages, not polity or church government.

FIGURE 23

# PROBLEM-SOLVING PARADIGM

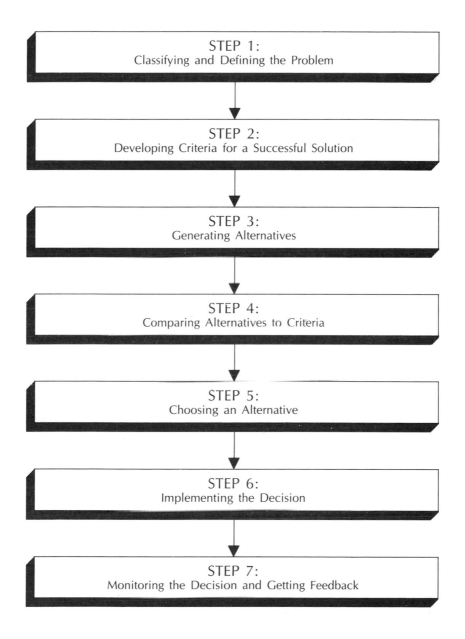

STEP 1:
Classifying and Defining the Problem

STEP 2:
Developing Criteria for a Successful Solution

STEP 3:
Generating Alternatives

STEP 4:
Comparing Alternatives to Criteria

STEP 5:
Choosing an Alternative

STEP 6:
Implementing the Decision

STEP 7:
Monitoring the Decision and Getting Feedback

## FREEDOM FROM PRESSURE AND PUBLICITY

One wonders how the President of the United States can make any executive decisions. Long before he announces most decisions the press has scrutinized them from top to bottom and suggested the pros and cons of every alternative. An efficient decision-making team may not operate entirely behind closed doors, but it certainly feels free from external pressure forcing it to do something it does not believe to be in the best interests of the organization.

Decision-making can be corrupted by unwillingness to share it with others, feeling one has to be in total command of every situation. It also provides the most obvious badge of that command. *Psychology Today* describes this as a compulsive organization, one marked by "inward orientation; indecisiveness due to the fear of making mistakes; inability to deviate from plans; overreliance on regulations; difficulties in seeing the big picture."

> The compulsive organization is exceedingly hierarchical, a reflection of the leader's strong concern with control. The compulsive person is always worried about the next move and how he is going to make it. Such a preoccupation has often been reinforced by periods when the firm was at the mercy of the other organizations and circumstances.[4]

*What we do with decision-making authority says a great deal about our own leadership styles and our management patterns.*

# VALUES OF EFFECTIVE TEAM DECISION-MAKING

Let's take brother Earl Anderson into a different dimension than the case study in which we find him. Suppose you are his pastor, shocked to hear such a radical viewpoint so bluntly stated in such a sensitive place. Imagine that you get through that moment and perhaps the whole board meeting without any further disasters so you take this question home with you. What should you do about Anderson's way to operate? What impact does this have on the rest of the board? How many people really feel like this? What kind of a noncohesive group have you got going here?

Obviously you need the answers to questions to bring order out of chaos at least with brother Anderson if not with the rest of the team. If we turn the question around we might learn more from it. How could you have averted the kind of scene which proffers such a pastoral nightmare? Answer: You could have created a decision-making administrative leadership team in which the members engaged in conscious, voluntary, group effort centering on interaction and including God's viewpoints geared to developing new perspectives (Noetic process). Or more to the point, what values are to be found in effective team decision-making?

## GREATER RESOURCES

The Book of Proverbs makes this point very clear.

> Do not rebuke a mocker or he will hate you; rebuke a wise man and he will love you (9:8).

> For lack of guidance a nation falls, but many advisers make victory sure (11:14).

> The first to present his case seems right, till another comes forward and questions him (18:17).

> Make plans by seeking advice; if you wage war, obtain guidance (20:18).

> For waging war you need guidance, and for victory many advisers (24:6).

> He who trusts in himself is a fool, but he who walks in wisdom is kept safe (28:26).

Chief among the values of effective decision-making is a wider source of options, a broader scope of wisdom, and a better opportunity to understand what God really wants from you and from His people at this particular time. So it was in the New Testament that "they" appointed the servants of Acts (chap. 6) and "they" selected the missionaries (chap. 13)—the New Testament believers trusted each other to make mutual decisions.

That increases the risk and, says Ellen Siegelman, "Although people are rarely consistent in their decision-making styles, most of us can detect some regularity in the way we make decisions ... for each dimension, choose the one response out of three that best describes how you usually respond in making a big decision" (Fig. 24).[5] The answers can be found on pages 199–200.

## INCREASED SUPPORT

It stands to reason. The more people participate in making decisions, the more those people will support them. One major study detailing this reality in educational leadership takes a rather interesting view of the concept of *consensus*. Normally consensus is thought of as the opposite of authoritarian decision-making and I am using it that way in this chapter. These writers, however, prefer the view of consensus as the "end of the continuum that ranges from authoritarian decision-making through consultive decision-making" and offer the very familiar rectangular representation of the viewpoint (Fig. 25).

Notice several things about the diagram. The pastor may make some decisions in which the board has no influence at all, but the reverse seems never possible. At the extreme right of the rectangle, the pastor delegates the authority to the group and the group actually becomes a decison-making consensus body. The authors correctly conclude: "Leadership by consensus is not for everybody. Consideration of LBC (leadership by consensus) cuts deeply into one's values and assumptions about the purpose of management, the qualities of people, the advantages and limitations of various management styles, and the nature of management systems." This volume is highly recommended reading for pastors, corporate executives, heads of mission boards, school principals, and college presidents.[6]

## EASIER ACCEPTANCE

Let us not confuse "increased support" (which refers to other members of the leadership team) with "easier acceptance" (which refers to general agreement by the public). It all fits together. When one gathers effective information, uses appropriate paradigms, calls forth maximal participation, exercises decision-making processes in freedom from pressure and publicity, taps access to greater resources, and increases support of the leadership team, easier acceptance is the only possible result.

Why would we bother to emphasize that a certain report was "unanimous" on the part of the recommending body if we didn't expect that unanimity to carry weight in making the project work through the implementation stage? Unity of the brethren is first and foremost a spiritual quality and therefore an organismic end; but it is also a pragmatic basis for getting the job done and, therefore, an organizational quality.

## ENHANCED TRAINING

Since a major portion of the book deals with this theme I'll not spend much time on it here. Every time we allow a growing leader to participate in a decision of some consequence he takes one giant

FIGURE 24

# WHAT KIND OF RISK-TAKER ARE YOU?

*Although people are rarely consistent in their decision-making styles, most of us can detect some regularity in the way we make important decisions. Think of the important life decisions you have made (e.g., marriage, major moves, career changes), and then answer the following questions. You may not answer some with complete confidence, but give the answers that come closest to what you believe. This is not a test; it is just a device to help you understand your own decision-making behavior. For each dimension, choose the one response out of three that best describes how you usually respond in making a big decision.*

I. Attitude toward change
   1. I prefer security to novelty.
   2. I value security and novelty about equally.
   3. I prefer novelty to security.

II. Search strategy
   1. I make a quick overall survey of possibilities hoping that something will hit me.
   2. I keep producing and then going over my possible choices.
   3. I think of a number of alternatives but stop after a reasonable search.

III. Attention to feelings
   1. I decide among alternatives not only by reasoning but by taking my feelings into account.
   2. I make major decisions almost exclusively on the basis of my feelings.
   3. I mistrust my feelings as a basis for a major decision; I try to use reason almost entirely.

IV. Decision rule
   1. I believe there is one right decision, and it is my job to dig it out.
   2. I believe there is no one right decision; I just need to find one that is good enough.
   3. I believe in choosing the first decision that really grabs me.

V. Sense of consequence
   1. I don't try to predict the consequences of my decision because I expect things will work out OK.
   2. I do think about consequences, tending to focus on the bad things that might happen.
   3. I try to think of both the good and bad consequences of my decision.

VI. Predecision emotions
   1. In thinking about taking a risky step, I feel mostly anxiety.
   2. In thinking about taking a risky step, I feel a mixture of anxiety and excitement.
   3. In thinking about taking a risky step, I feel mostly excitement.

VII. Time expended in decision-making process
   1. I usually make decisions—even big ones—quickly.
   2. I usually take a fairly long time to make big decision.
   3. I usually take a very long time to make big decisions.

VIII. Attitude toward new information
   1. I will consider new information even after I've arrived at a probable decision.
   2. I'm not interested in getting

new information after I've made a probable decision.

3. I feel compelled either to seek out new information or to shut it out after I've made a probable decision.

IX. Postdecision strategy
1. Once I've made a decision, I usually don't think about it before launching into action.
2. Once I've made a decision, I often experience serious doubts and may change my mind.

3. Once I've made a decision, I usually rally behind it after rechecking.

X. Evaluating the outcome of a risky decision
1. After I have acted on the decision, I tend to worry or regret that I didn't do something else.
2. After I have acted on the decision, I tend to put it out of my mind.
3. After I have acted on the decision, I tend to think about what I have learned from it.

step forward in leadership progress. If that leadership decision affects his own area and he takes major responsibility for researching it, praying it through, making it work, and evaluating it, he has learned a great deal about leadership while on the job.

Leaders must never allow their subordinates to make their problems the problems of the leader. How easy to have the subordinate (let's say an assistant pastor) come in to explain, "Chief, we have a problem," which translated from the original means, "I had a problem until I entered this room; now I'm dumping it on your desk." The wise leader listens sympathetically, may ask one or two poi-

FIGURE 25

# TEAM LEADERSHIP BY CONSENSUS

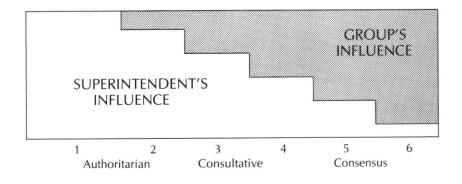

gnant questions, but never allows that growing assistant to forget that the problem and the decision belong to him and he will have to live with the outcomes. Of course there are those occasional moments of crisis when the chief executive officer has to take something in hand, to make a decision which only he can make. But if that happens with any regularity, he displays an autocratic leadership style, not based on consensus decision-making.

# PROCEDURE OF EFFECTIVE TEAM DECISION-MAKING

There is no magic here, perhaps not much more than common sense. But mix this common sense with a few ounces of integrity and spiritual maturity and you'll be amazed what emerges at the other end. Please remember that we are talking about a small leadership team that makes consensus decisions. It could be an elder board, deacon board, or administrative council—probably no more than ten people and likely a group whose members have worked together for three or four years. It takes time to develop a leadership team.

## *EACH MEMBER HAS ONE VOICE*

The word is "voice," not "vote." To be sure, even a friendly consensus meeting might deal with a specific legal or emotionally charged issue when votes must be counted; then each member has one vote as well. But we're not interested in his vote nearly as much as we are his voice. It's wisdom, maturity, experience, and spiritual sensitivity that will help us make wise decisions among the people of God, not the fact that he can write somebody's name on a piece of paper.

We can look at this item two ways. We could argue each member has *only* one voice, meaning that no member should dominate the consensus discussions. Or we could argue that each member has *at least* one voice; therefore, everybody needs to be actively involved.

## *EACH MEMBER HAS A RESPONSIBILITY TO EXPRESS HIS OR HER OPINION*

Not a week later! Not out in a parking lot after the meeting! Not in a whisper to the person next to him! Carefully, lovingly, clearly, and gently *in the meeting* where all the concerned, interdependent decision-makers have gathered to deal with the issue!

Here the chairman becomes crucial since there may be some developing leaders who have not yet understood this responsibility and, therefore, fear to exercise it. Rather than breathing a sigh of relief at getting through another business meeting without a quarrel, the chairman knows that Earl does not favor an item which appears to be the consensus opinion of the rest of the group, so he deliberately asks him to explain why he opposes the issue. This is not a congregational meeting at which sides can be formed and a church split developed. Within a carefully controlled, deliberately designed, spiritually selected group of leaders, good decisions rest on the will of God and unity of the body.

The mature leader, knowing his efforts might be futile, makes one last stand to explain why he does not believe the church ought to go into a building program rather than start a branch church on the other side of town. Lovingly and carefully he explains one more time all the arguments be believes to be in his favor. Lovingly and politely the other members listen one more time just to make sure they haven't inadvertently devalued this logic though they may have heard it many times before.

Sound like heaven? That's right; if we behave this way in business meetings they may be more like heaven than hell.

## EACH MEMBER MUST LISTEN RESPECTFULLY TO ALL OTHER OPTIONS

This kind of posture takes maturity as well. But nobody has a corner on God's truth—not the chairman and not the pastor. Just because this might happen to be a building committee item the local contractor on the board has no greater voice. We're seeking the mind of the Spirit of God as He gives each one of us wisdom; and we know truth could come from anyone (remember the disciples discounting Mary's record of the resurrection of Jesus).

## EACH MEMBER MUST DETACH HIMSELF EMOTIONALLY FROM HIS OWN IDEAS

Ideas and people are not organically connected. In fact, the less maturity one displays the more he demonstrates a complete linkage between attitude and the ownership of material or nonmaterial things. Picture the fury of a five-year-old when a neighborhood rival jumps on his new bike and takes the first ride. He had equated that bike with himself. It belonged to him and no one else. Or consider the anger of the young man whose new convertible gets crinkled in a senseless inner-city pileup. It's almost as though the car next to him had hit and injured him physically, so closely has he linked his automobile to his person.

Once again, those are marks of immaturity. The mature person can suggest an idea, "place it on the table," and deliberately allow his fellow decision-makers to weigh it, evaluate it, attack it, build on it, and take it in different directions because that is precisely his role as a member of the decision-making group. When they attack his idea he understands full well they are not attacking him.

This might be found in a book on introduction to psychology, but every pastor knows if he could just change this one attitude in board and congregational meetings, there would be a whole new flavor to these gatherings. Right here it's worth coming back to the brilliant words of the Apostle Paul in the Book of Philippians.

> If you have any encouragement from being united with Christ, if any comfort from His love, if any fellowship with the Spirit, if any tenderness and compassion, then make my joy complete by being like-minded, having the same love, being one in spirit and purpose. Do nothing out of selfish ambition or vain conceit, but in humility consider others better than yourselves. Each of you should look not only to your own interests, but also to the interests of others. Your attitude should be the same as that of Christ Jesus. . . . Do everything without complaining or arguing (Phil. 2:1-5, 14).

## EACH MEMBER MUST PUBLICLY SUPPORT THE GROUP'S DECISION

I suppose we could also say he must do it privately, but I'm thinking now of the group meeting together as a decision-making body (elders, planning team, administrative council, Christian Education Committee). On certain rare occasions there may be necessity for and value of a "minority report." Under normal conditions, however, consensus means that the group has agreed to do something and they now stand as one in making that announcement.

Consensus does not mean total unanimity. It means that a group of people operating in informed, spiritual accountability has made a decision which they will now present to the larger group of people who have authorized them to make that decision. From Moses and the elders wandering around the wilderness, to Paul and the missionaries wandering around Asia Minor—that's the way God's people were designed to work.

## EACH MEMBER MUST KEEP GROUP PROCESSES CONFIDENTIAL

Exactly how the group arrived at a decision is its own business. Imagine the following horror story after a building committee announces the decision to build a half-million dollar addition.

> "Helen, you were at all the committee meetings. Do you favor this decision?"
> "Well, not really, but we're not supposed to talk about what went on in the committee meetings."
> "Come on, Helen, I know you better than that. You would never vote for the kind of financial constraints this project will put on this church. What do you really think?"
> "Well, I was opposed to it until Bill explained that. . . ."

No! Never! The committee stands together and group process is known to committee members only. The same kind of "leaks" that practically render this country ungovernable can remake a calm congregation into a chaos of confusion. Helen's behavior confirms one thing—she was not qualified to be a member of the committee in the first place!

Surely it's obvious that team decision-making is essentially a matter of leadership style. *Autocratic leaders tend to make singular decisions; participatory leaders tend to involve other people.* The close linkage of decision-making and leadership style sometimes confuses the research. Yukl strongly advocates increased emphasis on situational variables in leader effectiveness research. He complains that few studies take situational variables into account.

> A major limitation on participation has been the conception of participation as a general management style rather than as a set of specific decision procedures that differ from each other as well as from autocratic procedures . . . most of the correlational studies define participation as the overall amount of influence allowed subordinates in decision-making, without any concern for the particular mix of decision procedures used by each leader . . . the experimental studies also show little concern for comparing differing participative procedures . . . in some studies, participation means consultation, whereas in other studies it means a group decision or delegation.[7]

Let me close this chapter by offering some survey results suggested by James Berkley in *Leadership* magazine. He titles his article, "How Pastors and Associates Get Along" and explains the results of the random sampling conducted by *Leadership* magazine, dividing leaders into Schaller's "shepherds and ranchers." Generally speaking, senior pastors picture staff working environment more positively than asssociates (over 20 percent of whom express some discontent with their present position). What do they want from associate staff? Cooperation, loyalty, and ability.

What about the associates' responses? What do they want from their pastors? Latitude, individuality, recognition, and support. Berkley's conclusion on all of this? Hire carefully, delegate thoughtfully, jump patiently, and communicate regularly. The pastor and his associate(s) may very well offer us the very best example of a leadership team adequately handling the decision-making task as descibed in the pages of this chapter.[8]

# STUDY QUESTIONS

**1.** How does Noetic decision-making differ from more traditional patterns?

**2.** Of all the values that might be attributed to group decision-making, which would you consider most important?

**3.** Describe "consensus" by suggesting what it is and what it is not.

**4.** Why do autocratic leaders experience difficulty with consensus/group decision-making?

**5.** In what ways can we help people detach themselves emotionally from their own ideas?

Scoring: Tally the number of A responses, B responses, and C responses using the following guide to see which decision-making style appears most often.

|       |       |       |       |
|-------|-------|-------|-------|
| I.    | —1. A | 2. B  | 3. C  |
| II.   | —1. C | 2. A  | 3. B  |
| III.  | —1. B | 2. C  | 3. A  |
| IV.   | —1. A | 2. B  | 3. C  |
| V.    | —1. C | 2. A  | 3. B  |
| VI.   | —1. A | 2. B  | 3. C  |
| VII.  | —1. C | 2. B  | 3. A  |
| VIII. | —1. B | 2. C  | 3. A  |
| IX.   | —1. C | 2. A  | 3. B  |

X. —1. A    2. C    3. B

Style A. The anxious risk-taker makes big decisions with great effort, is afraid of making mistakes, takes lots of time, and tends to ruminate and worry about the outcome.

Style B: The balanced risk-taker makes big decisions fairly slowly, is more concerned with reasonably good outcomes than with fear of failure or the need to make a good decision, and tends to plan and to review but without worrying too much.

Style C: The careless risk-taker makes big decisions quickly with little experience of mixed feelings, may feel "inappropriately optimistic," and spends little time in introspection or evaluation.

Most people evidence a mixture of styles. The average number of A responses is 6.7. The average number of B responses is 2.3. And the average number of C responses is 1.0 The goal is to be balanced.

—*Ellen Siegelman*
*New York, New York*

## ENDNOTES

**1.** Gloryanna Hees, "Split Devotion," The Case Study Institute (Boston, Mass.: 1979), p. 1.

**2.** William Rosenbach and Robert L. Taylor, eds., *Contemporary Issues in Leadership* (Boulder, Colo.: Westview Press, 1984), pp. 138–39.

**3.** Carl R. Anderson, *Management* (Needham, Mass.: Allyn and Bacon, 1984), p. 127.

**4.** Manfred R. Kets DeVries and Danny Miller, "Unstable at the Top," *Psychology Today* (October 1984), pp. 31–2.

**5.** Ellen Siegelman, "What Kind of Risk-Taker Are You?" *Personal Risk: Mastering Change in Love and Work* (New York: Harper & Row, 1983), reprinted in *Leadership* (Winter 1987), pp. 50–1.

**6.** Richard Wynn and Charles Goditus, *Team Management: Leadership by Consensus* (Columbus, Ohio: Charles E. Merrill, 1984), pp. 46–54.

**7.** Quoted in David R. Powers and Mary Powers, *Making Participatory Management Work* (San Francisco: Jossey Bass, 1983),

p. 134. Taken from G. A. Yukl, *Leadership in Organization* (Englewood Cliffs, N.J.: Prentice Hall, 1981), p. 219.

**8.** James Berkley, "How Pastors and Associates Get Along," *Leadership* (Winter 1986).

CHAPTER 13

# RELATING TO PEOPLE IN CHURCHES AND CHRISTIAN ORGANIZATIONS

Every Christian leader needs to answer the question, "Whom do you think you are?" Phenomenologists remind us that people tend to behave in accordance with the self they think themselves to be. But more to the point the Bible tells us we live in constant danger of overevaluating our own importance (Rom. 12:3; 2 Cor. 3:4-6; 4:7). *How we view ourselves directly affects the way we view other people* and therefore the way we behave toward them.

Immediately preceding Paul's beautiful *kenosis* hymn in Philippians 2, we find five verses emphasizing people relations.

If you have any encouragement from being united with Christ, if any comfort from His love, if any fellowship with the Spirit, if any tenderness and compassion, then make my job complete by being like-minded, having the same love, being one in spirit and purpose. Do nothing out of selfish ambition or vain conceit, but in humility consider others better than yourselves. Each of you should look not only to your own interests, but also to the interests of others. Your attitude should be the same as that of Christ Jesus (Phil. 2:1-5).

Dominating the landscape of this Pauline paragraph is the concept of *unity* in the body. Since believers have unity they can also anticipate encouragement, comfort, fellowship, tenderness, and compassion. All of that appears just in verse 1 establishing *the central idea of human relations in Christian organizations—the unity of the body in Christ.* All management techniques, programs, church growth

202

formulas, and other efforts to advance the work of the kingdom fall flat if we are unable to find encouragement from being united with other believers in Christ.

The second idea stands very close to the first—*like-mindedness.* The unity of verse 1 represents not just some general ambiguous theme but a practical working out "in spirit and purpose." What could be more practical in relationship with other Christians than Paul's reminder in the early verses of Ephesians 4:

As a prisoner for the Lord, then, I urge you to live a life worthy of the calling you have received. Be completely humble and gentle; be patient, bearing with one another in love. Make every effort to keep the unity of the Spirit through the bond of peace. There is one body and one Spirit—just as you were called to one hope when you were called—one Lord, one faith, one baptism; one God and Father of all, who is over all and through all and in all (Eph. 4:1-6).

A third idea in our Philippians passage is *humility* and it surfaces in verse 3. The Christian leader, unselfish and unconceited, sees himself as relatively unimportant. Let's not get confused with poor self-image and unwillingness to launch out into visionary leadership. Paul is talking about the difference between worldly conceit and spiritual humility, the genuine willingness to be third in the God◊others◊me triangle. I'm told that General William Booth was once unable to attend a meeting of the Salvation Army. He sent a one-word message by telegram: "Others."

Still a fourth idea in human relations stands out—*consideration.* In verse 4 Paul assumes that everyone will look to his own interests, but looking to the interests of others requires a reminder. The word translated "look to" in the NIV is the word from which we get our word "scope," also a portion of the New Testament word for "bishop." In other words, a Christian leader is a bishop who looks out for other people as well as for himself.

The final key is *attitude.* What more could be said than what Paul says in verse 5 followed by the brilliant Christmas hymn of verses 6-11. The congregation of Christian organizations behaves as a family in which these five components are essential ingredients of basic reality. We ought always to be praying, "May the mind of Christ my Saviour live in me from day to day, by His love and power controlling all I do and say" (A. Cyril Barham-Gould, 1925).

# WHY ARE HUMAN RELATIONS PROBLEMS OFTEN MORE DIFFICULT IN THE CHRISTIAN ORGANIZATION?

Someone dumped this question on me in a management seminar in Southern California. It prompted some thinking I had not been forced to do before. I doubt one could prove that human relations problems *are* more difficult in Christian organizations, perhaps they just seem that way because we are more sensitive to people's feelings and the outcomes in their lives. But if the proposition is valid, what might be some of the causes?

## *BECAUSE OF UNREALISTIC EXPECTATIONS*

Picture a secretary who has worked in a secular organization for ten years and now, at decreased pay, has accepted a position as secretary in a church, mission board, or Christian organization. After foul language, abuse, and duplicity in the office of her former employer, she anticipates almost millennial conditions in the Christian organization, forgetting that sin stains the whole world. Soon unkind people or unreasonable work demands provoke her to complain in disappointment, "I never expected this!"

Meanwhile, her Christian employer may cherish idealistic expectations for her commitment to the task. After all, this is not just work, this is ministry. He puts in sixty and seventy hours a week, why shouldn't the rest of the staff? Don't they understand that serving the Lord requires sacrificial commitment?

You can already see the scenario for human relations agony unfolding. Unrealistic expectations present an all too common problem for Christians who work together.

## *BECAUSE OF IGNORANCE IN MANAGERIAL PROCESS*

Christian organizations hold no monopoly on ignorance of managerial processes but often we allow "spirituality" to substitute for correct procedure, an irrational and unbiblical surrogate indeed. Let me raise again the nagging question: Why is the tenure of associates in ministry (youth directors, Christian education directors, assistant pastors, etc.) so brief? Can it be attributed to a scheme whereby these people go to a church for a year or two just to learn the ropes and then go on into other places of "more significant leadership"? That certainly happens in some cases, but I can assure you after more than a quarter century of training people for posts like this, such an explanation proves inadequate. Problems of advancement, finances, and ministry overload, though real, do not strike at the heart of the issue.

*The core problem is that many senior pastors do not know how to work with subordinates and many subordinates do not know how to work with a superior. One's failure to lead and the other's failure to follow renders a team relationship virtually impossible from the first.* Such a result is not inevitable as the long tenure of many in these positions has shown us. But where destructive breakdown in human relations occurs (and it occurs with agonizing frequency) the conflict usually comes from leadership style, organizational confusion in goals and objectives, and general administrative incompetence.

## WHAT ARE THE ROADBLOCKS TO POSITIVE HUMAN RELATIONS?

Like the Katzenjammer Kids of ancient comic-strip fame, we tend to bring our troubles on ourselves. One assignment I regularly use with graduate students at both Masters and Doctoral levels sends them out interviewing Christian leaders, asking about their "three biggest problems in human relations." The assignment proves so effective I have retained it over the years and by now certain patterns are predictable. For example, *poor communication inserts a constant irritant in the human relations process.* We'll get to that in just a moment. Another shows that *leaders rarely take responsibility for causing human relations problems.* They identify everything from the unspirituality of people to lack of commitment in churches; but only in the greatest rarity does a leader emerge with enough courage to admit like Paul, "I am the chief of sinners."

As long as we remain unaware *that* we cause the problems, and *how* we cause the problems, and *why* people respond the way they do, we will be unable to take corrective action and move toward positive human relations in the group. What specific issues are at stake? What "roadblocks" might we expect to find?

*THE WORDS WE USE*

Sometimes we create problems by sheer carelessness. Speaking too quickly or unkindly; judging a person's motives and responding the way we think he ought to be dealt with at that time; throwing in emotive terms like "loyalty" or "commitment" or "faithfulness."

The Book of Proverbs is full of warnings about using the tongue unwisely and most of them warn us to say less and think more. Even the folklore of our own language contains necessary phrases repeated with such constancy that they have become clichés: "I didn't mean to say that," or "Whoops—that came out wrong," or "Let me try to put it another way." Sometimes we leaders hinder rather than help positive human relations simply by the words we use.

## INEFFECTIVE NONVERBAL COMMUNICATION

Picture a Sunday School superintendent listening to an idea on room rearrangement presented by one of his teachers. As the teacher speaks the superintendent repeatedly looks at his watch, stares off into space, and even occasionally shakes his head in a slow but menacing gesture. Without a word he has accurately communicated his attitude: "Don't bother me with this; I'm not interested and furthermore your ideas are always useless." Leaders who promote positive human relations are leaders whose faces display openness and acceptance to the ideas of other leaders and subordinates. They know when to listen; they know how to listen; and they understand their people need to talk to them. Indeed, they encourage it regularly.

## HIDING MECHANISMS

The threatened, insecure Christian leader lies like an open pit into which someone will soon stumble. Already defensive, he says things which ought not to be said in ways which communicate hostility. He consistently projects images he thinks will advance his own status rather than practicing transparency and vulnerability in the leadership role.

In sociological parlance we call him an other-directed rather than inner-directed leader, swayed by forces outside himself rather than by what he really believes God wants him to be. His status symbols fit a stereotypical pattern as he polarizes his attitudes to agree with whatever group he happens to be in.

What may seem like normal hiding mechanisms in a threatened leadership role can quickly become neurosis as the leader's personality changes focus more and more on himself and less and less on others. Having abandoned his leadership by default, he multiplies his problems at home as well as in public ministry.

## IMPROPER CONCEPTS OF MOTIVATION

Conflict will always be with us but it takes a particularly nasty turn when people feel they are being manipulated rather than motivated by their leaders. Motivation comes when people believe their leaders really care about *them* and not just the work they do. Peters and Waterman in their now famous book *In Search of Excellence* claim that the best-run American companies care about their customers, communicate well in interdepartmental affairs, and show concern for their employees.

Part of the problem lies in training. If teachers teach as they were taught not as they were taught to teach, then it may very well follow that leaders lead as they were led not as they were taught to lead. We may be constantly perpetuating improper concepts of motivation, unaware that such behavior corrupts the human relations process. In an interesting article which appeared in *Hardcopy*, Schlesinger and Tiersten argued that a major difference between American management and Japanese management is training: "The average training period in an American firm takes one week. In Japan it takes fifty weeks, and thereafter training is regarded as a continuing process."[1]

Implications for training? Along with teaching our pastors and Christian leaders *orthodoxy* we need to teach them *orthopraxy*—the right way of doing things; in this case, how to motivate people in ministry groups.

## PERVERTED VIEWS OF LEADERSHIP

We keep coming back to this same issue. Leadership style affects every aspect of administrative behavior and certainly looms large in the area of human relations. Conflict often starts here because autocracy can produce resentment and as we have noticed in earlier chapters, independent congregations with autocratic pastors are headed for troublesome conflict. The goal is not absence of conflict; disequilibrium in the organization often leads to creative results. How we resolve conflict demonstrates whether we are advancing the cause of Christ or our own personal careers and goals.

A provocative issue of the *Christian Leadership Letter* explored "The Wrongness of Being Right." It included this paragraph:

Being right can be a losing proposition. If you are right all the time, you will intimidate people, and make it all the harder for them to remember the facts or attempt to share them with you. "No sense in telling old So-and-So. He has his mind made up before you begin." People don't really believe old So-and-So is right all the time. They just believe that that is what he thinks about himself. People in this situation easily become isolated. And the tragic consequence is that they continue to believe that they are right (most of the time) when in fact the number of opportunities they have to interact with important events becomes fewer and fewer.[2]

These are five roadblocks—five pitfalls to avoid if we as leaders genuinely want to improve the quality of human relations in the Christian organization. As in all problem-solving, we don't start with solution but with recognizing the problem and how we may be contributing to it.

## HOW CAN WE BUILD BETTER HUMAN RELATIONS INTO OUR LEADERSHIP STYLES?

The new loyalty, writes Harry Levinson in *Think* magazine, cannot be based on blind allegiance to other people or organizations. Rather, the "bonds of affection are the true bonds of loyalty. Affection and respect arise when people feel that others care about them. We feel that others care about us when they teach us fruitful ways to live and how to solve our problems."[3] Human relations center in the capacity of the Christian leader to be a team facilitator rather than a superstar.

In autocratic leadership, Sunday School teachers serve their superintendent and church members, their pastor. In biblical leadership, the leader functions as one of the players, though he may carry more responsibility than the others. Can we pick up a metaphor from modern professional football? A modern contemporary quarterback carries the ball as little as possible. He sets up the play, initiates its functioning, hands off, or throws the ball to another one of his teammates, then steps back safely to watch the play unfold. *Cooperative team ministry is the essential goal.*

### HELP FOLLOWERS UNDERSTAND YOUR GENUINE CONCERN FOR THEM

Let's get back to Levinson's idea again—"We feel that others care about us when they teach us fruitful ways to live and how to solve our problems." In a leadership-followership situation, an openness is required with subordinates as is some structure whereby leaders and followers can get together as responsible adults to solve mutual and common problems. One step toward the solution of that pastoral staff dilemma mentioned several paragraphs ago is a weekly staff meeting in which all members of the staff share problems and ask questions. They don't just gather to hear orders from headquarters or to find out how they can carry out the chief's directives for the next few days.

Cooperative ministry offers people the responsibility and opportunity to be accountable for their own ministry and the fate of the organization. *What happens in the church must not be viewed as the success or failure of the pastor but the collective outcome of congrega-*

*tional teamwork!* Levinson is right—genuine loyalty cannot be equated with blind obedience. Jesus alone could ask for that kind of commitment because He is God. Paul by contrast, always worked with members of the missionary team explaining why decisions were made and how plans were to be carried out. He listened to their viewpoints and on many occasions subjected his own will to what other people thought (Acts 11; 13; 15).

## HELP FOLLOWERS UNDERSTAND THE CREATIVE AND POSITIVE VALUES OF INTERPERSONAL CONFLICT

Earlier I suggested that conflict is not all bad because it produces the kind of necessary disequilibrium out of which new ideas are generated. Of course there will be disagreements in business meetings and planning conferences! Of course staff members will have different viewpoints about how certain goals can best be achieved! But the work of the body of Christ, carried out by spiritual people, must be conducted in an atmosphere of constant mutual trust and respect.

Dependence on group decision-making, perhaps even reflected in consensus rather than formal voting, reflects a genuine commitment to working toward outcomes. Small wonder the family provides a prototype for the church. If we can't work out squabbles and differences among husbands, wives, and children, how can we carry out the work of the Lord when our commonalities and opportunities to work together are much more rare than in the family?

Students so often ask how effective decisions can be made taking into consideration both the will of God and the leading of the Holy Spirit on the one hand, and a genuine commitment to proper managerial procedures on the other. The answer is simple though the process may at times be painful: *adequate information plus sanctified judgment equals good decisions.*

Too often human relations go awry when we attempt to make decisions purely on the basis of "sanctified judgment" without satisfying ourselves as to the adequacy or accuracy of the information (Prov. 18:15). An even worse problem finds us depending purely on secular procedures and making decisions only on the basis of information without appropriate concern for sensitivity to the Spirit's leading.

## HELP FOLLOWERS DEVELOP AN IDIOGRAPHIC LEADERSHIP STYLE

That's right, it's the task of the leader not only to develop his own leadership style but to help followers (subordinates) develop leadership styles of their own. We've already talked about the idiographic style which demonstrates concern for other people. *In the functioning of biblical responsibility in the church or Christian organization, people must know their tasks and believe them to be important; they must understand and support the objectives of the ministry in which they serve; they must be conscious of their relationship to other people in that ministry; they must be free from an atmosphere of intimidation; they must have a significant role in group process (what Schaller calls "ownership"); and they must be constantly alert to the maintenance of spiritual unity and community between and among themselves.*

Leadership is learned by modeling. Only as we demonstrate teamwork with our subordinates can they reflect that behavior in working with those whose ministries they supervise.

There should be no organization on the face of God's earth more eager to develop team leadership style than the church. In the book *Teambuilding: Issues and Alternatives,*[4] William Dyer assumes that team-type qualities are necessary for an effective organization. He makes the point that we already understand teams since all of us belong to some kind of group and that group had to learn to work together. Teambuilding brings order out of chaos and conflict, overcomes the unhealthy atmosphere of selfishness and conceit, and builds better human relations into Christian leadership style.

## MASTER THE DYNAMICS OF TEAM LEADERSHIP

A team leader knows how to involve others in the decision-making process, can articulate goals and objectives, understands the characteristics of groups in general (and particularly the group with which he serves), has a good grasp of the process of communication, and demonstrates sensitivity to the feelings and values of other people. That's very different than authoritarian (autocratic) administrators who must maintain dominance over other people to really feel they have control of the organization. Autocrats love the lone-wolf role and feel uncomfortable in give-and-take team meetings. They view the hierarchy as a protection of their own power whereas team leaders see organizational structure as something that protects the people who serve in the organization.

## LEARN HOW TO LISTEN TO SUBORDINATES

Human relations depend heavily on our ability to listen, a major part of communication. Are there some practical guidelines here? Can pastors, deans, principals, directors, and organization leaders actually relate to subordinates in ways that will change their listening habits? You bet; and they're really quite simple!

**1.** *Feedback.* Restate what you've been told so both you and the speaker understand precisely what he is trying to tell you. Always remember that we comprehend messages through our own emotional grids and therefore tend to corrupt the other person's meaning.

**2.** *Pay attention.* Sure you're the boss; but that doesn't give you the right to offer less concentration than you expect.

**3.** *Admit preconceived ideas.* Let people know where you're coming from so they'll be able to better understand you and the background that goes into the decisions you make.

**4.** *Discipline yourself, especially your emotions.* Mature leaders rarely (never?) show anger, hostility, or bitterness in a conversation with a fellow worker. There may very well be good reason to share mutual grief or joy. It's not a question of never showing emotion, but controlled self-discipline.

**5.** *Don't interrupt.* Sometimes leaders tend to think they know what subordinates are going to say so they just break in and finish the sentence for them. This not only disconcerts a subordinate who may have had to build up her courage to approach the boss; it is also downright rude. Most of us listen better with our mouths shut; then we may be prepared to respond in some appropriate way.

Positive human relations are built by one who seeks the good of other people and wants to see them rewarded for all they've done in the service of Christ. That's where our chapter began and that's where it ends. The facilitating leader sees responsibility diffused because it rests with the group not the person. Finding someone to blame or scold becomes counterproductive behavior.

Effective human relations may require us to look away from some short-term goals in order to place our focus on long-term values. The authoritative, inerrant Scriptures remind us repeatedly that relational development and nurture stand at the heart and core of all we do in leadership; if we fail here, the rest doesn't matter much.

## STUDY QUESTIONS

**1.** The author emphasizes Philippians 2:1-5 as a major biblical passage dealing with human relations. List three or four similarly valuable passages.

**2.** Do you agree that human relations are often more difficult in

Christian organizations? Evaluate his reasons in light of your own experience.

**3.** Evaluate the balance between orthodoxy and orthopraxy in your own seminary or college background.

**4.** Briefly describe how idiographic and nomothetic leaders would handle human relations issues differently.

**5.** Carry out the assignment described in the "Roadblocks" section. Interview five Christian leaders to discover their three biggest human relations problems—and how they go about solving them.

# ENDNOTES

**1.** Robert J. Schlesinger and Sylvia Tiersten, "Japanese Management: Is There Anything New?" *Hardcopy* (April 1986), p. 134.

**2.** Ted W. Engstrom and Edward R. Dayton, "The Wrongness of Being Right," *Christian Leadership Letter* (March 1980), p. 2.

**3.** Harry Levinson, "Whatever Happened to New Loyalty?" *Think* (IBM Publication, Jan.–Feb. 1967), p. 8.

**4.** William Dyer, *Team Building: Issues and Alternatives* (Reading, Mass.: Addison-Wesley, 1977).

CHAPTER 14

# COMMUNICATING—
# LEADER TO LEADER

In view of some of the crass marketing procedures we have seen in evangelical circles during the 1980s we would probably say that marketing has nothing to do with ministry. But if we can get over the hurdle of business terminology like manufacturing and marketing, we may recognize that it has a great deal to do with ministry. In the parallel metaphor, manufacturing is producing ministries that can really meet the needs of people, can really help them in areas where they need help. Marketing, on the other hand, lets them know that these opportunities exist.

More to the point, in this chapter we confront the issue of interpersonal communication. You and I can lead in the church and Christian organization by better understanding the scientific concepts of communication—interpersonal relationships between people.

Essentially "communication" describes the process whereby ideas are transmitted from one member of a group to another. In "organizational communication" (the interrelationships of people who work together) this must be a two-way process. Indeed, we can see it as a multi-way process which moves downward, upward, and laterally throughout the organization.

This chapter assumes that a propositional rather than relational view of communication accounts for a great many of the interpersonal problems we have in the body of Christ. Certainly the Bible offers propositional revelation but the pastor who thinks that he can solve all the problems in his church by "preaching the Word" has misunderstood both the Bible and the process of communication. The simplest definition of communication I ever heard came from

Joe Bayly who used to refer to it as "meaningful exchange." He wanted to distinguish genuine communication from the mere exchange of facts or information.

In the field of sociology, general semanticists argue that communication must always be viewed as containing *mutuality, presentality,* and *simultaneity.* These terms of social interaction emphasize that the communication process always involves more than one person, it is always ongoing existentially, and it always operates on two tracks at the same time. It's not my purpose to get into the detailed analysis of such a study, but it certainly bears understanding in our introductory thoughts.

## REVIEWING BASIC COMMUNICATION COMPONENTS

Numerous models have been used to demonstrate the communication process. I have commonly preferred the Ely model which is hardly new, but simple enough to be helpful.[1] The Ely model emphasizes that communication only takes place when decoding overlaps encoding. Let's review some couplets of communication.

FIGURE 26

# ELY COMMUNICATION MODEL

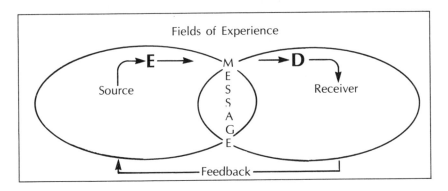

*SENDER/RECEIVER*

The sender (communicator) indicates his ideas by means of words, gestures, posture, attitude, appearance, and other symbolic gestures. The receiver represents the person for whom and toward whom these ideas were directed. Technically he does not become a receiver until decoding overlaps encoding.

## ENCODING/DECODING

These terms, once peculiar to mechanical hardware in communication, now refer commonly to the way the receiver perceives and understands what the sender has "said." Encoding simply means putting ideas into some kind of form such as words, signs, or symbols. Decoding means transferrring those words, signs, or symbols back to the meanings of the ideas.

As in studying the Bible, so in listening to someone speak in everyday conversation, "authorial intent" is crucial. The message must be understood in terms of what the speaker meant when he spoke. It must be understood in terms of what it means in the life and experience of the person to whom it was communicated. That leads us to a third couplet.

## MESSAGE/FEEDBACK

Feedback describes the means the sender designs to obtain evaluation of whether the message has been properly perceived. This proves just as true in preaching as it does in organizational communications and staff relationships. Lee Yih shows us a comparison of the traditional model to what he calls the ICCN model (Integrated Church Communications Network) showing how one-way communication differs from a network of communication in the teaching of God's Word (Fig. 27).[2]

Yih's point is that the training, feedback, response, and Bible discussion sessions all support the sermon so that preacher, lay leaders, and general congregation are all involved in the communication process and in the learning and activating of the Word of God. This plan is implemented by the way, on a weekly basis, not just as an occasional experiment.

## SUPERVISOR/SUBORDINATE

A good bit of the process of human relations depends on communication. Through communication, leaders either improve or endanger the quality of their human relations. In the third part of our chapter we'll talk about how to improve communication with staff and volunteer workers, but let's review here the kinds of principles which help us strengthen communication components.

1. Be open-minded when first meeting a person.
2. Familiarize yourself with his background, understanding that he will listen to you through his own emotional grid.
3. Focus on the individual in the singular rather than the plural.
4. Try to see the people you work with in varying situations.
5. Understand the psychological factors that motivate behavior.

FIGURE 27

# MODELS OF
# CHURCH COMMUNICATION

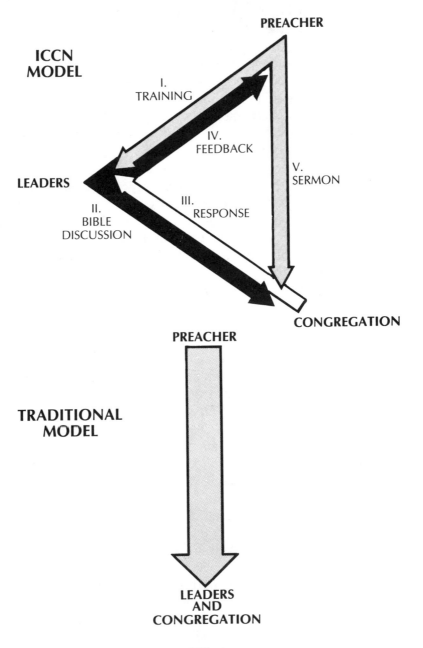

J.B. Phillips once said, "If words are to enter men's hearts and bear fruit, they must be the right words, shaped cunningly to pass men's defenses and explode silently and effectually within their minds" (*Letters to Young Churches,* New York: MacMillan, 1947). That may be true in Bible translation and preaching but it is also true in the simple day-to-day communications involved in organizational life.

Let me conclude this first section of the chapter by using one more model entitled "Intervention in Interaction" (Fig. 28). The key idea in this model demonstrates that words and events continue all the time. If we keep in mind a general communications model, we could argue they come from the "sender's side."

On the right side of the diagram we see the "receiver's context." He listens, he talks, presumably he thinks logically, he applies what he knows about social factors and his own emotions to interpretation. Somewhere between the words and the events of the sender and the interpretive activity of the receiver there occurs a *perception point* which is the heart and core of communication, or the point where decoding overlaps encoding.

# GUARDING AGAINST THE BARRIERS OF COMMUNICATION

Charlie West has been a Minister of Education for two years. Not a veteran to be sure, but enough experience to recognize when the beginning of a conversation is eventually going to end up with the words, "I quit." Like last week when Norma Simpson came to his office immediately after the morning service. After some small talk about the weather and Charlie's two young children she dropped the bomb: "I know I made a commitment to teach in the Primary Department throughout the entire year but things are really tough at home and I'm here to tell you this is my last Sunday."

How should Charlie respond? Well, before he responds at all, he needs to recognize that each word from that point on will take him through a mine field and he had better walk it very carefully. Here are some of the mines (barriers) he's up against in handling this seemingly simple situation with Norma Simpson.

## THE PERCEPTUAL BARRIER

How Charlie perceives Norma in this situation is important, but not nearly as important as how Norma perceives Charlie. Furthermore, her past perceptions will not only color her thinking regarding what he will say, but will frame all their relationships in the future. If

FIGURE 28

# "INTERVENTION IN INTERACTION"

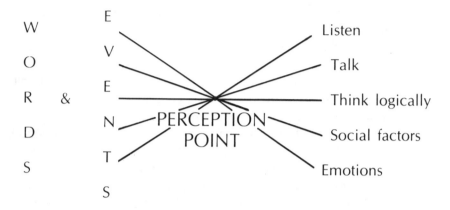

Charlie immediately sees Norma as a typical "quitter," one of those people who marks the lack of evangelical commitment in today's world, he will handle the situation one way. If however, he perceives her as a frustrated middle-aged mother who may very well have enormous problems at home which complicate her ministry at church, he will handle it differently.

Stickler and LeFever warn us to avoid what they call "communication blocks." They claim that each of the following "blocks the free flow of communication."

1. Moralizing, preaching—"You should. . . ." "You ought. . . ." "It's your responsibility."
2. Advising, giving suggestions—"What I would do is. . . ."
3. Persuading with logic, arguing or lecturing—"Do you realize. . . ?"
4. Reassuring, sympathizing—"Don't worry. . . ." "You'll feel better."
5. Withdrawing, distracting—"We can discuss it later."[3]

The authors argue that when a leader throws up communication blocks, the person he might have helped is no longer open to sharing.

## THE ESTEEM BARRIER

A person's image of himself dramatically influences how he sees his world. Has Norma been successful in teaching up to this point? Is quitting a habit or something she's never done before? Might this moment be as traumatic for her as it is for Charlie? At stake in this brief discussion is her self-esteem and if Charlie wants to retain a potential worker for the future, he had better protect her self-esteem.

## THE HIERARCHY BARRIER

Protestants claim Roman Catholics operate according to a hierarchical system; but we ourselves are hopelessly bound in lines and levels of authority through which communication must pass to get its job done. Charlie, because of his position—"Minister of Christian Education"—is more than likely to put his foot in the mine trap of hierarchical politics on this one. He really needs to show accessibility, warmth, understanding, and the ability to convince Norma that he is not some official aloof from the real problems of her world.

While we're on the subject let's talk about the problems of hierarchy in evangelical churches such as the strict separation of clergy and laity (with which I have dealt at length in other chapters); failure of some ministerial staff to speak on a layman's language-level; hesitation regarding the quality of work that the laity can do. He must show faith in Norma's ability and spiritual maturity to overcome this problem and work out the will of God for her and her family.

## THE PERSONALITY BARRIER

It's quite possible that his two years of experience have taught Charlie the difference between people and programs. If he's still giving his life to programs, he will lose Norma Simpson. If he has managed to shake his program orientation he may be able to bring together the nomothetic and idiographic dimensions in her resignation to work out the best solution.

Ahh, you argue, you still haven't told us how to hold onto Norma. No, because I'm not convinced that, in this situation, holding onto Norma is the right thing to do. We don't know enough about the situation to make any judgment at all. Charlie needs to find out what those "problems at home" really consist of, how the church can help Norma solve them, and then slowly work her back into a ministry position sometime next year. The best thing is the right thing; and the right thing is what is best for this individual child of God at this time, not the overall *advancement of the program.*

## THE POLARIZATION BARRIER

This issue surfaces repeatedly in evangelical churches. We have such a grasp of "right and wrong," "good and bad," that we immediately categorize (polarize) questions and answers, positions and stances into one or the other. Such generalization is useless in all of ministry and particularly in the kind of problem Charlie West now faces. Things are hardly ever completely right or completely wrong, especially in dealing with people. Flexibility and a willingness to think in terms of continuum lines rather than boxes offers the only way to ameliorate the barrier of polarization.

# IMPROVING COMMUNICATION WITH VOLUNTEERS

Since the national tenure of associates in pastoral ministry remains very short and Charlie has already lasted two years, we can assume he'll handle this in the right way. He has already established lines of communication with Norma which enable her to feel comfortable explaining her need to resign a ministry position at this time. It also means he has learned how to activate the following general principles related to communication with other people in general and with volunteers in particular.

## PRACTICE VULNERABILITY

In the conversation between Charlie and Norma, Norma seems to be the vulnerable one. Yet we all know that she can walk away leaving Charlie days of work in finding, training, and placing a suitable substitute. In that sense he appears already vulnerable regardless of what he says; so if he really wants to practice 2 Corinthians 3, he shares with Norma that they both serve from a common position of weakness and therefore she can feel comfortable telling him about her family problems. Rather than, "I'm OK, you're OK," we use the biblical version—"I need help and you need help."

Charlie and his team of leaders need to be establishing personal relationships between volunteers and themselves which make both groups feel they can work with each other toward goals which they hold in common. The way to start that (or continue it) at the present point of contact centers in listening.

## PERCEIVE ENVIRONMENTS

We won't go back to the sociologists again except to remind ourselves that Norma doesn't approach the question of resigning her ministry position in the emotional environment of Charlie's office. That may be the literal environment, but they might as well be standing at a railway station in France. Useful feedback must be helpful to the recipient. What Charlie says to Norma does not aim to advance the church's educational program but rather targets the advancement of Norma's personal spiritual life and family well-being. Norma needs to understand what Charlie is about to say; she needs to be willing and able to accept it; and she needs to be able to do something about it if she chooses to.

Charlie may decide to say virtually nothing at the moment but suggest a later more casual meeting where they can discuss it in a less time-pressured setting. Roger Gray reminds us that leaders retain leadership with volunteers only as long as they generate cooperation, and cooperation is generated through communication.

> Establishing the personal relationships between volunteer and leader makes both feel they are working *with* each other toward goals which they hold in common. *Listening* gives meaning to speaking . . . helping individual volunteers see how each is related to a larger structure of volunteers, to a project, and to the organization; making volunteers feel that they are a part of something greater than themselves.[4]

## PLAN INSTRUCTIONS
Now it's time for a much more sophisticated model which shows communication as the heart and core of the linkup among three crucial dimensions of the administrative process—policy, resources, and execution (Fig. 29).[5]

As you study the model notice that these five small circles represent the same component in each of the three segments of the chart. Whether one is engaged in policy-setting, resource allocation, or the execution and implementation stage, one must be concerned with controlling, reappraising, decision-making, programming, and communicating. But these three basic functions of administration do not come together at the point of controlling or decision-making, but at the point of communication!

Let's say that Charlie has a moment of prayer with Norma and agrees to visit her at her home on Tuesday. No decision has been made and they have not really discussed the issue at hand. Now Charlie brings this issue into staff meeting on Monday morning. At what point does he seek advice from senior colleagues? Decision-making? Programming? Controlling? Reappraising? None of the above. Decision-making comes close but the point of contact is clearly *communicating*. Love may make the world go 'round, but communication makes the organization go 'round and when it comes to relationships between leaders and volunteers, that's no silly sentiment but a very practical reality.

## PRAISE PARTICIPATION

Reinforcement provides a major part of feedback in the communication process. To be sure, some feedback may be negative, a critical evaluation of what the volunteer has done improperly. But whenever possible, the wise leader seeks to build in some kind of praise participation to reinforce at least the effort if not the product that the beginning volunteer has attempted. Let's assume Norma Simpson does quit. Let's assume the situation may have been less than satisfactory (meaning Charlie felt she should have stayed on). The church's chances of obtaining Norma's services at sometime in the future may depend on how Charlie handles her "exit interview." Will she leave with guilt? Will she leave with regrets? Will she leave with some question mark about whether she should have stayed? Will she understand that she is welcome back when those family problems get sorted out? How many thousands of people are currently "unemployed" in our churches because they once "quit" at the wrong time and the way that "quitting" was handled left such a bitter taste that they convinced themselves never again to try.

## PURSUE FEEDBACK

Charlie needs to know everything he can about Norma's situation, more than just the factors which occasioned her resignation. Was she happy with the support the Christian Education Committee gave her while she was teaching? Did she get along well with her staff? Did she feel she was properly supervised? Did the church purchase adequate materials? How might Charlie have been a better helper, a better resource person for her during the time she served? Remember, even though Norma may never again teach Sunday School in that church, she has dozens of friends who will be influenced directly or indirectly by her feelings.

When getting his feedback Charlie should be careful to make sure he has the real meanings, not just a set of words. He should restate what he has been told. He should pay attention to everything Norma says. He should avoid preconceived ideas he may have about her, her department, or the quality of her service.

Listening gives background for decisions. The more time a leader spends listening to people, the more input data he will have to make effective decisions. Intelligent decision-making comes from discov-

FIGURE 29

# COMMUNICATING—
# ADMINISTRATIVE LINKUP

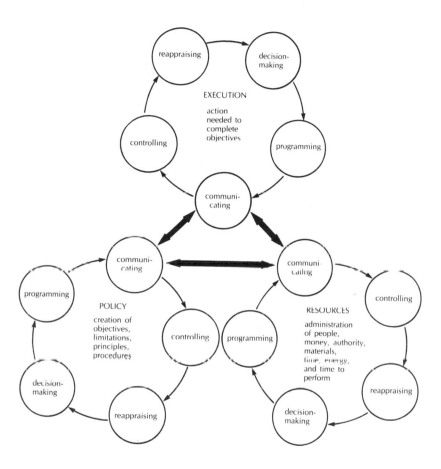

ering what one needs to know. The value of the feedback Charlie gets will be determined by how much he knows about what he needs to know, and how skilled he is at listening to get it.

Let me close this chapter in something of a different vein. We have been talking almost exclusively about how leaders communicate with their subordinates and vice versa. Yet many who read this book will be in subordinate positions (assistants, superintendents, directors), people who are not chief executive officers. In fact it could be argued that we all have bosses and therefore we all need to learn how to manage the boss.

Since managing the boss is largely a matter of communication, it may fit as well in this chapter as anywhere else in the book.

# HOW TO MANAGE THE BOSS

### RECOGNIZE HIS COMMONALITY OF WEAKNESS

No, you don't work for superman and never will. Your boss has moments of struggle, doubt, physical discomfort, emotional conflict, and spiritual struggle just the way you do. Try to understand that when dealing with him.

### LEARN WHETHER HE IS A LISTENER OR A READER

Someone once remarked that the universe could be divided into two kinds of people, those who divide the universe into two kinds of people and those who don't. I don't know about that, but I do know that the Bible commonly divides world population into two classes of people (such as saved and unsaved). In this particular situation it's valuable for us to learn about listeners and readers.

Listeners get their information by listening—in person, on the phone, in small groups—and somehow they mentally register what they hear and (much to the amazement of this writer) it sticks. The rest of us are readers. When people want to contact us they need to do so by memo because we remember what we read not what we hear. If a student passes me in the hall and asks me to make a certain change on a paper or jot down a certain appointment I simply smile and say, "See my secretary." How foolish I would be to keep my own appointment book or to think that I would act intelligently on some piece of conversation passed along in a hall.

### UNDERSTAND HIS LEADERSHIP STYLE

Oh, no, we're not talking here about something as complicated as the stylistic patterns dealt with earlier in the book, but the simple practice of how one goes about doing his job. What are his working hours? Is he a night person or a morning person? If he's a morning person, you'd hardly want to call him at 11:45 P.M.

How about thinking patterns? Is he a logical linear thinker or does he like firecracker ideas that just pop one after another in a meeting? What about his results orientation? Does he want to see a written report of what you've achieved measured by some specific fairly objective evaluative tool or is he going to make subjective judgment about whether he likes the way you're doing your job? How about his commitment to people or planning? Will he spend most of his leadership time working directly with people or is he more of a charts-and-plans man?

Let's stop right here and point out that we're not describing a good or a bad leader but merely distinguishing two different kinds. You need to know your own preferences so you can teach your subordinates how to relate to you; but more importantly, you need to understand your boss so you can communicate with him. You could argue that it's his responsibility to teach you how best to communicate with him but that's not going to solve any problems you might have in your job as a result of his failure to do so.

*NEVER UNDERRATE HIM*

Overrate him if you must; the worst that can happen is you can be personally disappointed. Underrate him, and you may be on your way to another organization.

*MAKE SURE HE UNDERSTANDS YOUR JOB, YOUR GOALS, AND YOUR NEEDS*

He may not know about your job, goals, and needs unless you tell him in a way he'll understand.

*DON'T BEGIN A CONFERENCE ON A NEGATIVE NOTE*

No boss, however experienced or hardnosed, likes to have a subordinate come and "dump." Yes, you may have some bad news and, yes, it may be necessary to tell the boss. But work up to it in a positive to negative format which doesn't make the dropping of the other shoe quite so obvious.

So who's responsible for quality of communication in an organization? Say "the leader" and you'll receive a great deal of support in the current literature. I have a much simpler answer—you are!

# STUDY QUESTIONS

**1.** Explain the meaning of the words, "mutuality," "presentality," and "simultaneity."

**2.** Review the Yih model. In what specific ways does this diagram apply to your church?

**3.** Describe a situation Christian leaders have to face which is different than but similar to the Norma Simpson story.

**4.** How does a person's self-concept help or hinder communication?

**5.** Evaluate yourself. Are you a listener or a reader? How will you help people communicate with you?

# ENDNOTES

**1.** Donald P. Ely, "Are We Getting Through to Each Other?" *International Journal of Religious Education* (May 1962), p. 4.

**2.** Lee Yih, "The Integration of Preaching, Teaching and Discipleship into a Church Communications Network" (Unpublished Th.M. Thesis, Dallas Theological Seminary, 1983), p. 36.

**3.** Kent Stickler and Marlene LeFever, *Creative Leadership Communication* (Elgin, Ill.: David C. Cook, n.d.), p. 21.

**4.** Roger Gray, "Communication: Leader—Volunteer," *Hillsdale Report* (Vol. 11, No. 7, 1973), p. 4.

**5.** Source unknown.

# CHAPTER 15

# WORKING WITH PEOPLE IN GROUPS

Jack is an average Christian. No one doubts his relationship with Christ and though his attendance seems somewhat spotty, he generally brings his family to church at least once a week. In the broad environs of the congregation itself or even a large Sunday School class, Jack seems quite comfortable and unthreatened. In any small group setting, however, different personality traits seem to manifest themselves. He becomes tense, defensive, irritable, and unable to function in a positive way to help the group achieve its goals. In simple terms, Jack fears being in a small group.

And he certainly need not feel lonely. This common problem plagues Christians and non-Christians alike. Christians, however, *should* be different because the Bible elevates the concept of small groups (consider the disciples). The Book of Mark barely gets underway before Jesus selects the Twelve and commences the leadership process of working with people in groups. Michael Wiebe says it plainly.

> To achieve the level of edifying relationships described in the New Testament, smaller groups are almost essential. Often the open and honest sharing and the process which begins in smaller groups can overflow into a larger body. Small groups offer an opportunity to know fewer people more deeply. This leads to the mutual trust that allows us to share our lives with one another. Then we can truly bear each other's burdens and encourage and even admonish each other when necessary. This is what small groups are for: knowing ourselves and each

other better through a Bible study, prayer, and sharing so that we can grow to be like our Lord and to know Him more fully.[1]

Certain theological foundations underlie group work among believers. Don't view group work as some kind of psychological voodoo to gloss over deeper problems in the body. Believers have been sovereignly placed in the body of Christ (1 Cor. 12:13) and the functioning of that body is described in numerous New Testament passages, like Ephesians 4:11-16. But practical function doesn't always follow positional placement of people into the body. Sure the Bible teaches that every member of the body holds an important and distinctive role, but actualizing body life may be something else.

The doctrine of sovereignty applied to individual situations suggests that God places people in various groups—families, churches, Bible study groups, Sunday School classes, etc. God's program and purpose extend to specific individuals, even to the details of their lives. When we look at people in a group we can enjoy *comfort* that only God could have put them there; *concern* when we realize the carelessness with which we treat His plan; and *challenge* to develop all the resident potential of every person in the group and produce what God wants from us collectively.

Add to all of this the gift of leadership, the role of the Holy Spirit in teaching us the Scriptures, the spiritual results that can come from the group, and we see something of group dynamic potential.

When the Holy Spirit controls a Christian group each member links up with a common Person—the Lord Jesus. This moment-by-moment relationship with the Saviour provides unity and harmony to the group and draws them together into a oneness unlike anything that can be achieved outside the supernatural atmosphere of a group of believers.

"But," you say, "how does that relate to leadership and administration in the church? Groups are fine for people whose personality problems and insecurity require others as crutches in their lives but I intend to be a visionary leader who makes things happen; what does all this have to do with me?"

We evangelicals tend to divide our understanding of groups just as we divide our understanding of sacred and secular truth. We see a group meeting for Bible study or prayer as a spiritual activity, a ministry group, something to be cultivated and sought after. A group meeting to discuss plans for the expansion of the parking lot, however, is a board, a committee, or a task force which seems to have little or nothing to do with the spiritual functioning of the church. In so doing we again confuse *organization* and *organism*, failing to see that all people working together in the service of Christ are in ministry.

Most theologians would say the goals of a Christian group are *theocentric* not *anthropocentric*. We concern ourselves with what happens to people in the group and structure specific patterns to induce those happenings (as we shall see). But Christians subject themselves to God's absolute revelation, so the group, whether study or business, is obligated to follow truth, to obey God, and glorify Him. *A Christian group can be defined as a gathering of believers with mutual interests working toward a common goal.*

# WHAT GROUPS ARE NOT

Church leaders have a bad habit of searching for and finding "cure-alls" for congregational problems. Perhaps they'll start a new youth program or a different approach to outreach evangelism. Maybe if we restructure the morning service or put the announcements and offering early in the hour before people get sleepy we'll get greater response.

Unfortunately we've done that with group work. In some places it has become a fetish, a substitute for carrying out other meaningful types of ministry. Small groups and group ministry should be many things and we will look at those in detail. But before we do it, let's explore what groups are *not*.

## GROUPS ARE NOT A CURE-ALL FOR ORGANIZATIONAL PROBLEMS

Once we recognize the value of a small group, we dare not expect more of it than it can deliver. If a pastor puts insufficient study time into his sermons, leading two more small groups during the week will complicate, not solve the problem. If the church waffles on some basic theological issues such as the inerrancy of Scripture or the deity of Christ, vibrant sharing groups meeting every Thursday evening can't salvage the situation. If the chairman and vice-chairman of the board (or congregation) are unable to prepare agendas, lead meetings, control discussion, and answer questions from the floor, small-group sessions will not enhance those kinds of administrative skills. The extract of apricot pits apparently does not cure cancer and exacting commitment to small-group work on the part of a congregation will not solve all of its organismic and organizational problems.

## GROUPS ARE NOT AN END UNTO THEMSELVES

In one sense the above statement needs qualification. Certainly positive human relations among believers offers one of the major goals of the church; to the extent that small-group activities serve that aim, they may be viewed as an end in themselves. But normally, we're trying to get at some other kinds of goals through the strategy of small groups. Groups might be pulled together for Bible study, prayer, and sharing. Or they might have as their goal creative problem-solving and decision-making. In Em Griffin's extremely helpful book *Getting Together* he describes three types of small groups, asking, "Will your group accomplish a task, build relationships, or influence behavior? It's not an either/or question. All three go into every group. Rather it's a matter of emphasis."[2] His helpful chart appears in Figure 30.

## GROUPS ARE NOT A SUBSTITUTE FOR INVOLVEMENT WITH THE ENTIRE BODY

Have you ever observed the single adult ministry in a large urban church? Sometimes that group with its unique interests and lifestyle becomes a subculture of the congregation, carrying out its own specific types of worship and ministry without merging with the larger congregation. Certainly small groups should meet special needs that can't be met in the general functions of the larger congregation, but never by creating a subculture which becomes a church-within-a-church. Indeed, a major goal in working with single adults in any congregation should be to stimulate the melting-pot effect by which they are not only *served by* but begin to genuinely *serve* the full congregation.

I recall the same kind of problem in a different context some twenty years ago. The setting centered in a relatively small suburban congregation in which several key members had involved themselves in several parachurch ministries. I believe God has given us parachurch ministries for the building of His kingdom in the twentieth century. They have achieved many things that local churches apparently have not been able to achieve in their normal ministerial functions. But a parachurch group, however effective and dynamic, dare not become a substitute for a Christian's participation in and support of a local congregation. My difficult but necessary duty as a leader in that congregation included speaking to some of the other leaders about subgroup involvement that appeared to be injuring their commitment to the local congregation rather than enhancing it.

FIGURE 30

# THREE TYPES OF SMALL GROUPS

Will your group accomplish a task, build relationships, or influence behavior? It's not an either/or question. All three go into every group. Rather it's a matter of emphasis.

| TASK GROUP | RELATIONSHIP GROUP | INFLUENCE GROUP |
|---|---|---|
| **Definition:**<br>Task groups form to accomplish a job which can't be done by one person alone. The goal of the group can be to arrive at a decision, solve a problem, or reach a joint understanding of new material. We're quite familiar with task groups in our churches. Sunday School classes and Bible studies that concentrate on historical information or scriptural content fall into this category. Their task is learning. | **Definition:**<br>We are social animals. We often toss our lot with others not to accomplish any specific goal but for the sheer warmth of human companionship. We sometimes need the fiction of a goal to act as a catalyst, but the real purpose of the group is fellowship. This is the case for many of our potluck dinners, youth fellowships, Tuesday morning sewing circles, and even prayer meetings. These groups serve a vital function. | **Definition:**<br>The influence group is composed of people who admit the need for change in their lives. They voluntarily gather and request that others exhort them and have an impact on their behavior and attitudes. There must ultimately be a shared desire for change on the part of the membership. Discipleship classes and individual or group pastoral counseling often fall into this persuasive category. |
| **Issues:**<br>◊ What is the most effective style of leadership to organize our people?<br>◊ What is the optimum size for our group?<br>◊ Do all the folks really share the same goal or is there a hidden agenda?<br>◊ How can we draw out shy members to benefit from their ideas? | **Issues:**<br>◊ What factors create cohesiveness? What pulls people together?<br>◊ What can we do to foster trust and self-disclosure?<br>◊ How can conflict surface without tearing the fellowship apart?<br>◊ How can we unconditionally accept members so that they are free to be themselves? | **Issues:**<br>◊ What happens when a member breaks the group's norms?<br>◊ How do leader's expectations affect a member's behavior?<br>◊ How can the leader motivate the troops?<br>◊ What type of influence lasts the longest?<br>◊ Do some members of the group have more power than others? |

| | | |
|---|---|---|
| ◊ What method of decision-making will give us a quality solution which members will support? | ◊ Is it possible to create a climate where an honest expression of emotion is safe? | |
| **Leadership:** An effective task group requires a different style of leadership depending on which phase it's in. As the group moves from phase to phase, change leaders. | **Leadership:** Leadership by example is the name of the game in relational communication. | **Leadership:** To be effective, leaders must model the life their followers seek. True influential leaders ask for sacrifices from their followers rather than promising goodies. |

Taken from *Getting Together* by Em Griffin, pages 26–46. ©1982 by Inter-Varsity Christian Fellowship of the U.S.A. and used by permission of InterVarsity Press, P.O. Box 1400 Downers Grove, Illinois 60515.

## GROUPS ARE NOT A SUBSTITUTE FOR PERSONAL INTER-ACTION

Remember Jack? He found small groups unacceptable because they weren't large enough; there was no place to hide. Other people find small groups just the right size because they offer a "cop-out" for individual decision-making or accountability. Sometimes autocratic leaders criticize team leaders claiming small groups (committees, boards, task forces) only offer a smoke screen for weak leadership and an unwillingness to make decisions. Of course that's not always true but it can be. And when groups mask the leadership incapabilities of those who ought to be handling things on an eyeball-to-eyeball, interactional basis, they become a liability rather than an asset.

Leaders need to stimulate, guide, and develop the resources inherent in the group. The group must be led through the process of solving its own problems, discovering and meeting its own needs, and determining proper courses of action. Leaders should ask themselves several questions about their behavior within the framework of the group:

1. Do I really want the group to discover its own potential and objectives or merely to force my own on it?

2. Do I have the ability to follow the group as well as lead it?

3. Do I have a paternalistic attitude toward the group or am I willing to be a peer?

4. Am I able to apply the Word of God appropriately in group

discussions in order to help the group see its decisions in the light of that truth?

Our comprehension of following and leading can now be based on some interesting new research in leadership theory and I hope to get back to it before the book ends. For now, let's go on to talk about the kinds of ingredients or components we might find in a properly functioning group in a church or Christian organization.

# CHARACTERISTICS OF AN EFFECTIVE GROUP

To hitchhike on Griffin's idea that all groups accomplish tasks, build relationships, and influence behavior (with the only difference being a point of emphasis), we might note going into this section of our chapter that most groups usually get involved in some form of creative problem-solving. The Bible study group seeks to interpret various texts and how they apply to daily living. A prayer group struggles with the needs of members, the church, the community, and the world. A planning group wrestles with the best way to achieve goals and objectives.

So it's fair to ask how we can make our boards, committee meetings, and other group sessions more refreshing and stimulating. How can we make them efficient and effective? How can these groups function at peak capacity so dynamic group action can be demonstrated? Answer? Look for, identify, and emphasize the following five ingredients.

*PURPOSE*

Have you ever been in a group meeting where people casually smile and make embarrassing small talk, all the while wondering what they're really doing there? I've been in some board and committee meetings like that! Even in the most informal of sharing groups, different in atmosphere from a monthly board meeting, the issue of purpose has to be foremost—why are we giving ourselves to this activity? Why do we invest this time?

Wiebe suggests, "At the first group meeting spend some time discussing the goals of the group, why each person came, and what each wants to get out of the group. But don't do this every week. Start into something right away that will edify and encourage."[3] He's talking about informal sharing groups. Task force groups wouldn't necessarily talk about their purposes each week either, but they certainly would have them clearly in mind at every meeting. One could make a case for reviewing those purposes to some extent at each meeting.

## INTERACTION

Some kind of communication must take place among the members of the group to legitimately call a collection of people a "group." Members of a pen pal club may never see each other face-to-face, may never carry on verbal discussions. But their regular writing is a form of communication and therefore a form of interaction. That may be stretching a definition but it still legitimately applies and makes that collection of people a group.

Conversely, a group of people whom we have dubbed the "Committee on Finance" may or may not be effective as a group to the extent that they talk (or don't talk) to each other about the subject of finance. If they grudgingly gather in a room, listen to the chairman's preconceived ideas about what the budget should look like, nod their approval and leave, they may have a document to offer the board but they have not functioned as a group. *Groups interact*; and as we noticed in our chapter on change, the more they interact, the more flexible, pliable, and useful they become.

## PERCEIVED UNITY

Leaders often ask, "How do I get people to work together? Why do some groups function as a team and others as a crowd of disorganized individuals? Can leaders really develop team consciousness in a group of people?"

We see it almost every day of our lives—*e pluribus unum*—but we fail to apply the ancient Latin motto to simple procedures of working with each other in small groups. We seek more than unity; we seek *perceived* unity. People must understand what it means to be a part of a group and sense that a special kind of loyalty slowly but surely builds as the group works together.

To be sure, loyalty follows a mutually owned purpose and ongoing interaction. But studies in sociometry have identified the dynamics that operate in any group. For example, the secret of teamwork is *morale* which comes not only from effective leadership, but also when group members see the connection between the time they invest and genuine results.

*Production* relates to perceived unity since the work output directly links to the team concept. *Perceived unity enables a group to think about team objectives and focus on team goals rather than difficulties and problems which stand in the way of goal achievement.*

## INTERDEPENDENCE

Remember our earlier discussion about independent and interdependent congregations? The same thing seems true on a smaller scale in groups. Group members usually begin their group experience with an independent frame of mind. They focus on what expertise and knowledge they can bring to the group or perhaps in some situations, a complete focus on their own needs and problems and how the group will help meet and solve them. So unleashing group dynamics moves not toward dependence of the members in the group (that could be a disastrous result), but their *interdependence*.

Again the athletic metaphor helps. The achievement of a relay race in a track meet rests on the performance of all four members. They have chosen an "anchor" and each has been placed in his particular position because of certain strengths or weaknesses; but in the final analysis the team can't possibly win unless all four runners contribute.

How often do we hear locker-room interviews after a big football game in which the quarterback expresses appreciation to the receivers for "getting open down field" or a running back who just compiled a record 167 yards on the ground gushes his praise for the offensive line and other blocking backs who made all those gains possible. That's interdependence. The runner depends on the blocker to open the hole, but after he's done his part, the blocker has every right to expect the runner to see the opening, break for it, and move that ball upfield.

Baseball sluggers may be called on to sacrifice-bunt a teammate to second base in a tight game. Hockey players constantly fling the puck back and forth across the ice in hopes that one of them will get it past the opposing goalie. The Los Angeles Lakers are famous for their fast break in which the ball goes whizzing back and forth across the passing lanes as three or four players streak down the floor for a quick two points. Teamwork—a fitting analogy for interdependence in group ministry.

## BOUNDARIES

Like it or not, in every group somebody belongs and somebody does not. With everybody in or everybody out we have no group. When we understand group membership, and why some have chosen it and others have not; when we consider how God has brought together this particular group of people for certain purposes, then we are prepared to work together to overcome whatever difficulties stand in the way of goal achievement.

In addition to serving as pastor and assistant pastor, it has been my privilege to function as a lay leader in a number of churches. I think of one of those churches in which the Christian Education

Committee functioned in a holistic and effective way. The group clearly understood its purpose, there was regular interaction in the committee meetings once a month, and all the committee members knew precisely who belonged in the group. In putting together a unified program of education, we were interdependent on one another and there were clear-cut boundaries.

But the committee members did not view the boundaries as a negative feature, like barbed-wire fences to keep out undesirables. Rather the boundaries emphasized that the entire congregation was dependent on the nine of us to design and implement the entire program of church education. We saw our role and we carried it out.

## PRINCIPLES FOR DEVELOPING GROUP DYNAMICS

When we genuinely recognize the essence of the small group, the role and function of its leader, and the kinds of life change and goal achievement that it can produce, we can commit ourselves to advancing and enhancing this phase of the church's ministry. We've already emphasized purpose, example of the leader, the necessity of interaction, and the value of vulnerability and openness. But we dare never forget that group dynamics cannot be superimposed; they are unleashed. That unleashing takes place as a leader works on three central components of group activity—*values, purpose,* and *climate.*[4]

### CLARIFY THE VALUES OF THE GROUP

"Group attractiveness" describes not only how people feel about what's happening to them in the group, it determines to a large extent whether they continue to participate or not. Without sounding like a used car salesman, the leader must regularly emphasize the values of the group not only to present members, but also to potential members. A small group functioning in any of the three ways Griffin describes in Figure 30 offers the following:

**1.** *Growth toward maturity.* Perhaps not all the members will grow but enough of them should be making progress to demonstrate the validity of the group's procedures.

**2.** *Self-awareness.* Part of the vulnerability and open sharing in small group activity should help us learn more about ourselves.

**3.** *Spiritual control.* To be sure, one can yield oneself to the Holy Spirit in personal quiet time, private prayer, or while driving the car down a busy freeway. But the unity of the Spirit in the bond of peace translates into something special when people work at it together. My friend Gene Getz refers to this as "one-anothering."

**4.** *Discipling.* We have come to think of discipling in the late twentieth century as one-on-one development of a less mature believer by a more mature believer. Surely it can happen that way, but the much more common biblical pattern is small groups. Jesus spent very little time with the disciples as individuals but a great deal of time with them as a small group.

**5.** *Reinforcement.* A good group should be encouraging people to speak out and rewarding them verbally for their contribution. Hesitant, shy, retiring people who really don't believe their contributions mean anything in the work of the kingdom should learn otherwise after participating for a time in an effective group.

**6.** *Education.* The dynamic of interaction provides an obvious learning experience; anyone who has participated in an effective small group for a period of time understands the reality of learning involved.

Remember that the change prompted by small groups may not always be pleasant. Sometimes group process uncovers sin in the lives of the members. But all this can be carried out in a climate of support and love which makes the group very valuable.

## COMMUNICATE THE PURPOSE OF THE GROUP

Yes, I know we've said this several times before but most likely it cannot be overstated. Is the group's purpose clearly understood by all the members? Do the members agree with where the group intends to go and how it intends to get there? Have group purposes changed or do they need reviewing after a period of time? Review the Griffin chart to see the distinctive purpose of groups and how they target the emphasis of group activities.

## CREATE THE CLIMATE OF THE GROUP

The proper climate for group dynamics should be nonthreatening, nondefensive, and nonembarrassing. Sometimes little introductory exercises such as name tag games can break the ice and stimulate involvement. Interactional methods such as describing one's most embarrassing experience or most memorable Christmas build empathy as other group members think, "I remember a Christmas just like that." The example of the leader and the environment of the group create the climate. It's no accident that the most effective evangelistic home Bible classes meet in homes around kitchen or dining room tables, or perhaps in a den by the fireplace.

Creating the climate includes providing opportunities for genuine communication. If you don't think group communication is important even in business meetings, notice how small groups of people gather in the parking lot after those meetings to talk with each other. The more tense and controversial the business meeting, the more loitering and lingering goes on around those cars. If they could have or would have said in the meeting what they're complaining about later, you might have diffused an explosive backlash.

Group development offers the leader one of his greatest challenges. It contains potential for effective ministry which could also become heartbreaking failure. Group work is learned behavior. And like Christian leadership, it takes useful form and provides eternal value as we allow God's Spirit to pull His people together.

## STUDY QUESTIONS

**1.** Name at least three small groups of which you've been a part in your adult life.

**2.** Study carefully the chart entitled "Three Types of Small Groups." With which are you most familiar? Why? Which would you feel most comfortable leading? Why?

**3.** Using the material under the section "Characteristics of an Effective Group" write a one-paragraph definition of "group."

**4.** Doubtless you have spent some years as a follower at home, in school, at church, and on the job. Think back and suggest some ways memorable leaders helped you and others form strong team bonds for effective group functioning.

**5.** Make two lists noting your strengths and weaknesses as they relate to group involvement.

| Strengths | Weaknesses |
|-----------|------------|
| _____ | _____ |
| _____ | _____ |
| _____ | _____ |

## ENDNOTES

**1.** Michael Wiebe, *Small Groups: Getting Them Started and*

*Keeping Them Going,* (Downers Grove, Ill.: InterVarsity Press, 1976), p. 6.

**2.** Em Griffin, *Getting Together,* (Downers Grove, Ill.: InterVarsity Press, 1982), pp. 26–46.

**3.** Wiebe, p. 9.

**4.** James Westgate, unpublished class notes, Dallas Theological Seminary, Department of Christian Education.

CHAPTER 16

# TRAINING FOR GODLINESS
## AND COMPETENCE

Two deacons of a small church sat on the porch of a general store in their town considering a forthcoming church business meeting and the elections to be held. One turned to the other and said, "I gotta go with Lundeen for moderator; he's a strong natural leader, well connected with a professional staff, a real climber, a no-nonsense high roller with great instincts for the bottom line." That fictional paragraph based on a cartoon by MacNelly in an October 1986 issue of *The Chicago Tribune* is intended to convey the cultural bias and worldly value system which has crept into church leadership at the end of the twentieth century.

The issue of training is no longer limited to teaching people how to stand before a group, prepare a lesson, or go out on evangelism, though those are still all important. Now we must begin much earlier—with a foundational understanding of the very nature of leadership and how it functions within the biblical framework. We could all agree that any leadership training program's purpose is to develop "good workers" but we might not all agree on what is "good" and how hard they should work.

Ephesians 2:10 tells us that "we are God's workmanship, created in Christ Jesus to do good works, which God prepared in advance for us to do." The apostle surely has in mind much more than formal service through church ministry programs, but those types of "good works" must be included. To start out generally and work toward more specific understandings of training, let's borrow a list from *The Christian Leadership Letter* which attempts to identify some way to define "good work" in a useful form.

1. Good work is based on good relationships.
2. Good work is efficient.
3. Good work sees and includes all resources as gifts over which we are to be stewards.
4. Good work is effective.
5. Good work is done skillfully.
6. Good work is done consistently.[1]

Writers talk about efficiency as the optimal use of resources and effectiveness as the production of what one was intended to produce. How do we equip this kind of servant in the local church and other Christian organizations?

For one thing, Jay Hunton reminds us that volunteers will always serve better (more efficiently and more effectively) in ministries toward which they feel commitment and concern. In these areas they will also be more ready to receive instruction, more eager to profit from training, and therefore more productive in the ministry.

> It must be the pastor's intention to make the minimum change in what people normally and naturally enjoy doing. One of the most unmet human needs is "to do something one enjoys and does well; the need to experience the use of a satisfying skill." Because a volunteer has decided to work where he enjoys it most, do not accuse him of no self-sacrifice, for this is where he can be most effective in the system. A "people approach" is always better than a "job approach."[2]

Every volunteer must learn both the context in which he serves and the details of a specific job. The training program must cover both while at the same time imbuing that biblical-spiritual grasp of leadership mentioned above. As the first major section of our chapter indicates, we focus on what potential leaders need to *know* and what they need to *do*. *The key is a competency based program which emphasizes outcomes rather than inputs or processes.* To put it another way, we work back from the product we want to see in order to understand how that product can be produced.

## CONTENT AND SKILLS OF THE TRAINING PROGRAM

Presumably any adequate training program for church volunteers will contain knowledge commitments, attitude development, and skill emphases. Educators refer to these as *cognitive, affective,* and *conative* objectives. They come together in the biblical manifesto for an equipping ministry (Eph. 4:11-16). Equipping (training) is purposive directive action whereby we train believers to fulfill the ministry for which God has gifted them and to which He has called them. One writer talks about "the enabler philosophy," emphasizing that administrative process provides the base for all effective training in the church.

> . . . people are of supreme importance in the local church; and since they are different and their needs are different, policies should always be written in a flexible manner to do all possible to meet these needs. Flexibility helps undergird the enabler philosophy. The feeling conveyed by the enabler philosophy will build within the local church membership the desire to accomplish God's will and purpose for the congregation, and will draw them together in a positive commitment to each other and to the church.[3]

In our quest for content and skills of leadership, let's begin where we ought to, in the pages of Scripture.

## LEARNING FROM BIBLICAL MODELS

The contrast between Joshua 1 and Judges 1 shows what happens when a leader trains a successor and what happens when he does not. The transition from Moses to Joshua shows one of the smoothest transfers of leadership recorded anywhere in the Scriptures and possibly in all of history.

We find a similar flow of authority from Elijah to Elisha. Their story seems more dramatic, but the personalities of those prophets were considerably different from those of their forefathers in the leadership of Israel.

The text of 1 Kings 19 offers evidence of a personal call, an important component in the recruitment process. This context differs considerably from that surrounding the call of Moses' successor, Joshua. Joshua's call came directly from the Lord but we can surely conclude that Moses and Joshua had frequently discussed what would happen in the future. I suspect that the message Jehovah recorded in Joshua 1 was not a surprise to His servant.

Consider the way Jesus called and taught the Twelve. Anyone harboring doubts about the importance of leadership development among the servants of the Lord need look no further than A.B.

Bruce's important book *The Training of the Twelve* (Kregel). Bruce describes the long, patient process far removed from the crowds.

The content of Mark 9 alone identifies how crude the disciples could be and how often they disappointed their Lord. Make no mistake about it—*leaders are not born; they are trained!* Church leaders do not just fill staff positions; they develop quality ministries which honor Christ in every way.

## LEARNING FROM EDUCATIONAL MODELS

We have already looked at the educational cycle. Another type of educational model appears in the image or word picture common to both Old and New Testaments. For example, in 1 Peter alone we see believers referred to as aliens and strangers (2:11), newborn babies (v. 2), obedient children (1:14), free men (2:16), living stones (v. 5), chosen people (v. 9), royal priesthood (v. 9), holy nation (v. 9), God's people (v. 9) and God's flock (5:1-4). Add to that images of new wine, the physical body, and the family, and we can see numerous educational models which the Bible itself provides.

Jesus used a significant image when He talked about the yoke (Matt. 11:28-30). As a carpenter Jesus doubtless fashioned many a yoke. As a Teacher He urged people to take the yoke with Him, thereby calling for discipline, obedience, and commitment.

> *Decision* and *commitment* are the chief characteristics of this style of learning. Persons learn by choosing to take on the yoke of responsibility and vocation. We decide to respond to Jesus' call to take up our cross and follow Him, and to link our lives to His kingdom come what may. We learn to be like Him, to identify with His people, and to follow in His way of love and service. Through making this commitment, many of the uncertainties and worries that concerned us earlier are resolved, and a new sense of peace and purpose sustains and guides us. By taking on His yoke, we learn of Christ and His will for our lives. We find definite aims for our learning and pursue them with intentionality. We readily acquire skills, information, and attitudes that contribute to our goals. We have become self-initiated learners out of our desire to faithfully carry the yoke of Christ.[4]

## LEARNING FROM PERSONAL MODELS

This form of training appears so obvious one hesitates to give it special space in a book of this type. Nevertheless, what we claim almost automatically in parents and children, we practice a bit more slowly in local church leadership development. Leaders and potential leaders live in constant shepherding relationships often brought about by the very nature of the professional tasks and assignments they hold.

Furthermore, they sustain frequent informal relationships (particularly in the smaller church) through church socials, visiting in each other's homes, informal chatter, and coffee breaks. So the ministry of friendship becomes an important aspect of the modeling program and one attested with great power in the biblical text. A significant example appears in the first chapter of the Book of 1 Thessalonians.

> Brothers loved by God, we know that He has chosen you, because our Gospel came to you not simply with words, but also with power, with the Holy Spirit and with deep conviction. You know how we lived among you for your sake. You became imitators of us and of the Lord; in spite of severe suffering, you welcomed the message with the joy given by the Holy Spirit. And so you became a model to all the believers in Macedonia and Achaia (1 Thes. 1:4-7).

In the New Testament church the fledgling congregation at Antioch stands out as a leadership-producing body. After only one year of intensive teaching, they came up with five candidates for missionary service, all of whom served as elders in the church. Larry Richards is right when he says, "In the Scriptures, spiritual leaders have two primary tasks to which they are called. One of them is to build up the maturity of the body, and they must also be involved in people's everyday lives, constantly teaching."[5]

## LEARNING FROM PROFESSIONAL MODELS

The necessity of training flows naturally out of an understanding of needs and the availability of recruits who lack the background to carry out their tasks. But when we begin to talk about training programs we have to sort out various kinds of professional models.

For example, we could consider *individual or group training.* Individual training on a one-to-one basis (such as a regional sales representative might do for his replacement) has obvious benefits but is not cost-effective. Group training (a class for new Sunday School teachers) enables us to reach more people in a shorter period of time but may not cover all the issues and problems that might be a part of the ministry.

We have already alluded to *skill, attitude, and knowledge training.* Knowledge training relates closely to formal schooling and·therefore pastors tend to gravitate toward this dimension first and sometimes exclusively. Skill training we relate to equipment or the carrying out of specific activities or programs in some phase of ministry. For example, knowing the Gospel of John falls under cognitive development but leading a Bible study on the Gospel of John is conative skill. In a church we must always remember the affective dimension; the attitude and spirit in which people serve (what they are) is probably far more important than what they know and what they can do.

Still a distinction must be made between *internal and external training.* Should you train teachers "in-house" using the kinds of programs we'll describe in the next section of the chapter? Should you bring in special consultants, experts in curriculum use and age-group understanding? Should you send your teachers out to the denominational or regional Sunday School conventions and seminars? Probably the best answer is twofold: "Some involvement in all of these approaches" and, "Whatever works best in your situation."

Let's add one more professional model here, a model designed by Kathleen Graham Wilson which attempts to take a step beyond the linear educational cycle to demonstrate ongoing processes. Figure 31 describes types of activity at the base of the cube, subsystems along the side and questions across the top. According to Wilson's own description:

> The four types of activities (designing, implementing, evaluating, modifying) found at the bottom of the cubicle model are at work with each sub-unit. The design processes lead to an orderly development of the blueprint for the unit's actions. The implementation activities set the unit into motion toward the accomplishments of that unit's goals. The evaluation activities monitor each unit's efforts and their effects. The modification activities help the unit adapt to the changes that occur within people and the church's life so that each unit can be in close harmony with the body's needs, interests, and abilities.[6]

Wilson also offers some helpful questions which assess the strengths and weaknesses of any current training procedures and launch us into the second portion of our chapter.

1. What are the current ways you use to train your leaders?

2. Whom do you spend most of your time training?

3. What are the results of that time spent?

4. Who needs to be trained?

5. How do those responsible for the training of leaders relate procedurally to the people who need to be trained?

6. How do those who need to be trained participate in the learning experiences?

7. Under what limitations are you performing the task of training leaders?

8. To what extent do present training procedures help to reach those whom we want to reach?

9. How do these procedures need to be improved?

And I would add yet a tenth question, what will be the time and type of the training programs?

## TIME AND TYPE OF THE TRAINING PROGRAMS

Dale Stine has just been called to Fellowship Baptist Church as the Pastor of Christian Education. The senior pastor, deacons, and congregation have numerous duties in mind for Dale and chief among them is development of lay leadership for virtually all the church's educational programs. Dale, a Christian education graduate of a reputable seminary, has had minimal experience but comes highly recommended and the church has significant expectations of him, particularly in the dimension of leadership training. They have also determined that the training will begin with a focus on in-service workers and proceed to a discovery and recruitment of new people.

Fortunately, Dale has been gathering resources for precisely this kind of equipping ministry and intends to walk carefully and successfully through the minefield of obstacles Lowell Brown so clearly enunciates in the ICL *Teaching Training Manual*—lack of vision, lack of pertinent training, lack of available time, lack of materials, lack of finances, lack of unified philosophy.[7] In this same helpful manual Brown and his colleagues emphasize the five crucial characteristics of an effective in-service training program.

a. It is related to the age-level taught.

b. It is practical.

c. It is related to the curriculum taught.

d. It is experiential.

e. It is regular and systematic.

Dale intends to apply every one of them.

246

FIGURE 31

# WILSON LEADERSHIP DEVELOPMENT CUBE

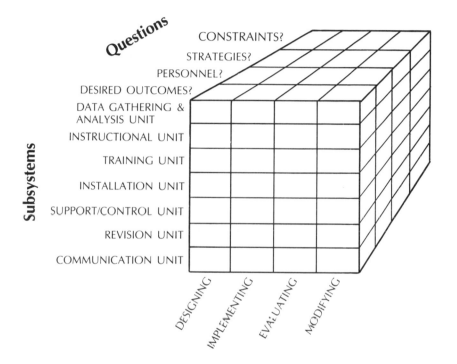

## WHEN SHOULD WE SCHEDULE TRAINING?

A few decades ago it seemed wise to conduct all training programs the hour before the evening service on Sunday. Some churches still find that time effective, but others have switched to a weekday evening or perhaps use one of the Sunday School class slots. Others set aside a specific month or several weekends each year. The only "best" way for a church to train leaders is the way that works in that congregation.

In all likelihood, each church will resort to a hybrid combination of these familiar plans. Not all teachers can attend a specific time-and-place program so we sweep the net more widely in order to catch as many as we can. My personal experience finds the Sunday morning plan quite effective simply because people are already there. Add to that a weekend concentration with high-level seminars, video backup, and hands-on planning (the experiential factor) and you're off and running with an effective training program.

We begin with the assumption that every volunteer needs training, continue with a clear philosophy of leadership, build in those three crucial types of learning (cognitive, affective, and conative) and only then get to specific programs and patterns.

*WHAT PATTERN SHOULD TRAINING TAKE?*

Douglas Johnson warns us that we must "customize the training" to the individual.

> Everyone may have been created equal, but each one is certainly different. There are differences between persons and rates of comprehension and abilities to accomplish tasks, and the amounts of discipline they can exercise on themselves and in the limits to their desire to continue to work in the church. The differences are evident in the rate at which trainees absorb whatever skills are being taught.[8]

Customizing means to direct individual people into training patterns that will meet their particular needs. Creating programs, as we have noted, can be internal or external, one time or ongoing, emphasize skill, knowledge, or attitude, focus on one person or a group, and held at virtually any time. Let's review some of those common training patterns.

1. Modeling—the trainee learns by watching the behavior and ministry of existing leaders.

2. Instructional classes—the trainee learns in formal settings structured at the most appropriate times.

3. Media—the trainee learns through the use of video, film, filmstrips, or slide programs designed to produce the maximum exposure.

4. Guest trainers—the trainee learns by exposure to experts who are brought into the church for periods of time to conduct professional sessions.

5. Conventions—the trainee learns through attendance at seminars and workshops.

6. Internship—the trainee learns through carrying out the ministry under the supervision of qualified leaders.

## WHO WILL LEAD THEM?

Four out of the six items above require local supervision. Only the use of guest trainers and sending people out to conventions relieves us of finding the people to do the job in-house. The ultimate responsibility rests with the highest board of the church, the elders or deacons and the pastor. Pyles carried out an extensive lay leadership training program and evaluated the results concluding:

> Successful training for the laity needs the complete support of the pastor. If the pastor personally leads such experiences, concentrated effort is required for research, planning and implementation. Unquestionably, this pastoral leadership will demand a reordering of priorities. His seminar experience has convinced the author that such dedication to equipping the laity has given increased credibility to his pastoral ministry.[9]

A great deal of interesting research has been done lately on the issue of followership. Some of it suggests that leadership may be chiefly an achievement of followers—that able leaders may emerge only from the ranks of able followers. Many implications for effective training programs rise from this research suggesting, for example, that any functioning leader's behavior could be contingent on at least four aspects of any given situation: the nature of the people being managed; characteristics of the work itself; the relationship between manager and employees, and the relationships among the employees and the manager's personality and preferred management style.[10]

This unique interdependence between leader and followers deserves much more attention in local church studies of leadership. Producing six chapters on this very theme, the editors of one outstanding secular leadership book published in this decade remind us:

> Followers' expectations are changing. Social, economic, and technological environments have created a better educated, more sophisticated constituency. Similarly, superior education, technical skills, and access to information are no longer solely within the purview of the leader. Today's leadership issues are more complex and leaders are expected to perform better. As a result, leaders are feeling the effects of a narrowing gap between their followers' competencies and their own abilities. Increasingly, leaders must actively involve followers in organi-

zational decision-making. All of this suggests a need to *train followers* in how to communicate their expectations and expertise, to enhance their willingness to participate. [11]

Before we leave this section it might be useful to reproduce an interesting chart offered by James Fidler showing the responsibility for reproducing leadership within the framework of the church (Fig. 32). [12]

# RESULTS AND EVALUATION OF THE TRAINING PROGRAM

Remember the earlier point that in training programs we work back from the desired ends to design the means? What results do you want to see at the end of leadership training programs in your church? Certainly, securing qualified people to teach the Bible in Sunday School will be a major concern in most churches.

But other areas of leadership must be dealt with. Have you considered group leadership—the ability to lead a discussion or a home Bible class without actually expounding the Scriptures as a part of the process? Another area we might call public leadership—the ability to go to the platform during the Sunday services, read the Scriptures, make announcements, or take part in the service in some other way. Consider also the issue of board leadership. We want to train elders and deacons to take responsibility for the spiritual growth of other people and to make intelligent decisions in line with biblical commitments.

These are different kinds of competencies and we need to decide what results we want. That's why *outcomes give birth to objectives as a forerunner of design.* The mere acquisition of a skill does not in itself guarantee mature leadership. Character quality provides the determining standard of growth and maturity.

Another church conducts an elder development program aimed at training two kinds of qualities—life and ministry. The first emphasizes the elder-in-training applying biblical priorities in his lifestyle and modeling those characteristics in his family, in his church, and on the job. The second aims at skill and fruit production in equipping other people to mature along biblical lines. The emphasis focuses on *serving* people rather than ruling them.

That congregation, after reaching a satisfactory level of success in elder development, expanded the program to develop Christian leadership in college and seminary students attending the church.

FIGURE 32

# TOWARD A TRAINED LEADERSHIP

these       will train       these

## Professional Leaders:
Pastor
Associate Pastor
Director of Christian
   Education
Choir Director
Organist-Pianist

## Leaders of Leaders:
Chairmen of Boards
Chairmen of Committees
Choirs
Counselors
Teachers
Officers
General Superintendent
Department
   Superintendents
Chairmen of Personal
   Groups
Community Leaders
Supervisors
Instructors for
   Leadership Education
   Schools

**C O M M U N I C A T I O N**

## Leaders of Leaders:
Chairmen of Boards
Superintendent
Teacher
Community Leader:
   Scouts, P.T.A., etc.
Personal Group Leaders
Instructors of Leadership
   Education Classes
Dean of Leadership
   Education School

## Members of Groups:
Church Boards
Workers' Conferences
Sunday Church School
   Class
Parent-Teachers'
   Association
Family
Scout Troop
Personal Group
Leadership Education
   Class
Leadership Education
   School
Church Membership Class

Everybody a Leader
(All Responsible Church Members)

## COMMUNICATES TO

### All Persons
In group, class, job,
home, school, community

*Our Church Plans for Leadership Education,* James E. Fidler, Valley Forge, Pa.:
Judson Press, 1962. Used by permission.

251

## QUALITY CONTROL OF TRAINING OBJECTIVES

Two key words dominate this last section of our chapter—"quality control." Preparing people for the highest calling on earth, service for Jesus Christ, even though it may be "part time" and "lay level," we dare not surrender excellence on the altar of efficiency or expediency. Once we understand the needs of the ministry and the kinds of people who can meet those needs, we are prepared to work back to identification of the objectives.

Objectives must be measurable and written. They must spell out precisely what we want to see happen in the training progam. Perhaps more useful is an actual model of the kind of objectives that might be used toward building leadership skills. This is somewhat detailed, but it can be reproduced for every area of ministry—teaching, evangelism, music ministry, etc.

Objectives for a Training Unit on
Building Leadership Skills

Upon completion of the training, each participant will be able to:

1.0 demonstrate he understands the biblical view of leadership.
  1.1 explain how a leader can be a servant.
    1.11 explain the biblical view of authority as it pertains to leadership.
    1.12 explain the biblical view of submission as it pertains to leadership.
    1.13 explain the biblical view of accountability as it pertains to leadership.
  1.2 explain the responsibilities of a steward.
  1.3 describe the personal qualities and devotional life needed by Christian leaders.
2.0 set goals and develop a plan for achieving those goals (within his sphere of responsibility in the church).
  2.1 write (in consultation with other leaders in his department) a mission statement for his sphere of responsibility within the church which derives from and is consistent with the mission statement for the church.
    2.11 delimit his sphere of responsibility within the church.
  2.2 write specific, measurable, realistic objectives stating the results to be achieved.

2.21 gather data needed to write objectives.
    2.211   determine what data are required.
    2.212   determine how data can be obtained.
    2.213   check data for accuracy and completeness.
2.22 analyze data to determine probable cause of problems or deficiencies.
2.23 determine the level of improvement desired or attainable within a specified time period for each problem area.

2.3  formulate a program for achieving agreed on objectives.
    2.31 generate possible solutions or courses of action intended to overcome the deficiency or eliminate the problem.
    2.32 analyze possible solutions to determine best solution(s).
    2.33 establish priorities for implementing solution(s).
    2.34 establish sequence and time schedule for implementing solution(s).

2.4  allocate resources needed for achieving objectives.
    2.41 identify what resources are required for reaching objectives.
    2.42 identify available resources.
    2.43 plan how available resources (i.e., space, money, equipment) will be used.

3.0 organize structure for effective accomplishment of objectives.
  3.1  review and/or modify existing organizational structure.
  3.2  create position descriptions.
    3.21 determine performance standards.
    3.22 delineate organizational relationships.
  3.3  establish position qualifications.

4.0 staff the program and manage all human resources.
  4.1  recruit qualified individuals.
  4.2  train recruited personnel.
  4.3  develop the capabilities of staff members.

5.0 direct efforts of team members toward achieving established objectives.
  5.1  assign tasks to team members and delegate authority needed to complete assigned tasks.
  5.2  motivate team members.
    5.21 explain motivational principles which are biblically valid.

    5.3   coordinate team efforts.

6.0 control team efforts to ensure progress toward objectives according to plan.

    6.1   gather data pertaining to results attained or achieved.

        6.11 determine what data are needed.

        6.12 determine how data can be obtained.

    6.2   measure results in terms of objectives.

    6.3   make corrections in individual or team activities.

        6.31 determine cause(s) of problems or deficiencies.

        6.32 give constructive feedback.

        6.33 implement changes in programs or job assignments.

    6.4. recognize the contributions of individuals toward achieving group goals.

NOTE: The following are five possible areas of additional training in leadership skills.

    7.0 demonstrate competence in time management and time effectiveness.

    8.0 demonstrate the ability to manage conflict and stress.

    9.0 use a decision-making process.

    10.0 conduct committee meetings effectively.

    11.0 communicate effectively in order to achieve desired results within his sphere of responsibility in the church.

## QUALITY CONTROL OF TRAINING PHILOSOPHY

Effective training programs derive from biblical principles of ministry. For example, if one believes the New Testament teaches plurality of leadership, he will approach training responsibilities differently than if he is comfortable with a one-man leader role in the church. Shared leadership is a central biblical axiom which dominates both didactic passages and practice of the early believers. Another point of training philosophy suggests that church leaders must be recognizable by character and consent, responsible for their tasks and the people they lead (1 Peter 5), and accountable to each other. Ministry must be done by all God's people and, as Menking reminds us, "Training will be needed as long as the ministry exists. To decide what training should be provided will require you to look at the laity in the ministry. . . . All will need different kinds of training."[13]

## QUALITY CONTROL OF TRAINING COMPETENCIES

Garland Bible Fellowship uses a manual entitled "Shepherding Shepherds" designed to develop biblical leadership in that congregation. Rather than focusing specifically on elders or the pastor, this congregation attempts to train what they call "minichurch pastors" who will be responsible to shepherd care groups. They have spelled out precisely what these leaders should do in carrying out their ministries. The competencies fall into four categories—pastoring ministry, teaching ministry, evangelism ministry, and overseeing ministry. The training program emphasizes six functions: shepherding the flock (Acts 28; 1 Peter 5:2); teaching and exhorting (1 Tim. 3:2; Titus 1:9); serving as an example for the flock (1 Peter 5:3); refuting those who contradict truth (Titus 1:9); managing the church (1 Tim. 3:5); and praying for the sick (James 5:14-15).

Obviously what the congregation in Garland is saying about minichurch pastors can be said of elders or pastors in other contexts. They should attempt to exert quality control over detailed training competencies.

## QUALITY CONTROL OF TRAINING PROCEDURES

Here we can succeed or fail in the whole process of leadership development. Like almost any other phase of the church's ministry, good programs administered by poor leaders will fail while even poor programs administered by good leaders can succeed. *The human ingredient is the key issue in leadership.* Pastors who function as ineffectual leaders are hardly candidates to direct leadership training programs. Churches in which intrastaff quarreling is a way of life can neither develop strong lay leaders nor emphasize the qualities of biblical eldership.

Each person monitors the quality of the persons for whom he is reponsible in the training program. The Chairman of the Christian Education Committee (in the absence of a Christian Education Pastor) must take the responsibility for quality control of training programs carried out by the Sunday School, youth ministry, club programs, and other facets of the church's educational ministry.

Recruitment and training can be done well but only if church leaders make training a priority and develop long-term goals. Imagine for example, a church of 200 people needing more Sunday School teachers and setting aside a special leadership development class for one quarter each year during the Sunday School hour. Church leaders provide twenty seats in the class and hope to draw twenty leadership recruits. On the first Sunday only sixteen people show up. By the end of the quarter, six of those have dropped out.

Instead of twenty people, the church now has ten who have completed the program. Only 50 percent of the set goal was attained; but such a count emphasizes weakness instead of strength.

Let us rather see a local congregation which may have never before done anything effective in training now actually working for a full quarter with ten potential ministry leaders!

Even if five more people drop out before they assume teaching posts, the remaining five probably represent more leadership than that church has ever trained before. That number represents an achievement for which we can be very grateful to God.

The joy of service can be a reality in any church but only when biblical patterns are followed. Techniques, media, and programs are important; but nothing can replace the congregation's commitment to lead (serve) as a response to God's love and grace.

## STUDY QUESTIONS

**1.** In your own words, describe what you think the author means by "a competency-based program which emphasizes outcomes rather than inputs or processes."

**2.** The chapter touches on the experiences of Elijah and Elisha. Find that passage of Scripture and list three or four leadership lessons that can be derived from it.

**3.** Study Matthew 11:28-30 and suggest what we learn about Christian leadership from the concept of the yoke.

**4.** If you are currently a church leader, how would you answer the nine questions at the end of the first portion of our chapter? If you are not, how do you think you would answer them?

**5.** What things need to be built into a local church training program in order to protect quality control?

## ENDNOTES

1. Ted W. Engstrom and Edward R. Dayton, "Goodness," *The Christian Leadership Letter* (October 1986), p. 2.

2. Jay Hunton, "Horse Sense Cannot Be Taken for Granite," *Preachers' Magazine* (March–May 1986), p. 33.

3. Robert A. Young, *The Development of a Church Manual of Administrative Policies* (Louisville, Ky.: Bel-Air Church Directory Publishers, 1975), p. 14.

**4.** Douglas E. Winglier, "Biblical Images of Learning" *East Asia Journal of Theology* (April 1984), p. 6.

**5.** Lawrence Richards and Gene Getz, "A Biblical Style of Leadership," *Leadership* (Spring 1981), p. 72.

**6.** Kathleen Graham Wilson, "How to Facilitate Leadership Development within Your Church," *Church Leadership Development* (Wheaton, Ill.: Scripture Press Foundation, 1977), p. 6.

**7.** Lowell E. Brown et al., *Teacher Training Manual* (Ventura, Calif.: International Center for Learning, 1982), pp. 85–7.

**8.** Douglas Johnson, *The Care and Feeding of Volunteers* (Nashville: Abingdon, 1978), p. 112.

**9.** William K. Pyles, "A Training Seminar in Roles and Functions of Lay Leadership within the Local Church," (Drew University Doctor of Ministries dissertation, 1980), p. 105.

**10.** William F. Zierden, "Leading through the Follower's Point of View" in *Contemporary Issues in Leadership*, William Rosenbach and Robert L. Taylor, eds. (Boulder, Colo.: Westview Press, 1984), p. 145.

**11.** Rosenbach and Taylor, *Contemporary Issues in Leadership* (Boulder, Colo.: Westview Press, 1984), p. 135.

**12.** James A. Fidler, *Our Church Plans for Leadership Education* (Valley Forge, Pa.: Judson Press, 1962), p. 70.

**13.** Stanley J. Menking, *Helping Laity Help Others* (Philadelphia: Westminster Press, 1984), p. 84.

CHAPTER 17

# PLACING GOD'S SERVANTS IN GOD'S SERVICE

My own failures in placing staff have been numerous, but none stands out in my memory like the time a local church Christian Education Committee which I was chairing asked Bob to teach a Junior boys' class. The class had no teacher, Bob was willing, so we performed the marriage without so much as asking whether the bride and groom knew each other. The fact of the matter is they did not and within a few weeks we had to assist in divorce proceedings—Bob and the boys were not going to make it.

What now? Assume that Bob is either incompetent, unspiritual, or ungifted? Shove him aside to some unfruitful corner of the congregation assuming we have no ministry for someone who can't function in a simple Junior boys' class? Nonsense! But that's what churches do with regularity—place the blame on the worker, not on the bosses.

In this case *we* had made a terrible error. Our assessment had been negligible, our recruitment totally inadequate, and our training of Bob for the task completely invisible. We had predetermined his failure in virtually any ministry and to top it all off, we put him in the wrong place!

After some heart-searching prayer and long discussions, we invited Bob to work in our weekday boys' club program. Within the first year he became the head of the whole operation and did a magnificent job in a very strategic ministry role. We had finally placed God's servant at the proper point in God's service. All of this emphasizes one more time the strategic importance of leadership attitude relating to lay workers in the church. According to Doohan:

Laypersons do not *belong* to the church, nor do they have a *role in* the church . . . *they are* the church, and in union with Christ, their mission is the mission of the church itself. There is no particular vocation for laity in the church, no need of a quest for lay identity. Being church in its fullness is the spirituality for laity.[1]

Lay leader Bill Garrison of Fort Worth claims that lay people want just five things from pastors.
1. An orientation to the glory of God rather than competition.
2. Love.
3. Humility.
4. The willingness to be a learner.
5. A model of the servant leader.
If he is right, we may have been complaining about the wrong deficiencies—deficiencies in the laity rather than the real deficiencies in their leaders. People serve either where we ask them to serve or where we allow them to serve and generally function at a very low level of motivation, a problem we'll deal with in another chapter. Ted Ward observes that:

Leadership is not what one *does* so much as what one *is* within the given context of the development of the body of believers. Leadership is not so much bringing people out of the wilderness as it is sharing in a journey. This sharing is as a peer . . . and sharing is to be done as would a servant. In the church, those who lead (better to say *minister?*) are to serve as agents of the Holy Spirit's gift to the church. Perhaps there are points of similarity between the Christian and the secular definition of leadership, but they are much less important than the points of dissimilarity . . . we must change the *induce, motivate,* and *congratulate* model of leadership into *accept, share,* and *grow together* or we have no business at all putting the word *Christian* ahead of the word *leadership.*[2]

## HOW TO HELP PEOPLE FUNCTION WHERE GOD PLACES THEM

Note the shift in emphasis. Rather than focusing on where *we* place people, we emphasize that issue of call we discussed earlier in an attempt to determine where God wants them to serve. But the process is not mystical, God works through existing leaders to facilitate His will in the recruitment, placement, and development of new leaders. Certain practical strategies can be identified, giving us a means to achieve the goal of helping people function where God places them.

## WISE LEADERS HELP PEOPLE FIND WHERE THEY BELONG

Staffing decisions must center on emphasizing strengths. Sunday School teachers, youth sponsors, visitation workers, and other lay leaders tend to be ineffective for various reasons. Perhaps they are unhappy with that particular ministry and therefore serve from a position of frustration. Or they may be ill-trained for the post and confused about how to go about the ministry. It's possible that a given lay leader does not have the temperament for a given task. The Peter Principle reminds us of the dangerous habit of elevating people to the point of their incompetence. An aggressive college teacher, for example, may make a poor dean and a worse president.

In the church as organism we fall back to an understanding of gifts and call. In the church as organization we recognize that it is administrative irresponsibility to allow an ineffective worker to stay in that ministry. Constant evaluation is necessary to guard against both the Peter Principle (putting a person in the wrong place to begin with) and the Paul Principle (allowing a person to stagnate as the ministry grows beyond his capabilities).

## WISE LEADERS MINISTER WITHOUT THREAT OR INTIMIDATION

This principle works two ways. Pastors, professional staff, and elders must learn to minister without being intimidated by the awesome responsibilities of their posts. In the other direction, however, they minister without intimidating those who look to them for servant models of leadership. The Christian leader does not hide under some kind of mask (2 Cor. 3); he does not try to be someone else; and he does not try to force others to become what God has not made them.

Once again the inseparable link between leadership and followership reminds us that leaders should attempt to reproduce themselves and can only do so to the extent of their own spirituality and competence. Bill Lawrence points up the difference between "personal power" and "social power."

> The servant leader. . . . has a radically different motivation from the "Gentile" leader (cf. Matt. 20:25-28; Mark 10:42-

45). This distinction has been suggested by the terms "personal power people" and "social power people." Personal power people want positions of influence for their own personal aggrandizement and status and put others down in the process. Social power people use their power on behalf of others and act to build the confidence and self-worth of the ones whom they lead.

Social power is simply a contemporary way of describing what a servant leader does: he uses his gifts and abilities as a leader with the capacity to influence and direct others to build their confidence and self-worth, not to destroy their confidence and self-worth in order to build his own. Such a leader is very unique.[3]

## WISE LEADERS ANTICIPATE AND HANDLE CONFLICT

Mature leaders are not afraid of conflict because they know how to make it productive. They have learned first of all that conflict is not necessarily confrontation—it does not have to be negative and destructive. Secondly, they have learned that conflict can be dealt with and redirected to actually help the ministry. A good leader tries to ascertain what people need from him and gives them a chance to explain those needs. Since conflict largely stems from misunderstanding, he listens and communicates well to break through misunderstanding to the real source of the conflict.

Often we leaders tend to be insufficiently flexible to cope with the vast variety of ministry situations which abound even in the smaller church. Our understanding of ourselves and our leadership is deficient and we project that on others, often causing conflict.

Many Christian leaders seem so unprepared to exercise administrative responsibility or leadership functions that they have developed totally distorted pictures of the needs and tasks of the ministry. If something doesn't fit, it is obviously the fault of the laymen.

In the source cited earlier, Lawrence details five different conflict management styles—avoiding, accommodating, collaborating, compromising, and competing. He selects collaborating as the proper style for the Christian leader, calling it an "effort to get all conflicting parties fully involved in determining the cause and nature of the conflict and working to resolve it agreeably."

In this style the person emphasizes equally the achieving of everyone's goals, the interests of the organization, and the well being of the relationships affected by the conflict. This person believes that everyone's goals must be sastisfied if relationships are to last. From his perspective he must be both assertive and flexible, working to keep communication flowing, and confident that the conflict can be used to strengthen both the organization and the relationships now under stress.[4]

*WISE LEADERS WORK TOWARD MINISTRY CONTROL*
Let's be careful here. We're not talking about controlling people, but controlling our tasks (ministries) and helping new leaders control theirs. Control deals with measuring results against the objectives, what we sometimes call "getting a handle on the job." Let's tap an authoritative secular source for a formal definition.

Controlling consists of three steps that directly follow the four other management functions: establishing performance standards, measuring performance and comparing it to standards, and correcting deviations . . . performance standards are what the manager expects from each unit and individual in the organization.[5]

The entirety of our next section details this important dimension of administrative leadership. Let's keep our perspective, however—all of this has to do with placing servants in the right ministries.

# HOW TO HELP PEOPLE GAIN MINISTRY CONTROL
Lay leaders gain ministry control in precisely the same way the professional staff achieves that goal. First of all, it's a process rather than an event; secondly, control can be identified by several specific factors. To put it very simply, you know you have ministry control if you have adequate understanding of objectives, access to resources, reason for confidence, and motivation to excellence. Let's look at each one individually.
*PROVIDE SUFFICIENT UNDERSTANDING OF OBJECTIVES*
Dr. Richard Patterson, President of the Evangelical Teacher Training Association, has observed the same thing I have seen through frequent working with experienced pastors. My contacts have been through informal speaking in churches around the world and working with Doctor of Ministry students at several graduate theological seminaries. Patterson calls the problem, "mission obscurity."

The incidence of this issue was overwhelming. It was nearly unanimous. In the ministries in which they served, the members had little current recognition of "ownership" or why their organization existed. In most cases the implementation of this project was the first time they had ever experienced mission assessment. Constitution and bylaws had been in some obscure drawer for years and the church or organization simply perpetuated what it had been used to doing or thinking.[6]

People can never serve adequately in any particular place of ministry unless we provide them an understanding of the objectives of that ministry. Earlier I dealt in detail with the process of identifying mission, setting goals, objectives, and implementation steps. Let me just remind the reader here that delineation of objectives must be in writing, clearly understood, and mutually agreed on. Anything less can never lead to ministry control.

This kind of goal orientation (Phil. 3:10-14) keeps us tuned to biblical imperatives and alert to God's plan for our churches and schools. We can defy the fear of failure and be careful not to assume too much responsibility when we set realistic goals and objectives. Rather than complicate ministry, clarity in objectives leads to simplification and achievement.

## PROVIDE SUFFICIENT ACCESS TO RESOURCES

"Resources"—one of those helpful words that enables us to gather all kinds of variegated things under a single umbrella. Obviously, ministry achievement depends on adequate human resource. One of my doctoral students noted that he spends ten–fifteen hours a week as a pastor just handling secretarial and clerical duties since the church "can't afford to hire a secretary." My response took virtually no thought or hesitation: that church can't afford *not* to hire a secretary. No church can afford to squander its pastor's time in clerical duties. Precisely that kind of situation provides a clarion call for the necessity of lay leadership and volunteerism at all levels in ministry. In my opinion only ignorance or stubbornness can create counterproductive blockades like that one.

But other kinds of resources include equipment, supplies, and time. If we assign a lay leader a task which takes fifteen hours a week and he has only five hours to give, we have doomed him to frustration. Subordinates do not find these things for themselves; they are provided by their leaders. And when as leaders we do not provide adequate resources, we have said in effect, "Do the best

you can but we really don't expect you to succeed."
## PROVIDE SUFFICIENT REASON FOR CONFIDENCE
When a worker has a sufficient grasp of objectives, and a sufficient access to whatever resources he needs, he begins to have a reason for confidence in his ministry. To be sure, he repeats with regularity the important words of the apostle in 2 Corinthians 3:5. "Not that we are competent to claim anything for ourselves, but our competence comes from God."

We lead people to confidence by how we treat them in ministry. A basic rule of delegation (see chap. 11) requires that we demonstrate our confidence in the capability of lay leaders. Let's draw a parallel here between a teacher and students. It is not difficult for teachers to convince students they are unable to do satisfactory work in a given course. True, some will "come out fighting" determined to prove the teacher wrong. But many will assume the teacher's assessment correct and fail by default.

We want to set high standards of achievement for local church ministry but we also want to place servants so carefully that we can honestly affirm our confidence in what they can be in their service for Christ. Let's listen to Lawrence one more time.

> This means that to be a servant leader under the Lord Jesus Christ is to gain the highest honor since it enables the one who occupies the position to share in the very glory and prestige of the Lord of the universe. The following definition conveys the concept of servant leadership: A servant is someone under the authority of another who voluntarily serves for that one's benefit with a spirit of humble dependence and who finds his freedom, fulfillment, and significance in the limits of his service. [7]

## PROVIDE SUFFICIENT MOTIVATION TO EXCELLENCE
Perhaps folks seem to serve the Lord so halfheartedly on occasion because they do not grasp the significance of their roles in the wider scheme of things. They may even view themselves as serving the pastoral staff or the organization rather than rendering their service directly to the Lord. J. Ralph Hardee calls on churches to turn the pyramid upside down. Rather than operating a church which exists to support the staff's ministry we should design our resources and programs so that the staff's ministry supports the body (Fig. 33).[8]

Hardee describes the church as:

The arena for the laity to learn to do their ministry. Thus, the role of staff ministers becomes to provide help and give support to the ministry of the laity. This view places the church staff in a position of ministering *under* lay persons and tends to set a pattern of equipping ministry *through, with,* and *to*— rather than *for* the laity.[9]

The lay leader who understands what God wants him to do and believes he is called to do it; whose ministerial staff and lay supervisors have provided for him all the resources essential to effective ministry; who has found confidence in the power of the Holy Spirit and an understanding of his own spiritual gifts—that lay leader can move on to excellence in ministry.

# HOW TO HELP PEOPLE STAY IN THEIR MINISTRIES

What is the key to retention? How can we as leaders not only find, recruit, train, and place the right people in the right ministries, but keep them there for a reasonable period of time? Most of the surveys indicate the same kinds of conclusions—*retention is essentially built on service that meets needs and produces meaningful results.* Contrary to popular viewpoint, the cost of commitment does not appear as crucial as rewards of the task. People will pay a reasonable price to reach satisfactory ministry objectives when leaders emphasize accomplishment and achievement rather than duty and responsibility. And what do we offer in the service staff to retain them for ministry? I have selected four answers.

## AGREEABLE TIME FRAMES

A contract or service agreement should spell this out right up front. My preference is to secure workers for one year though we might often "contract" volunteers for a shorter time such as a quarter or perhaps six months. We do not want the aura of a life sentence. The word "agreeable" works both ways. Presumably we should not ask a person to commit herself to teaching junior high girls for the next ten years. Few people would respond with enthusiasm to that kind of challenge. However, it is also not agreeable to accept a volunteer to head Children's Church for one month if the Christian Education Committee has determined service periods in that ministry should be no shorter than thirteen weeks each.

Some suggest that recruiting should be spread out over the year in order to reduce pressure on recruiters and spread out the attri-

FIGURE 33

# STAFF SUPPORT PYRAMID

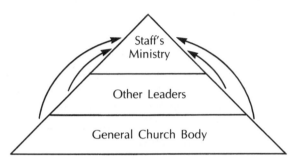

## CHURCH EXISTING TO SUPPORT
## THE STAFF'S MINISTRY

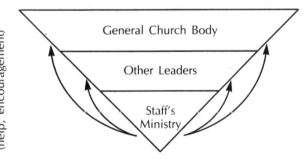

## STAFF'S MINISTRY EXISTING
## TO SUPPORT THE CHURCH

tion. Thereby a smaller proportion of the teaching staff would be replaced at any one time and recruiters could concentrate on quarterly recruiting. In an extremely large church with a great deal of population mobility this might be a highly desirable plan. My own preference continues to favor the one-year appointment with recruiting going on from time to time throughout the year but placement only occurring at the beginning of September. (Obviously we need to fill vacancies throughout the year.)

## APPROPRIATE REST PERIODS

The increasing demographic mobility of the North American population makes this less a problem than it was twenty or thirty years ago. People get "time off" between ministries simply by moving to a different church, a different part of the town, or even across state lines. But for those who stay occasional R & R is important. Sometimes people get discouraged and need a brief sabbatical just to have some time for spiritual refreshment and the regathering of enthusiasm for the ministry.

By the way, don't underestimate the importance of mandatory rest periods to break the stranglehold some people develop on certain ministries. Through annual appointments to all ministries and a required quarter off after six straight quarters of teaching we can create "positive interruption" in what sometimes becomes a fiefdom of one person's dominance in a certain ministry.

## ACCEPTABLE SUPPORT STAFF

Notice how one of the features of retention seems identical with an essential component of control—resources. Will the pastor I described earlier leave his church when that burden of ten–fifteen hours clerical work each week becomes unbearable? If so, he won't be the first to leave a ministry position because people who could did not provide sufficient support staff. Amazingly, when we talk about volunteerism, we are not asking for a decision which will bankrupt the budget. Three members of that congregation, each volunteering five hours a week, could solve the problem immediately and release their pastor for the kind of ministry God called and gifted him to do.

Perhaps the problem looms larger than clerical work. Maybe the church needs to hire a second full-time member of the pastoral staff, a Minister of Christian Education or Youth. When those decision points come along in the life of a congregation the leaders must act courageously and wisely in order to retain the staff they already have.

But "support staff" might be something even smaller than clerical volunteers. Perhaps the former Sunday School superintendent has warmly assured the new superintendent of his availability at any time to answer any questions and help the new leader feel comfortable in his ministry. That's support staff. Or, maybe a Sunday School teacher knows the Christian education program won't collapse and nobody will haunt her with guilt if she takes a weekend vacation because the Christian Education Committee has provided a list of substitutes on whom she can call to fill in when necessary.

All this leads again to our oft-repeated emphasis on team ministry. No lay leader need feel isolated or "cut off" in the ministry when he understands he is a part of the broad team essential to the functioning of any biblical congregation. In its philosophy of ministry one congregation has written:

The church must care for its members, not casually or superficially, but deliberately and intensively. Caring is the very cornerstone of our faith. It has its roots in God who cares for His creation to the point of suffering on our behalf. His caring is fully expressed in the life, death, and resurrection of Jesus.

In Him we see caring at its best. He cares for the world, but He focuses His caring love by giving freely of Himself to individual persons. He looks with compassion upon the masses but never loses the individual in the crowd. He calls His church to a caring vocation.

But what does it mean to care and to be cared for? How does one give specific expression to caring? One traditional answer has been the response of the pastor, trained to meet the serious needs of the congregation. The pastor responds to crisis, and serious needs in the lives of the church member. But deliberate and intensive caring is beyond the capability of any one person in a church with a membership in excess of 1,100. For our church to be the caring, loving fellowship which we desire it to be, a plan for Parish Lay Ministry is essential.[10]

## ADEQUATE REWARD SYSTEMS
People need to know they're appreciated. Wise leaders offer periodic encouragement and reinforcement all throughout the year. Certificates of recognition, plaques, and public acclaim are all important, but the genuine and regular appreciation expressed by super-

FIGURE 34

# APPRECIATION CHECKLIST

PURPOSE | Most of us need to develop a discipline of periodically reviewing our performance in expressing appreciation.

Look over the checklist and see if you are already doing the things suggested. If not, begin today. Add to the list. You may be surprised at how appreciative you can become.

## CHECKLIST

| yes | no | don't remember | Acts and Actions |
|-----|-----|-----|-----|
|  |  |  | I have written a personal note of appreciation to a staff member this week. |
|  |  |  | I have discussed a personal problem with a staff member. |
|  |  |  | I have had lunch or a meal with a member of my staff. |
|  |  |  | I am aware of problems of my staff members and help where I can. |
|  |  |  | I usually remember people's birthdays. |
|  |  |  | I know how long each person reporting to me has been with the organization and I recognize the anniversary date with a card of appreciation. |
|  |  |  | I discuss personal performances with each of my staff members at least once a year. |
|  |  |  | I have thought about and have goals for the personal growth of those reporting to me. |
|  |  |  | Our organization is continuously analyzing cost-of-living against present salaries. |

| yes | no | don't remember | Acts and Actions |
|-----|-----|-----|-----|
| | | | I supply training opportunities to qualified staff. |
| | | | I have allowed a member of my department to attend a training seminar on company time. |
| | | | I have prayed for my staff members this week. |

visors is crucial. Donald Bell reminds us:

A group leader is frequently discouraged because the group to which he belongs is not fully recognized. Just as some public school teachers have lost group prestige in America, Sunday School teachers in many of our churches are taken for granted. If the leaders maintain the prestige of such groups, the volunteer workers within them will have high morale. The establishment of definite standards of jobs like these will lead to better morale and a higher quality of job performance.

An interesting psychological factor is involved here. Since the volunteer church worker is not paid for his services, he may need some other personal satisfactions and rewards, in addition to his joy in service to God. The church staff worker receives a salary as part of his reward. The volunteer worker should be compensated with group acceptance and expressions of appreciation from his leaders.[11]

Marilyn Clinton describes "appreciation" as "a sensitive awareness of the worth and significance of the person's contribution to the organization and a personal communication of gratitude to that person for his contribution." She suggests a list that will help leaders evaluate whether they have shown appreciation privately, individually, or in a group—all of which are appropriate methods at different times. Figure 34 shows how you can design and use such an instrument yourself.[12]

Placing God's servants in God's service is important and eternal business. It assumes everything we have already studied about cultivating a biblical leadership style, assessing, recruiting, and training. The process never ends; it is both sequential and cyclical. Reward systems and rest periods are useless if we have not helped people find the right ministry in the first place. And don't forget, the model of the pastor in joyful, optimistic, visionary, enthusiastic ministry sets the standard for the rest of the team.

## STUDY QUESTIONS

**1.** What's the difference between the Peter Principle and the Paul Principle?

**2.** In your own words discuss the difference between "personal power" and "social power."

**3.** Do you agree with Lawrence in choosing "collaborating" as the proper style for Christian leadership?

**4.** The chapter contains a formal definition of "controlling." Rework that in your own words.

**5.** What ways does your church or organization provide "adequate reward systems" for people who serve in it?

## ENDNOTES

**1.** Leonard Doohan, *The Lay-Centered Church* (Minneapolis: Winston Press, 1984), p. 24.

**2.** Ted Ward, "Facing Educational Issues," *Church Leadership Development* (Glen Ellyn, Ill.: Scripture Press Ministries, 1977), p. 34.

**3.** William D. Lawrence, *Developing Lay Leadership* (unpublished Continuing Education Seminar booklet, Dallas Theological Seminary, n.d.), p. 10.

**4.** Lawrence, p. 85.

**5.** Carl Anderson, *Management* (Dubuque, Iowa: Wm. C. Brown, 1984), p. 22.

**6.** Richard Patterson, "What's Happening to Us?" *Christian Education Today* (Spring 1988), p. 8.

**7.** Lawrence, "Distinctives of Christian Leadership," *Bibliotheca Sacra* (June–August 1987), p. 327.

**8.** Bruce Powers, *Church Administration Handbook* (Nashville: Broadman, 1985), p. 309.

**9.** J. Ralph Hardee, "Perspective on Ministry" in *Church Administration Handbook*, Bruce P. Powers, ed. (Nashville: Broadman, 1985), p. 309.

**10.** Taken from the ministry philosophy statement of St. Paul's Church in Creve Coeur, Mo.

**11.** A. Donald Bell, "Counseling the Discouraged Group Leader," *Church Administration* (December 1973), p. 47.

**12.** Marilyn Clinton, "Appreciation Unit," Learning Resource Center (Worldteam, Coral Gables, Fla., n.d.), pp. 2–3.

CHAPTER 18

# CHAIRING BUSINESS MEETINGS

In 1983 an organization called Communispond, Inc. of New York conducted a survey of 471 U.S. executives, attempting to elicit their frank opinions about business sessions and meetings. Seventy-one percent of the respondents agreed with the statement that meetings are "a waste of time." It's just a guess, but after working with Christian leaders and pastors' conferences, doctoral seminars and consulting situations for about a quarter of a century, I suspect evangelical Christian leaders would say about the same thing in about the same ratio.

Our problem, however, rises as an even greater menace to ministry. It's bad enough to consider business sessions a waste of time when they exist for profit-making and the advancing of secular business or industry. It's even more tragic when those meetings constitute an essential part of the ongoing of God's kingdom work in the world. Herein lies the central problem of business meetings in the church: *we have viewed them not as essential service for Jesus Christ, but as a necessary evil to be dispensed with as quickly and painlessly as possible so that service can commence.*

How would the overall climate of ministry in your church or Christian organization change if every person who serves on a board or committee viewed that time and energy as much an investment in ministry as teaching Sunday School, door-to-door evangelism, or even pulpit preaching? Our purpose in this chapter deals with the nuts-and-bolts procedures of running a good business meeting (whether board or committee). But right at the outset I want to make clear that those sessions are subject in effectiveness

273

to the spiritual attitudes with which the participants approach their time together.

By the way, we'll make no specific distinction for our purposes between *boards* and *committees*. Generally speaking a board serves as a policy-making body and a committee, a recommending body. In a local church a Christian Education Committee or a Missions Committee might make recommendations to the official board, governing board, elder board, or deacon board, depending on church polity. The board might delegate some policy-making authority to the committee but essentially policy belongs to the board.

In a college the board of directors, trustees, or regents carries out its work through gathering information as its members serve on numerous committees in such areas as academic policies, student services, business and finance, public relations, and development. It should be already obvious that spiritual maturity provides a basic prerequisite for effective ministry on a board and/or committee. And the higher the authority of the body, the more necessary a well-developed level of spiritual maturity.

## FIVE DEADLY SINS OF CHAIRPERSONS

Obviously from what has already been said, there are at least "six deadly sins"—the first and most important being to view a church board or committee session as secular rather than spiritual activity. The ones we deal with now are adapted from a twenty-year-old article written by Gurnie Hobbs and copyrighted by the National Management Association. My intention is to take Hobbs' basic structure and redevelop it within the framework of Christian organizations.[1]

### AMBIGUOUS AIMS

Remember the old line, "I guess you're all wondering why I called this meeting"? One often hears it when three or four people are standing together perhaps waiting for an elevator or maybe they just accidentally met in a hallway or on a street corner. The line would be better spoken by some board and committee chairman about halfway through some business meetings.

Every chairperson must have a clear grasp on the intent of every meeting. What is it supposed to do? What goals are we here to accomplish? Can this meeting hold sufficient importance if its only purpose is consciousness-raising, i.e., a developing of increased awareness of issues and problems in the minds of the members? Perhaps; but if so, the chairman must understand that and quickly explain it to the members. One ought to ask about each potential meeting, "Can the goals of this session be accomplished by memos or phone calls, or do we really need to get together to discuss these issues?"

## CONFUSED FORMAT

Have you ever been in a meeting at which the group disagreed on who should chair or one without an agenda, either written or unwritten? Or perhaps one in which the time frames were totally unidentifiable? These format questions reflect primarily on the chair. But they also demonstrate that people attending the meeting have not done their homework and therefore cannot bring fertile minds capable of grappling with the issues. Format might also raise the question of who should attend the meeting. At some formal meetings guests and nonmembers might be invited, but at business sessions it is wasteful to have people in attendance who have no stake in the issues at hand and nothing to contribute to the deliberations.

## UNCLEAR BUDGET

What can we spend? How do we spend it? What procedures must we use to procure funds necessary to our projects? Decentralization is a factor here. The wise church board will delegate to its various committees (Christian Education, Missions, Evangelism, etc.) not only certain tasks, but an appropriate portion of the budget which they can spend without having to come back to the board for approval.

Another question on budget has to do with the funds necessary to carry out the meeting itself. Sometimes a task force or some temporary business group (such as a presidential search committee for a Christian college) operates totally apart from the normal budget of the organization and needs separate funds to carry out its function. It needs to transport members to meetings, carry on correspondence with potential candidates, bring the candidates to interview sessions, and perhaps hire secretarial services to handle the essential paperwork. Making bricks without straw was difficult in Egypt—for modern-day committees it's impossible.

## INDEFINITE RESPONSIBILITY

Though inseparable from the first item listed above, this one differs slightly. Here we're asking exactly what kind of body we have. For example, boards of reference may affirm the validity and integrity of the organization but their voices do not form policy. A board of advisers has no legal responsibility for the organization but serves because of general interest and technical expertise. A committee might be formed for advisement purposes or a task force sent to search out options and report back to the board which created it.

Remember, somewhere there resides someone responsible for doing all the things which contribute to a good meeting. In most cases that would be the chairperson, but not always. This leader must understand his responsibility in getting himself and others ready for the meeting, providing sufficient documentary backup, and exhibiting a clear-cut understanding of the responsibility of the body when its members come together.

## UNSTABLE DECISION-MAKING AUTHORITY

When I became President of Miami Christian College in 1974 the college operated according to a normal pattern whereby various department managers served on a president's cabinet advising the chief executive officer regarding college policies. One of my first administrative decisions changed the president's cabinet to an administrative committee, thereby making it a decision-making rather than an advisory group. That decision said in effect, "I am not asking you gentlemen to give me information so I can make decisions about the college; I am asking you to make those decisions with me as a leadership team."

In 1974 group decision-making was not a popular procedure. A great deal of research since that time, however, has established group consensus as not only viable but perhaps the preferred model in organizational leadership. The works of Em Griffin have contributed a great deal to our understanding of this, though a vast body of secular management resources has been building to affirm consensus decision-making.[2]

The chart in Figure 35 illustrates the kind of purpose awareness essential to keep meetings from becoming a waste of time. John Foskett has identified five types of meetings and suggests certain styles by which those meetings can operate. Obviously there must be a good bit of flexibility but the chart does help inexperienced chairpersons get a grasp on the kinds of things they should be doing in planning for meetings.[3]

The *Christian Leadership Letter* suggests:

Too often a committee is appointed for a particular purpose, but as the weeks and months go by, it becomes obvious that the committee is not going to act. The problem probably emanated because of oversight in giving the committee a proper charge. However, it could also be that no follow-up system was instituted. Follow-up is important, both for those for whom the committee is working and for the committee itself. Such an interchange with the leadership of the organization, either through personal contact or through correspondence, gives both sides a sense of direction.[4]

Consider these test questions for analyzing your boards and committees. Obviously you're striving for the greatest number of affirmative answers (on a 1–10 scale rating), but if you're serious about improving board and committee performance, be critically honest in your appraisal.

1. Do you conduct meetings only when there is a distinctive purpose rather than just because of schedule?

2. Do members do their homework by analyzing documents and setting the agenda prior to the meeting?

3. Does the person in charge know how to conduct a meeting and keep things moving?

4. Is the meeting held in an atmosphere conducive to good discussing and decision-making?

5. Are the time boundaries of the meeting properly controlled so that it doesn't last too long?

6. Is the agenda prepared and distributed in advance with appropriate documentation?

7. Do committee members get copies of the minutes as quickly as possible after each meeting?

8. Are action items appropriately marked for follow-up by specific people within a specific time frame?

9. Does each committee chairman understand his or her role as convener and presider?

10. Are actions of the committee reported to the appropriate authorities, preferably in writing?

Let's conclude this section by linking meeting chairmanship and leadership style. The principle of decentralization carries through to the leadership of a business session. There may be a time for autocratic leadership in meetings (as Fig. 35 identifies), but that should be the exception rather than the rule.

## THE AGENDA AND HOW TO PREPARE IT

Ever try to drive through a strange city without any map? You can quickly lose your sense of direction and spend valuable time driving

FIGURE 35

# TYPES OF MEETINGS

| IF THIS IS THE TYPE OF MEETING... | | ...THIS STYLE IS BEST SUITED |
|---|---|---|
| 1. INFORMATION GIVING—  | Such as: addressing a civic group, making year-end report to employees, explaining a directive to the staff. | AUTOCRATIC: Because it's from you to them with little need for reaction from them or further explanation. |
| 2. INFORMATION COLLECTING—  | Such as: interviewing new employees, hearing union committee opinions, getting staff member reports. | SHARED (a better word for "democratic"): Because lots of participation is important to get the facts out. Members stimulate each other. |
| 3. DECISION-MAKING—  | Such as: establishing new pricing policy, planning a cost-reducing program, setting up the work schedule. | SHARED: Because almost every member can perform useful functions and members need to become committed to follow-up action. |
| 4. DECISION-SELLING—  | Such as: getting staff members to accept new organization set-up passed down by the board (not open to questions); getting subordinates to go along with your decision on capital-equipment policy. | AUTOCRATIC: As far as any questioning of the decision (which has already been made) but SHARED as far as carrying out the decision—because intelligent, individual commitments to action are needed. |
| 5. PROBLEM-SOLVING—  | Such as: figuring out how to handle a difficult customer, helping each other on best ways to hold talks with subordinates. | SHARED: Because it calls for flexibility and the use of all resources available. |

in the wrong direction, around in circles, through the wrong part of town, and eventually end up frustrated and confused about the whole trip. The problem intensifies if time is a factor and each wrong decision costs precious minutes in arriving at your intended destination point.

That's what it's like to run a meeting without a properly prepared agenda, because the agenda provides the map of a business meeting. Sometimes even when you have a map it can be frustrating if the accuracy is questionable. One of my pet peeves has to do with maps drawn with some direction other than north at the top of the page. Frequently people who draw such maps aim the page in the direction they're going and fill in the map accordingly. Every professional map, however, has north at the top and topographers have adopted that principle so map-reading carries some reasonable standard for the users.

No agendas, upside-down agendas, agendas with items missing, agendas arranged with improper understanding of priorities—all of these and more lead to failure and frustration in business meetings, and you've probably seen them all at one time or another. *If the key to a good meeting is the chairperson, the key to a good chairperson is a good agenda.* Let's look at it in greater detail.

## WHO PREPARES IT?

One would think the answer to our question quite obvious—the chairperson prepares the agenda. And in many cases, perhaps even in most cases, that would be correct. It is not uncommon, however, for the chief executive officer to have the responsibility for agenda planning.

Think about a quarterly college board meeting for a moment. Board members come in from a wide range of geographical locations and distances. Quite possibly the chairman lives locally, but not necessarily. Even if he does, his day-to-day contact with business events on campus is minimal at best. Probably the agenda for the quarterly business meeting is put together by the chief executive officer (the president) subject to the approval of the chairman and perhaps in constant consultation with him.

Whoever prepares it, it should be designed well in advance of the meeting, and distributed along with support documents and all essential information necessary to an effective meeting. The agenda might include a list of the members and an estimation of the length of the meeting. Procedures and preparation should be clearly understood between the chair and the chief executive officer.

## HOW IS THE AGENDA PREPARED?

Some leaders use the "bingo method" by pulling agenda items out of a bowl or hat and sticking them on paper in any order. Such folly leads to an imbalanced meeting in which items of mediocre importance grab valuable early meeting time while crucial decisions might be pushed into the later hours with participants already in a state of fatigue.

Others choose the "department method" quite common to board meetings of colleges and schools. The board might first discuss academic issues, then move on to business and finance, later student services, etc. Each section of the meeting might be preceded by a report from the appropriate committee chairman advising the board on the present status of that portion of the operation and decisions or issues the board must deal with as a result of committee recommendations. This system offers much more order to an agenda than the bingo method. The problem lies in the possibility of the same area grasping prime time at every meeting. The solution? Rotate the order in which the different departments appear on the agenda.

Some chairmen use the "hopscotch method," switching back and forth from tough to easy items. This has psychological value to cut down on tedium and stress but does not lend itself to coherence or flow in the agenda.

The "pyramid method" builds to a peak of importance and interest in the meeting. The general idea is to get the "Mickey Mouse stuff" out of the way first so we can really give our attention to the major decisions before us. The rationale seems sound, but the implementation often fails. Those "Mickey Mouse" items have a way of clogging up precious committee/board time which should have been invested in the group.

My preference would be an "inverted pyramid" approach built on a semidepartment method. Keep the issues of the agenda within the department so we can deal with them in coherent form. But within each department, put the most important issues first so they get the primary attention. Add to that a fixed time limit on each section (and maybe on each issue), and you have the makings of a productive meeting.

## WHO RECEIVES THE AGENDA AND WHAT DOES IT INCLUDE?

We've already partially answered the second part of that question. The agenda should include as much information as possible, arranged in the best order for a maximal goal achievement. *A good agenda focuses on goals rather than problems*, though almost all business meetings will have to deal with some problems, major or minor.

Who receives the agenda? All board or committee members. But there may be other people who should see the agenda. A senior pastor for example might be an *ex officio* (by virtue of office) member of all boards and committees in the church, but does not normally attend 75 percent of them. He could never decide in advance whether he should attend a certain meeting unless he sees the agenda and knows what will be discussed. It is more than common courtesy to include such a person in the distribution of the agenda.

Or perhaps the Christian Education Committee of a local church plans to deal with an item in the realm of music or missions education. If the church has a music director who is not on the Christian Education Committee, he might be advised of this particular agenda item by seeing a copy of the agenda and the same for the chairman of the Missions Committee. Get the idea? Government in the sunshine—no surprises—open transparency which lets everybody know what's going on.

In *Claw Your Way to the Top*, humorist Dave Barry pokes fun at business meetings by pointing out two major kinds of meetings— meetings held for basically the same reason we observe Arbor Day—tradition, and meetings which really hold some alleged purpose. He notes:

> The modern business meeting, however, might be better compared with a funeral, in the sense that you have a gathering of people who are wearing uncomfortable clothing and would rather be somewhere else. The major difference is that most funerals have a definite purpose. Also, nothing is ever really buried in a meeting. [5]

## MINUTES—THE RECORD OF YOUR COMPETENCE

Interesting, isn't it, that we continue to use this strange word to describe a document which records the transactions of a business meeting. Webster's *New Intercollegiate Dictionary* offers that as only the fourth choice in its list of definitions of *minute*. Spelled the same but with different pronunciation is the word *minute* which is defined as "very small, of small importance, or trifling." Someday we may wish to choose a new word to describe what we're talking about here but minutes of a business meeting are neither trifling nor of small importance. Engstrom and Dayton warn that:

> Minutes are probably the most abused and misused part of any meeting. How much the minutes need to recount all of the details of the meeting is generally dependent on the time between meetings on the same subject and whether such a meeting is ever going to be held again. But, in general, minutes should be limited to statements of decisions that were made, problems that are still open and actions that need to be taken before the next meeting.[6]

Since the chairperson does not keep minutes of a meeting, he must appoint (or the group must elect) an exacting and wise secretary. In some cases the chair may have to instruct the secretary on the proper procedure for taking minutes. In no case, however, does he have the authority to change the minutes; they are signed by the secretary, the legal custodian of the minutes. During the meeting the chair may direct the secretary to include or not include something in the minutes and presumably do minor editing of grammar and spelling. But the substance of the minutes remains the exclusive property of the secretary and should those minutes ever be used in court, the secretary alone is the legally responsible party.

Having your business minutes used in court seems far-fetched, but it was my experience for seven years. As a prosecution witness in a federal trial, I had to repeatedly affirm or deny the intent of the board of directors of a Christian organization with respect to meetings that took place while I served as its chief executive officer.

The secretary of the board at that time was an astute and fastidious gentleman who recorded with great exactitude precisely what went on in those board meeings. Years later on the witness stand (under oath) I was able to say numerous times, "I have no independent recollection of the events of that meeting, but I am confident that the secretary has accurately portrayed them in the minutes which make up the prosecution's exhibit I have just been shown."

Consider a few simple but practical guidelines for improving the minutes in your board and committee meetings.

## USE A TIME-SAVING CODE

Sometimes this code could deal with the separate departments we discussed earlier in the chapter so that college or Christian school board minutes might identify academic policy actions with an AP, business and finance matters with a BF, etc. In a local congregation the Christian Education Committee could label all its minutes with a CE, missions with an MI, music with an MU.

The value is obvious. When discussing an action item from the source of the action is quickly discernible. A Building Committee, for example, discussing the size of Sunday School classrooms can immediately refer to CE126 which might describe the square footage the CE Committee determined for the classrooms assigned to the Primary Department. The number leads us to another idea.

*NUMBER THE MINUTES CONSECUTIVELY*

How many times have you been in a meeting in which a participant wished to refer to a previous action (let's say a decision made by the same committee six months earlier), only to describe "that meeting sometime last spring when we discussed this and agreed to proceed as long as the cost didn't exceed $1,000. Seems like Jack

FIGURE 36

# SAMPLE MINUTES

GRACE CHURCH
Minutes of the Christian Education Committee
November 16, 1987
7:30 P.M.

Present:    Barnes, Dalton, Fendley, Lyndsey, and Rose
Absent:    Mitchell and Wickham

After a time of prayer, Chairman Dalton presented the agenda. Adjournment time was fixed and committee work began.

*Singles Ministry.* Acting on the recommendation of the *ad hoc* committee studying this area, the committee determined the following:

CE 139 MSC—To begin a singles ministry at Grace Church by January 1, 1988 using existing lay leadership with the director responsible to the C.E. Committee. Meeting location, 1988 budget, and other details will be fixed at the December meeting.

*Sunday School.*    This being the third meeting at which the committee discussed changing the curriculum to Scripture Press, the decision was made.

CE 140 MSC—To begin Scripture Press in all departments through high school effective December 6. The Superintendent will order all necessary materials immediately and. . . .

FIGURE 37

# A PRACTICAL GUIDE TO
Lee H. McCoy
(For more information refer to
*Robert's Rules of Order Revised*)

| CLASSIFICATION OF MOTIONS | ORDER OF PRECEDENCE[1] | MOTIONS |
|---|---|---|
| **I. PRIVILEGED MOTIONS** The highest in rank and of such importance that they permit the main business of the body to be set aside. | 1 2 | To fix the time to adjourn To adjourn |
| | 3 4 | To take a recess To raise a question of privilege |
| | 5 | To call for the orders of the day |
| **II. SUBSIDIARY MOTIONS** Used to modify or help dispose of other motions. They can be offered only in the order of their rank and must be voted on before returning to the original motion. | 6 | To lay on the table |
| | 7 | To call for the previous question |
| | 8 | To limit or extend limits of debate |
| | 9 10 11 12 | To postpone to a definite time To refer to a committee To amend To postpone indefinitely |
| **III. THE MAIN MOTION** The lowest in rank. All other motions take precedence over it in the order of their rank. | 13 | To make a main motion[5] |
| **IV. INCIDENTAL MOTIONS** These arise "incidentally" out of discussion of pending business. They take precedence and must be decided before voting on the question from which they arise. They are lower in rank than privileged motions and generally yield to the motion to lay on the table. | All incidental motions are of equal rank. None can be displaced by one of the others. | To raise a point of order To appeal from the decision of the Chair To call for a division of the body To call for a division of a question To object to the consideration of a matter To make a parliamentary inquiry To withdraw or modify a motion To suspend the rules To make nominations To close nominations |
| **V. MISCELLANEOUS MOTIONS** Have characteristics of their own. Do not fit into any of the other classifications. | See footnotes 6 and 7. | To take from the table[6] To reconsider a question[7] |

# PARLIAMENTARY PROCEDURE

| INTERRUPT A SPEAKER? | A SECOND REQUIRED? | MAY BE DEBATED? | MAY BE AMENDED? | VOTE REQUIRED? | PURPOSE OF MOTION |
|---|---|---|---|---|---|
| No | Yes | No | Yes[2] | Majority | To set a time (and place) for the next meeting |
| No | Yes | No | No | Majority | To terminate the meeting (to the next regular meeting time) |
| No | Yes | No | Yes[2] | Majority | To secure an intermission in the proceedings |
| Yes | No | No | No | None[3] | To protect the rights of the body or of an individual |
| Yes | No | No | No | None[3] | To insist on conforming to the order of business |
| No | Yes | No | No | Majority | To postpone temporarily so as to attend to other matters |
| No | Yes | No | No | Two-Thirds | To stop debate and bring the pending question to vote |
| No | Yes | No | Yes | Two-Thirds | To decrease or increase the allowable time for discussion |
| No | Yes | Yes | Yes | Majority | To delay action until a later time |
| No | Yes | Yes | Yes | Majority | To place in hands of a small group for study |
| No | Yes | Yes | Yes[2] | Majority | To change the wording of a pending motion |
| No | Yes | Yes | No | Majority | To prevent a vote on the main question |
| No | Yes | Yes | Yes | Majority | To bring a matter before the body for its consideration and action |
| Yes | No | No | No | None[3] | To call attention to a violation of the rules |
| Yes | Yes | Yes | No | Majority | To obtain opinion of the body on the ruling of the Chair |
| Yes | No | No | No | None[3] | To determine the accuracy of the voice vote |
| Yes[2] | Yes[2] | No | Yes | Majority | To discuss by parts for more careful consideration |
| Yes | No | No | No | Two-Thirds | To prevent discussion of irrelevant questions |
| Yes | No | No | No | None[3] | To secure parliamentary information when in doubt |
| Yes | No | No | No | None[3] | To allow person making motion to withdraw or change it |
| No | Yes | No | No | Two-Thirds | To permit action prohibited by a particular rule |
| No | No | Yes | No | Majority | To present names for consideration to fill offices |
| No | Yes | No | Yes | Two-Thirds | To prevent other names from being placed in nomination |
| No | Yes | No | No | Majority | To consider business that temporarily has been set aside |
| Yes | Yes | Yes[5] | No | Majority | To reopen for discussion and decision a matter previously considered and voted upon |

1. When any one of the motions is immediately pending, those above it are in order and those below it are out of order (IV and V excepted).

2. Restricted. See *Robert's Rules of Order Revised.*

3. The Chair decides. If appealed, then majority decides.

4. An amendment to an amendment cannot be amended.

made the motion but I don't remember what meeting it was or actually how it was worded." As the secretary scrambles through pages of notes for something that approximates the wording just described, we lose valuable committee time.

In the example above, CE126 immediately identifies the committee and the action number. It can be tracked down and reentered into any discussion subsequent to the initial passing of the action. You can enhance the numbering system by attaching a list of action items to the minutes when they are distributed (see sample in Fig. 36).

## WORD THE BUSINESS ACTIONS PROPERLY

Normally the names of those who move and second need not be included in the minutes though one commonly sees minutes prepared that way. But let's be careful and accurate in our language. A member "moves"; he does not "make a motion." Again, a time-saving code uses the letters MSC (moved, seconded, carried). Minutes commonly contain both MSC and MS, the latter indicating a motion seconded but not carried. Obviously, one would never just record an M since a motion without a second has no life of its own.

## PERSONALIZE THE MINUTES FOR DISTRIBUTION

After the secretary has signed the original and copies have been made, the chairman or chief executive officer may want to personalize the minutes for each participant. In a Christian Education Committee meeting, the Sunday School superintendent may have been requested by the committee to carry out certain actions. Those could be circled in red on his personalized copy of the minutes along with a note from the chairman expressing appreciation for his work on the committee, his ministry as superintendent, and his contributions at the meeting.

We have said nothing throughout this chapter about parliamentary procedure or the difference between moving/voting and agreeing by consensus. I address that question in the chapter on decision-making. Suffice it here to say that I prefer to operate by group consensus whenever possible (if there are no pressing legal concerns).

5. Only one main motion can be considered at a time.

6. Take precedence over no pending question. It is in order only during that meeting or the next. It is proposed under "new business." It yields to privileged and incidental motion, but not to subsidiary.

7. Can be made only by one voting with the prevailing side. While having high precedence as to "entry," it has precedence only over other main motion and to take from the table.

8. Undebatable only when the motion to be reconsidered is undebatable.

Nevertheless, sometimes the bylaws require boards and committees to do business according to parliamentary procedure, and perhaps even according to *Robert's Rules of Order*. One of the best summaries of the Robert's system I have ever seen once appeared in an issue of *Church Administration* and is reproduced in Figure 37 by permission.[7]

Perhaps I could best close this chapter by offering "Ten Commandments of Committee Competence" which I have used in graduate-level classes over the past several years. Many of these items have already been discussed throughout the chapter and therefore the list may just serve as review.

1. The objectives of each meeting must be clear to every member.

2. Each member should understand how the committee serves the organization or board which created it.

3. The chairperson sets the tone, the tempo, and the tactics.

4. Like individual leaders, committees must be efficient (doing things right) and effective (doing the right things).

5. Most committees require skills in the functions of planning and problem-solving and, therefore, members should be appointed who can contribute to these tasks.

6. Accurate communication is imperative for effectiveness in any board or committee meeting.

7. Almost every committee decision or recommendation affects people who, in turn, affect the success or failure of the committee.

8. Achievement is increased when members work on assignments between meetings.

9. A committee report should be the product of the group, not the chairperson or secretary.

10. Realization procedures (implementation steps) must attend decisions and recommendations so the committee can achieve rather than just talk about actions.

We've emphasized the chairperson repeatedly throughout this chapter and, to a lesser degree, the secretary. In reality a board or committee is a team and the quality of each member affects the quality of the whole. The concerns and characteristics of effective group work discussed in the last chapter carry over to business groups as well.

# STUDY QUESTIONS

**1.** Try to recall a business meeting you attended (or chaired) recently. Which of the "five deadly sins" caused trouble in that meeting?

**2.** Plot the boards and committees of your church on an evaluation grid using the ten questions on page 277. A possible sample might look like this:

*Questions*/Elders/Deacons/CE  Committee/Missions  Committee, etc.

1. _____
2. _____
3. _____
4. _____
5. _____
6. _____
7. _____
8. _____
9. _____
10. _____

Rather than yes or no use a 1–10 rating scale with 10 indicating the highest performance.

**3.** Prepare a good agenda for a board/committee meeting. If you will be leading such a meeting soon, make this the actual document. If not, create a likely situation. Employ the agenda preparation guidelines offered in the chapter.

**4.** Pull out some old minutes of boards or committees you have worked with over the years. Grade them (A, B, C, D, F) on the basis of the criteria listed under "Minutes–The Record of Your Competence."

**5.** Digest the ten-item list at the end of the chapter and write three things you will do differently the next time you chair a business meeting.

# ENDNOTES

**1.** Gurnie C. Hobbs, "The Five Deadly Sins of Meeting Planning," *Management Magazine* (July 1978), pp. 37–41.

**2.** Em Griffin, *Getting Together* (Downers Grove, Ill.: Intervarsity Press, 1982).

**3.** John D. Foskett, "Do You Get Maximum Benefit from Your Executive Meetings?" *International Management* (McGraw-Hill Publishers: January 1966), p. 67.

**4.** Ted W. Engstrom and Edward R. Dayton, "Not Another Committee!" *Christian Leadership Letter* (September 1974), p. 3.

**5.** Dave Barry, *Claw Your Way to the Top* (Emmaus, Pa.: Rodale Press, 1986), p. 113.

**6.** Engstrom and Dayton, "Meetings! . . ." *Christian Leadership Letter* (September 1973), p. 3.

**7.** Lee H. McCoy, "A Practical Guide to Parliamentary Procedure," *Church Administration* (The Sunday School Board of the Southern Baptist Convention: August 1964), p. 5ff.

CHAPTER 19

# Supervising and Evaluating Volunteers

Of all the leadership terms we use to define offices in the church's ministry, the one which most often appears seems to be "superintendent." We have general superintendents, departmental superintendents, Vacation Bible School superintendents, children's church superintendents, and at the denominational level, district superintendents, etc.

The superintendent's task centers in supervision. Supervision might be defined as "the action, process, or occupation of critically watching and directing the activities of other people."

Most professional studies show little disagreement between what supervisors think they should be doing and what their subordinates think they should be doing. In order of greatest frequency, one firm suggests the following top ten tasks of supervisors:

1. Maintaining departmental cooperation.
2. Constantly being cost-conscious.
3. Administering union contracts.
4. Handling materials, both flow and storage.
5. Maintaining tools and equipment in proper condition.
6. Facilitating two-way flow of communication.
7. Designing new and improved methods.
8. Applying company policies and procedures.
9. Watching production and shipping schedules.
10. Planning the work and following through.

In a different study subordinates were asked what they looked for in a good supervisor. In this case researchers divided the qualities into five categories and, while they roughly approximate the general list above, some striking differences appear.

A. Must maintain efficient operation so as to meet production schedules.

   1. Must know each job as well as his employees.

   2. Must be a good leader.

   3. Must cooperate with other departments.

B. Must maintain good employee relations.

   1. Must handle personnel problems in best possible way.

   2. Must properly indoctrinate and train employees and plan their advancement.

   3. Must keep up-to-date on incentives and payroll policies and administer them.

C. Must accept his personal responsibilities and try to improve on them.

   1. Must set and serve as a moral example.

   2. Must have confidence in self and others.

   3. Must maintain proper attitude toward employees and company.

D. Must maintain proper communications.

   1. Must help maintain customer relations.

   2. Must act as company representative on policy matters.

   3. Must maintain liaison between top management and employees.

E. Must be responsible for safety and housekeeping in his area and should strive to improve working conditions.[1]

Somehow the second list strikes me as much more relevant to our purposes. First of all, it emphasizes more what the supervisor should *be* in relation to his employees than what he should *do* for the company. Secondly, it maintains a balance between getting the job done (nomothetic) and relating to people (idiographic).

From these and other studies I have made up a checklist for supervisors in the church. It's not ideal and may not adapt well to your particular situation, but at least it's a start to measure the kind of quality supervision you need. You might want to read the rest of the chapter before coming back to the chart in Figure 38.

## IMPLEMENTING SUPERVISORY PRINCIPLES

The effectiveness of any organization depends largely on its leaders and the effectiveness of the leaders depends largely on those they supervise. Consequently, everyone gains when we improve the supervisory system and the effectiveness of any leader increases.

FIGURE 38

# CHECKLIST FOR SUPERVISORS

| ITEM | Excellent | Good | Average | Fair | Poor |
|---|---|---|---|---|---|
| 1. KNOWLEDGE OF JOB—Familiarity with the various procedures of the work | | | | | |
| 2. EXPERIENCE—Skill and practical wisdom gained by personal knowledge | | | | | |
| 3. GENERAL COMPANY INFORMATION —Knowledge of major and minor company policies and procedures | | | | | |
| 4. HEALTH—Soundness of body and mind and freedom from physical diseases or disability | | | | | |
| 5. ENTHUSIASM—a positive, ardent, and eager response | | | | | |
| 6. PERSONALITY—The external mannerisms consciously or unconsciously displayed in meeting situations | | | | | |
| 7. APPEARANCE—Outward general impressions made by a person | | | | | |
| 8. CHARACTER—Integrity of an individual | | | | | |
| 9. MENTALITY—Quality of mind, mental power, and creative intellectual ability of a person | | | | | |
| 10. SOCIABILITY—Sense of mutual relationship, companionship, and friendliness with others | | | | | |
| 11. ABILITY TO GET THINGS DONE—Ability to perform, execute, and achieve an assigned task | | | | | |
| 12. COOPERATION—An appreciation of collective action for mutual profit and and common benefit | | | | | |
| 13. ACCEPTANCE OF RESPONSIBILITY— Willingness to assume and execute duties | | | | | |
| 14. JUDGMENT—Ability to grasp a situation and draw correct conclusions | | | | | |
| 15. INITIATIVE—Desire and ability to introduce a new course of action | | | | | |
| 16. EXPRESSION—Ability to articulate and state orally and in writing one's thoughts and feelings | | | | | |
| 17. RATE OF WORK—The time taken to properly finish a specific assignment | | | | | |
| 18. ACCURACY—A high percentage of freedom from mistakes | | | | | |
| 19. BUDGET ACCOMPLISHMENT—Ability to hold costs to an absolute minimum | | | | | |
| 20. CONDITION OF DEPARTMENT—Orderly and clean | | | | | |

| | | | | | |
|---|---|---|---|---|---|
| 21. HANDLING PEOPLE—The ability to appreciate, understand, and direct individual differences | | | | | |
| 22. DEVELOPING ASSISTANTS—The ability to delegate responsibility to the right individual | | | | | |
| 23. DELEGATING WORK—The assignment of specific responsibilities for proper results | | | | | |
| 24. PLANNING AND ORGANIZING—Success in delegating authority to organize and plan work | | | | | |
| 25. VISION—The power to see and imagine | | | | | |
| 26. CREATIVITY—Looking for new and useful ways to improve self and the work | | | | | |
| 27. PROFESSIONALISM—Attending available meetings, conferences, workshops, and checking magazines and other publications for new ideas | | | | | |

**CONCLUSION** If organizations are to remain competitive during these trying times, then the members of the MANAGEMENT TEAM, in particular, must know their purposes, programs, and their personnel. All must work harmoniously together to attain the worthy goals of BETTER RELATIONSHIPS; GREATER EFFICIENCY; LOWER COSTS; and INCREASED PROFITS.

Several checkpoints help us specify the crucial areas of supervision and serve as an analysis of "vital signs" for the supervisory health of the leader.[2]

*PERSONAL ATTITUDE*

Not all employees will like their employers and not all subordinates will think about their supervisors with warmth. But in the Christian organization, and particularly the church, we ought to make every effort to ensure that supervisory problems are not caused by our own negative attitudes. Facing the last decade of the twentieth century, the evangelical church stares at a virtual crisis of accountability and authority. To be sure, part of that has come about through the ignorance and inefficiency of leaders untrained in administrative and group process, but even more dangerous is the spirit of the age, an anarchy which rebels against authority (2 Thes. 2).

The Christian leader understands this and starts his analysis of the supervisory situation by looking at his own failings. How do my workers feel about approaching me on various problems? Do I fog the leadership air by sarcasm or an occasional loss of temper? Can people under my direction depend on my support and confidence in what they share with me? Violations of these principles in secular organizations create serious pitfalls, in some cases, cause for dismissal. In the Christian organization they represent sin and a guarantee of the removal of God's blessing on the ministry.

## IMPARTIALITY

George Youstra writes about what he calls "The Christian Approach to Supervision. That is, assistance in the development of a better teacher-learner situation." In the context of Christian elementary or secondary school he emphasizes Galatians 2 and says, "The administrator who takes it to heart will leave his office and observe faculty in their classrooms for the purpose of assisting them to be better teachers—not to spy on them or to gain the derisive reputation of being a 'snoopervisor.' "[3]

The supervisor behaves somewhat like a parent who must treat all his children alike. There can be no showing of favoritism, no allowing of personal likes and dislikes to change treatment of certain individuals. The supervisor must be careful not to spend undue amounts of time with people he thinks are pleasant and inadequate time with workers whose company he might not enjoy but whose work clearly needs more of his input.

## CLEAR-CUT GOALS

When properly used, supervision can produce significant benefits for any organization. It can make that organization effective (people doing the right things) as well as efficient (people doing things right). When viewed as an end rather than a means, supervision tends to close in on itself; but when used as a tool it can be the major facilitator in the achievement of goals.

What about the selection of objectives and priorities?

1. Know your objectives. Hyperactivity cannot substitute for decision-making and long-range planning.

2. Choose the right strategy. Compromise in objectives and plans may sometimes be necessary but choosing the *right* compromise represents a supervisory skill. Half a loaf may be better than none; half a baby is not.

3. Help your staff (however large or small) understand and agree with the priorities of your collective mutual ministry.

4. Are you willing to bring others into the decision-making process and allow them to set the kinds of standards which will govern the supervisory process of the organization?

## JOB CLARIFICATION

Each person in your department or organization needs to know exactly what he must do. Job descriptions set up personal interviews in which you talk with each subordinate about his portion of the total ministry and how it contributes to the whole. Every person must know what you expect of him and what he may expect of you as his supervisor. Mutual trust and respect can only stem from frequent and open interaction; that means staff meetings on a regular basis.

Of course you'll always have sweet old Clara who comes Sunday after Sunday and, when asked about her ministry will respond, "Oh, I just show up and do what needs to be done." But that is not an administrative statement as much as casual conversation. Major principles of supervision require supervisors to help every individual understand precisely what he is expected to do. The supervisor establishes a warm climate free from tension, encourages each leader to work out his own solutions, and helps the leader accept problems as normal, viewing them as stepping-stones for learning. The supervisor freely shares what knowledge and understanding he might have; he helps each worker set his own goals; and he periodically evaluates the worker's progress.

## RESPONSIBILITY

Here again we have a two-sided coin. On the one hand, the effective leader accepts full responsibility for successful completion of the work he supervises. He takes the "blame" for the mistakes in his department rather than constantly telling his superiors that the problems were caused by certain people under his leadership. There's a factor of consistency here too, in which the good supervisor avoids asking for too much work on some occasions and too little on others. To put it simply, the good supervisor leans as hard on himself as he does on any of his subordinates.

But we must also emphasize the proper acceptance of responsibility on the part of the workers. Several items seem crucial to this acceptance:

1. Each worker must know his task and believe it to be important.

2. Each worker must understand and support the objectives of the overall ministry program.

3. Each worker must be conscious of his relationship to other workers in the program.

4. Each worker must be free from an atmosphere of intimidation.

5. Each worker must have a significant role in group process.

6. Each worker must be alert to his responsibility toward maintaining a spirit of unity and community in the group.

## COMMUNICATION

The supervisor must keep his people informed. That means he must guarantee himself a way of getting the proper information from the higher echelons of the organization. For example, the Sunday School superintendent should be an *ex officio* member of the board or committee of Christian education because it gives him access to information about the total church program so he can keep all teachers and workers in tune with what is going on.

But communication also means a willingness to have subordinates come to their supervisor with suggestions, expecting that he will have a sympathetic ear to their points of view. Let me just add a few simple suggestions describing what should be happening when a supervisor listens to a subordinate:

1. Rephrase in your own words anything you hear which really sounds important.

2. Avoid exaggerating the good points—you might miss something the subordinate is really trying to tell you.

3. Learn to concentrate—especially in long conferences or meetings.

4. Listen for the unfamiliar. If you're an experienced supervisor, so much of what you hear sounds like so much of what you have heard before. So listen carefully for some new item.

5. Be extra careful when you disagree. Think before you speak and possibly, don't speak at all.

In communication you always want to be careful with the nonverbal area, what Ross Snyder calls the "the feeling strand." My personal preference calls for following up any significant employee conference with a memo which establishes in writing the kinds of things you have agreed on so there is no question weeks or months later.

## CONTROL

The supervisor must be in control of his situation at all times. That requires patience and a willingness to repeat instructions when some people seem slow to grasp new ideas. It also means discipline in a kind but efficient manner so that the supervisor learns to reprimand when necessary but never forgets that the goal is to prevent recurrences of violation. Obviously self-control represents the most important kind of control.

Very close to control is the issue of retention. The quality of any supervisor may be judged on whether he retains high quality subordinates. Obviously there always may be some he does not wish to retain, but a frequent "walk through" of qualified people tips an observer to problems in the organization. What we do in control and retention assigns people to results rather than just to posts. The issue of goals surfaces large once again.

Let's remember too that sometimes *abandonment* is a value not a failure. Like automobiles, institutional objectives and procedures have built-in obsolescence. Attaining one's objectives may be too dangerous because when we "arrive" we may discover we don't want what we attained or we may lose the dynamic of moving toward given goals. Abandonment can be viewed as positive in that we *abandon* mistakes, revise, and move on; we *abandon* obsolete objectives and substitute new ones; we *abandon* outdated procedures and methods and get in step with current needs.

## TRAINING

One could argue that everything the supervisor does leads toward the training of workers. Supervision means training and the supervisor is always responsible for his subordinates. Everyone must be growing on his job and that growth requires leadership on the part of the supervisor so that new resources and techniques can be mastered and effective results can be achieved.

In all of this the supervisor sets the spiritual tone for the ministry. He demonstrates the life of prayer; he displays commitment to the Scriptures; he develops a Christlikeness in all the activities of the organization.

It should be obvious in all of the above that supervisors must be groomed rather than just thrust into responsibility and expected to perform. I wince each time I attend or hear about an annual church business meeting in which some unsuspecting lay person is voted in as Sunday School superintendent for the next year. With no training, no background, very little experience, possibly minimal interest, he is expected to lead that Sunday School to effective ministry for fifty-two weeks. Small wonder we groan that our evangelical Sunday Schools struggle.

## USING ESSENTIAL TOOLS

Supervision, like a good play, requires props. Personnel files, job descriptions, an office or procedures manual, clear-cut statements of goals and purposes (sound familiar?), and the minutes of staff meetings all serve as the "stuff" which makes good supervision. These tools or props become skilled instruments in the hands of the wise administrator who genuinely wants to improve his supervisory skills and improve the quality of his team. What does he do with these tools?

When a supervisor delegates responsibility to people, he faces the necessity of encouraging them to solve their own problems rather than running to the boss every time something comes up. The more people you can make responsible for ministry the more successful that ministry will be. The supervisor who gets tied down by day-to-day details in spelling out exactly what subordinates should do and how they should do it will not only suffer from job fatigue himself, but will cause his workers' initiative in decision-making abilities to grow dull.

Consider the chairman of the Christian Education Committee at your church. He may see his task as exclusively related to drawing effective and responsible people together for correlation and direction of the overall church education program. He may not be an expert in every aspect of the program; in fact, there may be lay leaders in the church who know more about early childhood education than he does. But as an administrator, he leads each of the committee members to take responsibility for their particular areas. According to Levenson:

> If a subordinate shows evidence of creative problem-solving, he should be encouraged in every way possible, even if his idea is not as original or as brilliant as he thinks. Such an approach will get your people into the habit, when problems crop up, of consulting first with themselves, not with the boss.[4]

## HE EXPLAINS THE ORGANIZATION

I'm genuinely convinced that many of our people operate at subpar levels in ministry simply because they don't know what's expected of them. Part of the process of proper supervision deals with giving instructions on how the organization operates. In order to do so the superintendent (supervisor) should be sure he knows the results he wants, must write those instructions out, must select the right people for the right jobs, must match instructions to the situation, must show people what to do rather than telling them how, and must give latitude for new ideas and new approaches.

In addition he uses feedback to check for understanding, follow-through, and progress. We must catch and clip misunderstanding early. Follow these four rules:

1. Say what you mean.
2. Say it in a way to make sure you're understood.

3. Say it with feedback to include follow-up.

4. Say it in a way that the employee understands there is genuine delegation going on.

## HE FINDS THAT RIGHT-HAND PERSON

Effective supervision demands the creative use of your closest associate. For the pastor that might be the assistant pastor or the minister of Christian education. For the Sunday School superintendent it is probably the assistant superintendent. For the classroom teacher it may be the substitute or assistant teacher.

Yet, many times the person who ought to be the best help in the organization becomes an abrasive problem or perhaps even a competitor. Any executive who doesn't know how to work well with an assistant ruins what could be a positive force in the effectiveness of his own work. Certain rules describe appointing or accepting an associate relationship. The supervisor does not always have control over who will be placed in that position, but he certainly ought to have a major voice in the selection.

1. *Pay attention to compatibility.* You must be able to get along with your right-hand person. There must be some mutual attraction of personalities. Your very close association rests on rapport, mutuality, and ability to work together.

2. *Spend time with your assistant.* Though you need to be available to all your subordinates, you should spend most of your time with that key person. Tell him or her how you see the job in terms of overall objectives and effectiveness. Indicate responsibilities and be specific in areas in which you feel he needs improvement.

3. *Specify general and emergency communication channels.* In other words there needs to be a time when the pastor (or other leader) regularly meets with the associate, probably at least two to three hours a week. There must also be some way for the superintendent to contact the assistant superintendent on a moment's notice (and vice versa) rather than having to wait until he happens to see him again at church.

4. *Don't treat the right-hand person like a highly paid messenger.* The value of an assistant depends on passing on part of the heavy load that rests on your shoulders.

5. *Don't let him see his job as a stepping-stone to yours.* This touchy matter must grapple with the reality that he may very well be the logical successor. On the other hand, a subordinate fascinated by the attractiveness of your position may fail to see the challenges of his own.

When you deliberately groom a Timothy to take over your post, know your mutual values and design some kind of time schedule. But if you have no intention of vacating the post within the foreseeable future, you may be better off with a right-hand person who does not aspire to your role. That's one reason why a director of Christian education sometimes seems a more effective staff member than someone who carries the title of assistant pastor.

**6.** *Develop the capabilities of your assistant.* Keep a clear picture in your own mind of his skills and abilities and occasionally share with him those things you think he can achieve. This requires continual evaluation and a constant eye on the future.

## HE DEFINES THE TASK

The wise supervisor constantly asks the so-what questions. Sometimes this kind of attitude produces a defensive reaction because people like to run things the way they have always been run. But the staff meeting (crucial to any kind of supervisory effectiveness) is the place where those so-what questions need to surface in all their bare reality.

A good staff meeting brings people together. It's like a football huddle where team members literally put their heads together not just to figure out what they're going to do next, but why they're going to do that rather than something else. Until we define the task, people will not know how to do it and supervision will be a nightmare.

## HE COPES WITH PROBLEM WORKERS

Yes, receiving grievances constitutes a major part of supervision. The "heat in the kitchen" traditionally ascribed to Harry Truman can be related first to tough decisions and then secondly to taking the blame when things go wrong or when people don't like what's going on. The wise supervisor receives each grievance carefully, giving it his full attention and a fair hearing. He checks out the angles, relates the grievance to the organization's policies and practices (isn't it amazing how many times the handbook actually covers something we can argue about for hours?), and he examines the worker's records. Hearing a grievance from some dependable worker who rarely complains is one thing. Hearing a grievance from somebody who complains on a weekly basis is quite another.

Without getting into technical psychology (an area in which I would feel most uncomfortable) let me suggest that we are dealing here with self-concept. It could very well be the self-concept of a supervisor ill-fitted to his role. But assuming we have *him* in the right place, we examine the subordinate's view of himself in relation to other people and to the organization. Bob Tannehill says it best.

> After all, it is the subordinate's essential perception of self that must be changed. We can rest assured that whatever his behavior in the past, it made sense to him. From his perception of himself and his environment, he drew certain conclusions and acted in keeping with those perceptions. To help him gain new perceptions runs headlong into the concept that the ideas he had about himself were wrong. This is a decidedly difficult task for all of us ... and we defend ourselves vigorously against it until we can readily accept the fact that the person working with us is not a threat, but is trying to help us develop and grow and become more competent, help us achieve what we want, through better self-perception.[5]

That's a great paragraph describing the significance of the role of the supervisor in developing workers.

It may be necessary on occasion to "fire" volunteer workers. The very thought of this chokes many pastors and church leaders. After all, if a person volunteered his time, how can you actually ask him to leave a position! Because the overall ministry involves many more people than just the individual in question. We must protect the integrity of the body of Christ not just our relationship with a specific individual.

We resort to this only after every other redemptive scheme has been applied, and we carry it out only with a proper termination interview allowing sufficient time for emotions to stabilize. Having been in the position of releasing several employees, both volunteer and paid staff, let me offer you two checklists I like to use before that final decision is made. The first is simply called "Separation Checklist."

___ The job has been described.

___ The employee understands the job.

___ Evaluation criteria have been established.

___ The employee has been evaluated over a long enough period.

___ The employee understands the evaluation.

___ The job cannot be modified to make it possible for the employee to perform satisfactorily.

___ Consideration has been given to other jobs the employee might do.

\_\_ Adequate notice has been given.

\_\_ Job location assistance has been offered where appropriate.

\_\_ A termination interview has been held.

\_\_ Follow-up termination has been made.

That protects both parties in any termination and guarantees integrity and fairness, what some have come to call "due process."

Another series I like to go through with an employee who doesn't seem to be working out consists of four questions. I once heard Peter Drucker offer it in a speech and have adapted it to my own administrative procedures.

1. Can this employee do this job?

2. Can this employee do this job better than any other job?

3. Can this employee do this job better than any other job in this organization?

4. Can this employee do this job better than any other job in this organization under my leadership?

It's possible to get a "yes" on the first three items and discover that the real problem suggests the subordinate simply can't work for you. Sometimes that rupture can be healed; other times it cannot.

## ACHIEVING EFFECTIVE EVALUATION

Evaluation presents a key point in the improvement cycle of supervisory process. We appoint people to tasks; we go through the process of training, delegating, observing; and at the evaluation point we determine whether these people can carry out the tasks. Must revisions be made? Must substitutions be made? What steps must we follow in evaluating church educational programs?

*Establish standards.* Standards are necessary if evaluation is to be accomplished. These should be determined by the board of Christian education and/or church teaching staff.

*Evaluate in the light of the standards.* Any evaluation instrument should reflect the church's educational philosophy and standards. And once the standards have been established, there must be a meaningful and honest way to evaluate the degrees to which they are being accomplished.

*Design evaluation rating forms.* Once your list of standards is complete, rating forms should be prepared to be used in evaluating each program. It is best to work with others in developing the forms. This instrument lists questions or statements relating to the various program areas to be evaluated. Statements on the forms should relate to all areas of the educational ministry, leadership, staff, students, curriculum, space, and equipment.

*Complete the rating forms.* Before beginning to distribute the evaluation rating forms decide who should participate in the process (West suggests older teen and adult students, pastor, members of the board of Christian education, parents, and nonteaching staff).

*Assemble and analyze the data.* How the evaluation data will be assembled depends on how large the program is and how many forms were completed . . . prepare a summary report of the findings indicating strengths, weaknesses, trends, and suggestions for improvement. Share the findings with those who would profit from knowing them.[6]

## DIFFUSING THE CONFLICT

West's careful guidelines help us understand that evaluation can be a very threatening experience and we want to diffuse the conflict whenever possible. Confidentiality, inclusiveness, fairness, and all the usual factors must be taken into consideration. Somehow we must sort out genuine conflict from legitimate confrontation. Saul and David show us chaos produced through jealousy; Barnabas and Paul apparently demonstrate God-designed conflict and separation; Rehoboam and Jeroboam represent just plain poor judgment resulting in strife and agony.

Conflict can be diffused if evaluation is carried out properly. Some will always say, "Don't spy on me; I know what I'm doing"; but the generally effective worker will welcome anyone who wants to observe his ministry. I'm almost prepared to say you can tell in advance who is doing an effective job and who is not by their attitude toward proposed evaluation.

## EMPLOYING VARIOUS MEASURES

We work hard at Dallas to design systems of evaluation that are fair and geared toward the improvement of instruction rather than threatening faculty and administration. Various committees have designed instruments to evaluate faculty by students, faculty by their department chairman, department chairmen by faculty, and administration by faculty.

I'm sure these instruments are not used effectively all the time but let me concentrate on the one that concerns us most—evaluation of faculty by department chairmen.

The system works very simply. Once a year, I use multiple measures to fill out the proper evaluation form in accordance with the best information I have (student evaluations, classroom observation, general contact, participation in departmental activities, etc.). At the same time, the faculty member fills out his evaluation of me. Then we get together and invest time discussing where our collective strengths and weaknesses lie.

These sessions are nonthreatening because they have nothing to do with salary increases, hiring, or firing. Geared to mutual brotherly encouragement, evaluation helps teachers be better faculty and helps me be a better department chairman. The key lies in multiple measures and in *knowing in advance what you're looking for. Evaluation based on subjective consideration will always end in futility.*

*PERSONALIZING THE PROCESS*

Mere exchange of evaluation forms seems a useless endeavor, quite probably doing more harm than good. The person-to-person discussions I have mentioned in the above paragraphs make supervisory evaluation work. Fox develops an outline similar to those I have suggested and concludes:

> Building on the approach outlined above, the development program should stand a better chance than the typical merit rating system in fitting the motivational level and personality of the subordinate because it is primarily his program, tailored to his needs. At any given time he knows where he stands and has more control over how he will be evaluated. In fact, to a large extent he can evaluate himself through knowledge of his performance relative to his program.[7]

## COMBATING MINISTERIAL STRESS

We'll deal with this at greater length in another chapter but let me mention here that administration in general and more specifically supervision create problems for pastors who have not been trained in managerial process (which includes most pastors active today). We may cry "lack of commitment" or "everybody's too busy" but ministry stress presents a genuine factor. About 15 percent of the 100,000 occupational disease claims filed in 1985 were stress-related and that represents more than a 30 percent jump from the previous year according to the National Council on Compensation Insurance.[8] Effective supervision can reduce stress, and the way we

FIGURE 39

# OVERALL ELDER EVALUATION

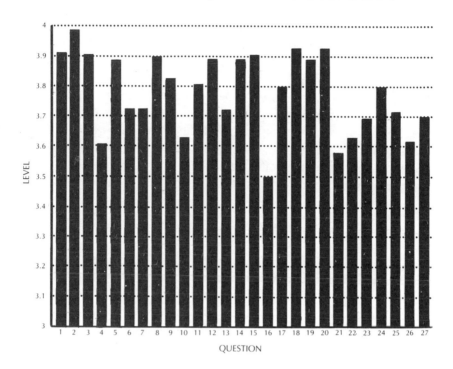

go about the task makes that difference.

## EMPHASIZING STRENGTHS

My favorite chapter in my favorite book among Peter Drucker's writings emphasizes strengths in the effective executive. Drucker makes a point that cannot be overemphasized in our discussion of Christian leadership—when dealing with subordinates, emphasize their strengths and capitalize on them; deal with weaknesses and inadequacies *later*. See the point? The constantly nagging supervisor creates an atmosphere of hostility by emphasizing weakness rather than strength.

In a church I pastored we designed an elder evaluation questionnaire to assess where we stood in the eyes of the congregation. A congregation responds to elders as they see them, not as they really are. That's another significant reason for evaluation at any point. The results of our survey are in Figure 39.

In my opinion every board of deacons, elders, administrators, and leaders must engage in some kind of evaluation like this on an annual basis. It affirms strengths—where God is really blessing our ministry—and it shows us where we need to work at ministering more effectively. Let me say it one more time. This survey does not indicate that our elder board was not prudent, but rather that the congregation did not *perceive* us at the highest level. Possibly we had strength that needed more public demonstration.

## REDUCE RESIGNATIONS

Recruiting students means big time business for every college and seminary, but retaining the students we have is an absolute imperative. Furthermore, it's cheaper than finding new ones. Good supervisors reduce resignations.

We end this chapter by offering a measure for supervisors, a self-evaluation. Read the directions carefully and follow through to mea-

FIGURE 40

# SUPERVISOR SELF-EVALUATION

1. How many people are you losing?

2. What are the differences between the people who survive in your ministry and those who do not?

3. What is it costing you in hours and dollars to replace workers each year?

4. Is there a pattern to the kinds of people who leave your church?

5. Could some of the losses have been retained with better supervisory processes?

6. Wouldn't transfer to another position rather than termination be an effective answer?

7. How many people are we keeping in ministry who really shouldn't be there?

8. What specific process do we follow when a person announces that he is leaving a certain kind of ministry?

9. What shrinkage has been due to deficiency on the part of the worker and how much due to the efficiency of the supervisor?

10. What program do we have for training supervisors?

sure your qualities as a supervisor and then adopt or adapt the scale to other supervisory personnel in your organization (Fig. 40).[9]

## STUDY QUESTIONS

**1.** Explain how the nomothetic and idiographic dimensions relate to the function of supervision.

**2.** Look again at the three self-evaluation questions found under "Personal Attitude." What answers can be given when you ask them of yourself?

**3.** Review your current job description for accuracy and adequacy. If you don't have a job description, write one.

**4.** Define "control," particularly as it relates to communication.

**5.** Check again the four questions which precede a termination. How do you answer them with regard to your present ministry?

## ENDNOTES

**1.** Russell L. Packard, "Management Team Relations," *The Hillsdale College Leadership Letter* (Vol. 6, No. 8, 1968), pp. 2–3.

**2.** Some of this material first appeared in my article "How to Supervise Workers," *Sunday School Times/Gospel Herald* (December 15, 1975), pp. 28–9.

**3.** George Youstra, "Supervision That Counts," *Excel* (Spring 1987), p. 10.

**4.** Robert E. Levenson, "Six Shortcuts to Stronger Management," *Business Management Magazine* (July 1966), p. 23.

**5.** Robert E. Tannehill, "How to Counsel the Problem Performer," *Hillsdale Report* (Vol. 11, No. 3, 1972), p. 3.

**6.** Robert R. West, "Evaluation: The Key to Success," *Profile* (Summer 1987), p. 3.

**7.** William M. Fox, "Evaluating and Developing Subordinates," *Business and Economic Dimensions* (February 1969), p. 20.

**8.** Susan Dentzer, John McCormick, Doug Tsuruoka, "A Cure for Job Stress," *Newsweek* (June 2, 1986), p. 46.

**9.** "Skills and Qualities for Supervisors," *Preacher's Magazine* (March–May 1986), pp. 36–7.

# CHAPTER 20

# REPRODUCING LEADERS
# WHO REPRODUCE

Win Arn asks a penetrating question: "Where are you on the church growth development scale?" He then offers his readers eight levels shown in Figure 41.

FIGURE 41

## GROWTH DEVELOPMENT SCALE

| I G N O R A N C E | I N F O R M A T I O N | I N F U S I O N | I N D I V I D U A L | C H A N G E | O R G A N I Z A T I O N A L | C H A N G E | A W K W A R D | A P P L I C A T I O N | I N T E G R A T I O N | I N N O V A T I O N |
|---|---|---|---|---|---|---|---|---|---|---|
| 1 | 2 | 3 | 4 | 5 | | | 6 | | 7 | 8 |

◄ DANGER: DROPOUT AREA ►
Growth Development Scale

Neither this chapter nor this book are about church growth but principles of reproducing leaders who reproduce follow very closely the principles of church growth, at least on this particular occasion.

According to Arn, the "dangerous dropout area" falls anywhere between the end of two and the beginning of seven.[1]

In a very real sense this chapter sums up the book and takes it beyond all earlier chapters. We're not just interested in producing leaders any more than Christian parents are interested only in producing Christian children. Those parents pray for the godliness of their grandchildren, great grandchildren and all who will follow until the coming of the Lord. Church leaders need to produce leaders who will reproduce leaders precisely as it is done in the family— through experience, instruction, and modeling.

As an educator I find it somewhat difficult to give those three terms as distinct a difference in church leadership development as I could in the nurture of children within a domestic context, but they are important. The true leader practices all of them all the time but especially with that immediate assistant.

We have dealt at length with philosophy and process through these chapters. We have attempted to demonstrate that the assumptions in training church leaders today must parallel the development of mature and committed disciples of Jesus Christ. One could ask with David Kornfield, "What would a training program look like that had no more and no fewer assumptions than those underlying being and becoming a mature disciple of Jesus Christ?"[2] I confess a genuine warmth toward the simplicity and essentiality of that question, but ours is a much more sophisticated age than the first century; in addition to spiritual maturity we deal with important skills and areas of knowledge in the cognitive, affective, and conative domains. So process, not only philosophy, is crucial to what we do.

Secular educators call what we have been describing, "competency-based education." In competency-based education a person "finishes" or "graduates" when he has acquired the ability to carry out certain competencies. It is not a question of time, nor credits, nor semester hours, nor accumulation of degrees. It relates rather to the achieving of New Testament goals, for example, those dealing with the development of elders or deacons.

## MODELING—BUILDING YOUR LIFE INTO YOUR STAFF

The leadership training process remains at heart a discipling process with modeling the first and indispensable part of the task. Deacons watch their pastor chair or moderate a congregational meeting and they understand something about participatory leadership, graciousness, two-way communication, and a concern for all viewpoints. As we look at the New Testament (Matt. 20:26-28; John 13:15, 34-35; 1 Cor. 11:1; Phil. 3:17; 1 Tim. 3:2, 10; 4:12-16) we see that modeling refers to non-classroom behavior. This leads Kornfield to raise the rhetorical question, "Which leaves a more lasting impression—being told what to do or being shown what to do?"

Let me not lead you astray. As an educator my tendencies probably wander more into the conative domain and edge too closely to the door of a room labeled "pragmatism." Nevertheless, a course in Old Testament and/or New Testament will not alone train Sunday School teachers—not even if they take it seventeen times! So how do we go about modeling Christian leadership in such a way that we build our lives into those of our staff, both professional and lay?

*SELECT COMPLEMENTARY STAFF*

Once again, I refer to earlier chapters in which I dealt with leadership styles and how they can be complementary. Figure 42 shows us the now familiar idiographic/nomothetic dimension recast in language which describes "providing supportive behavior" and "providing directive behavior." Some 100 years of literature in management science deals with these two dimensions in infinite variety and terminology while always speaking about the same behaviors.

But, you ask, how can you know in advance whether a staff member will be complementary? Herein lies the rub. Both churches who do the hiring and staff members who do the accepting; both congregations who do the asking and lay volunteers who do the accepting err by obtaining inadequate and sometimes inaccurate advance information. Engstrom and Dayton suggest:

> Hopefully you will be able to find more than one applicant for the job. If this is the case, go through the various applications and other information that you have and decide from what you read which ones you would like to talk to first. If the person does not have to travel far for an interview, it's best to set up an initial screening time in which you can get an overall feel as to whether you think it worthwhile to set up interviews with a number of other people. If the person is coming from a distance, then do some personal screening on the telephone.[3]

Yes, I realize they are talking about professional staff but the

FIGURE 42

# TWO ADMINISTRATIVE BEHAVIORS

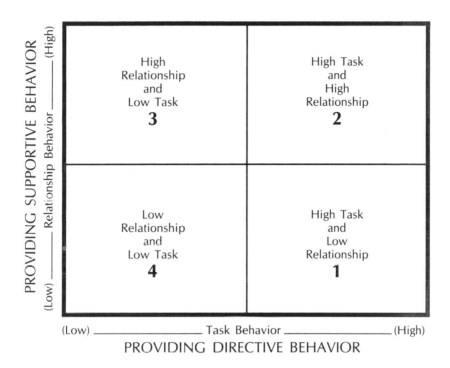

principles remain the same for volunteers. Know as much as you can; know precisely the kind of person you need; and double-check the responses in as many ways as you can.

*ADAPT TO OUT-OF-STEP STAFF*

Getting along with other staff members comes with ministry. If you have trouble with Joe Blake at Central Chapel, don't switch to Southside Cathedral because there's a "Joe Blake" there too. His hair will be a different color, he will be a different age, he'll hold a different position, but he'll be the same in relationship terminology. You need to adapt your leadership to people who seem to be out of step with you, and even out of step with others.

Few articles down through the years have dealt with this more thoroughly than Swan Haworth's "How Church Staff Members Relate." Haworth warns that "some staff members will actually be extractive and manipulative." He doesn't hide the fact that "your days will be filled with actions and reactions for and against your fellow staff members." He talks about the dependent staff member, the hostile staff member, those who are suspicious, angry, erratic, detached, despairing, apathetic, and of them all reminds us:

> It would be a comfort to you to know that these people will relate to God in the same characteristic ways. They will be angry with Him; they will suspect Him of persecuting them; they will remain uncommitted to Him, etc. . . . It will also help to remember that you are not bound and compelled to react in one way to all people. In fact, you have a good pattern suggested by the Apostle Paul, who learned that to become all things to all men gave him a much better chance to reach some.[4]

Of absolutely crucial nature here is the relationship between the chief executive officer and the professional staff. I emphasize this because their behavior becomes the model for everything that goes on in the church. The way the pastor treats his associates sets the standard for the way the Sunday School superintendent treats departmental superintendents and teachers, the way board and committee chairpersons treat the members of those boards and committees, and the way the members of the congregation treat each other. Groups have personalities just like individuals and a pastor must relate to a collective board (or a chairman to a collective committee) just as he or she must relate to each individual member of that committee.

## DEVELOP ACCOUNTABILITY IN STAFF

Virtually everything we've said so far deals with the modeling of individual leaders for other individual leaders. But what about groups? What about training committees? The First Baptist Church of Longview, Texas for example, harbors 268 committee members on 36 church committees! How do you keep track of all those folks? How do you apply any kind of competency-based measurement to their activities?

Associate Minister Larry Maddox says they train committee members at the beginning of each year. In short, they develop accountability as a part of the training process, not after a break-down and tragedy. They don't fuss about spiritual inadequacy when one leader has let down another on some major project; they plan in advance to teach people how to be accountable.

The two-part format at Longview includes a detailed briefing for all chairpersons and a complete training clinic for all committee members. The first (chairperson's briefing) provides overall information about the church, the committee, procedures, the usual nuts and bolts kind of information, and evaluation scales on how the committee has functioned during the previous year.

The committee training clinic itself deals with the nature of committee work, the specific task of each given committee, the opportunity to plan committee meeting times for the year, and a brainstorming session to get the committee rolling. That's not only a good idea, but the kind of thing that can be implemented in churches of any size.[5]

## DELEGATE RESPONSIBILITY AND AUTHORITY

Delegation links inseparably to the training process — building your life into your staff through modeling. Keep in mind what we're talking about in this chapter — reproducing leaders who reproduce. Sooner or later you will leave your present position either through resignation, death, advancement, or some other natural or super-natural means. The key to reproducing leadership is to clearly plan for it. How many churches and Christian colleges fall into disarray because leaders (sometimes founders) stay in their leadership positions too long? How many have fallen prey to the medieval practice of nepotism as foreign to the New Testament as the use of Urim and Thummim?

As I write these paragraphs, my present position as a department chairman finds me in charge of five full-time and two part-time faculty, all of whom are younger than I. One could reasonably assume that one of these gentlemen will succeed me, even though I will have no voice in that succession. My task, therefore, centers in delegating responsibility and authority, building up leadership qualities, and making every man a part of the operation. When the day comes that I step aside for whatever reason, the modeling of my role should have prepared one of my colleagues to assume it. I know the system works because I have done it several times before in other institutions.

Remember what professional athletic teams often call "depth." My personal view contends that the Boston Celtics lost the 1987

NBA World Championship because they had no "bench." Guard backup wasn't too bad (though compared with what the Lakers could produce it didn't seem like much); but any depth at forward or center was either invisible or nonexistent. Beaten and battered, Parish and McHale played far more minutes than they needed to, their aging, aching bodies trying to keep pace with the Laker fast-break.

Building one's life into one's staff is the opposite of waiting for leadership vacuums to arise and then searching for someone to quickly stuff in the empty hole! Depth, in terms of church staff, means that our training programs have produced people who are — yes I'm actually going to say it — waiting in line to take over a position when it opens. Laugh if you will; it can be done and has been done.

During the late 1950s I served as assistant pastor with primary responsibilities for music in a Baptist church in Northern Indiana. As I recall, the choir loft held a fixed complement of something like thirty-two or thirty-three seats with absolutely no room to add chairs. In short, we were limited to the number of people we could have in the choir. But the ministry of the choir was so important in that church, it had been so elevated as a means of serving the Lord, that auditions were necessary in order to be placed on a waiting list for possible vacancies in one of the sections! I take no credit for the situation; it was handed to me by a friend who had served in that position prior to me. That should be done for every ministry in the church.

## EXPERIENCE — REDUCING STRESS IN THE MINISTRY

But doesn't the experience cause the stress? Not necessarily. We would not consider it uncommon to find a veteran pastor with thirty–forty years ministerial experience who has experienced virtually no stress in the ministry. At the same time we could find a comparative neophyte who has learned nothing through his failures and successes and therefore is a ready candidate for burnout long before his time.

Both professional and lay leaders experience burnout. Sometimes it is self-induced as a result of workaholism, a syndrome of problems related to success addiction. Like other people in our culture, Christians become performance-dependent and when their performance no longer satisfies them, burnout results.

Recent research shows that pastoral stress disqualifies or drives people from ministry. One study identifies forty-three potential stressors with the top five listed as:

1. Proliferation of activities.
2. Perfectionism.
3. No time for study.
4. Role conflicts.
5. Unwelcome surprise.[6]

Yet another study (by Paul Robbins) named the top five as:

1. Problems with parishioners.
2. Overwork.
3. Local church problems.
4. Feelings of futility.
5. Conflicts within the congregation.[7]

Among professional staff leaders the most interesting survey I have seen was done by Craig Ellison in conjunction with *The Journal of Psychology and Theology*.[8] He divided respondents into three groups—senior pastor with staff, senior pastor without staff, and associate pastor. For all three groups "stress" was the number-one item but the arrangement of the other four differed widely.

| Senior Pastor/Staff | Senior Pastor/No Staff | Associate Pastor |
| --- | --- | --- |
| stress | stress | stress |
| disappointment | frustration | frustration |
| spiritual dryness | inadequacy | anxiety |
| inadequacy | disappointment | spiritual dryness |
| anxiety | fear of failure | fear of failure |

My premise for this portion of our chapter is very simple: *if ministerial stress poses a problem for pastors and associate pastors, it also creates a problem for lay leaders.* Lay leaders receive no remuneration for what they do, often labor longer in the same church than professional staff, and have little or no professional training for ministry. Stress could be an even more prevalent and dangerous factor among the laity than among professional clergy because of these factors.

## WHAT KINDS OF MINISTERIAL STRESSORS CAN BE IDENTIFIED?

One survey notes four categories identifying them as personality stressors, social stressors, spiritual stressors, and career stressors. Among the first one would consider such things as low self-esteem (ever talk to a Sunday School teacher who suffered from this?), perfectionism, status orientation marked by aggression, ambition or competitiveness, and a lack of personal identity or realistic self-concept. I think it's safe to say that I have seen these characteristics in church lay leaders in almost every congregation I have served.

Under social stressors we find things such as unrealistic expectations, time demands, family demands, and financial demands. Spiritual stressors can cover a multitude of sins or perhaps imagined sins and certainly the now famous pop psych concept, "guilt trip." Career stressors are less related to lay leadership but in this particular context they would refer to the kinds of things that cause anxiety "on the job" such as the inability to get along with another teacher or committee member.

## HOW DOES A LEADER WATCH FOR STRESS?

What does the Christian leader do about stress in lay leaders? Like many diseases, the analysis or diagnosis is a bit easier than the prognosis. However, we can employ some simple and biblical patterns to retain the good people we have and allow them to become reproducing leaders. Remember the following axioms about stressful situations:

**1.** *Stress is a mind/body response to imbalance and frustration.* When one of the people we supervise seems to struggle in some type of stressful situation, we assume imbalance or disequilibrium somewhere in that person's life.

**2.** *Stress is no stranger to Christians.* A worthless and simplistic homily suggests that because people belong to Jesus Christ they have become immune to stress factors in modern society. But reading Psalm 23 will not cure problems of bitterness and friction between Fred and Tom.

**3.** *Stress is a result of how we perceive problems and pressures.* Sometimes we perceive correctly indicating genuine stress. Sometimes, however, we guess wrong and the stress we imagine is not really there. At those points wiser, more experienced leaders can help us get around the stress problem.

**4.** *Stress lies within ourselves—not in inanimate objects or situa-*

*tions.* Flip Wilson's, "The devil made me do it," line may very well be true about some behavior of some people, but your lawnmower cannot "make you" angry. Failure of your car to start cannot "create" frustration. Frustration and anger lie within you and conflict with those obstinate motorized monsters merely offers it an occasion to erupt.

**5.** *Stress excess may be a matter of choice.* Some people serve on too many committees, serving the Lord in too many different ways. It may be better to burn out for God than to rust out, but better options are available. We can carefully, wisely wear out using spiritual and physical resources at a reasonable rather than foolish rate.

Remember our key learning idea here—experience. Stress will always come and if those stressful experiences teach us how to handle them, how to change and adjust our perceptions, and how to trust the God who can mold every situation and solve every problem, we have come a long way toward developing our own leadership.

Don Huddle may not be a believer; at least I have no reason to think that he writes from a Christian perspective. Nevertheless, he vividly describes a mature Christian leader counseling a subordinate under stress when he writes:

> The person in a stress situation needs support, and the best types are *understanding* (that the pain of emotional distress is real and not "all in your head"); *listening* (remembering that the superior can offer only emergency help and cannot hold himself responsible for other people's troubles); and *referring* (guiding the person with the behavioral problems to professional sources—not necessarily a psychiatrist).[9]

# INSTRUCTION—KEEPING YOUR BALANCE ON THE LEADERSHIP LADDER

We reproduce leaders who reproduce through modeling, experience, and instruction. Every leader is a teacher and must be aware of this instructional task at all times. As a teacher, he faces the responsibility of helping people carefully "climb" the leadership ladder without either missing a rung or trying to take too many in the same step. The key, of course, lies in balance.

*HOW CAN I BALANCE EXPECTATION AND REALITY?*

That question pertains to both leader and follower. A great deal of the frustration we create in our driven selves comes from imbalance between expectation and reality. Some lazy pastors may watch expectation and reality factors fall below what they should be, but that is not the common problem. More likely we will find a pastor whose expectations rise too high and therefore whose reality, not quite meeting those expectations, creates imbalance on the leadership ladder.

## HOW CAN I BALANCE NEED AND TASK?

Most of the pastors I know struggle with balance in their own lives and wrestle with the problem throughout the lay leadership in their churches. Sometimes the conflict shows up in what Carl George calls "the regrettable war" between leadership-gifted pastors and administration-gifted lay people. He argues that people, unaware of their own spiritual gifts, tend to assess everybody else's abilities in light of their own. ("If I can do it, why can't he?")

Believe it or not, one of the easiest ways to identify a person's giftedness is to examine what he or she criticizes! One thing an administrator surely knows how to do is spot the absence of administrative performance in other people. However, in our observation, he rarely realizes that his pastor might not have the gift of administration. He assumes the opposite and then criticizes the pastor for laziness, unwillingness to delegate, lack of confidence in lay leadership, distrust of newcomers, backwardness, or unwillingness to manage intentionally. If he were in the pastor's position he would surely handle matters differently. The only excuses he can think of are lack of humility, dedication, spirit, or commitment. These malignings are easy to radiate and difficult to overlook.

The pastor is naturally hurt by these criticisms and frequently launches a defensive action. How a leader wages war against administrators may take several forms.

He may devalue the administration gift and consider matters like planning, goal-setting, monitoring, controlling, and supervising to be mere details, unworthy of serious consideration by the truly spiritual.

He may insist that there are enormous differences between the business world and the church and the body of Christ does not admit to the same kinds of intentional activity for which successful businesses are known.

Pastors who are skillful in maneuvering can occasionally close out the business and administratively trained people from having any particular say, either at the church board or department leadership level.

Where the leader's defenses are successful, administratively gifted lay persons start compartmentalizing—turning off their brains and gifts at the door, having learned that to attempt to offer insights from their business life will only raise defensiveness from the minister and other leaders. This effectively blocks them from applying their gifts.[10]

## HOW CAN I BALANCE MINISTRY AND MEDITATION?

Pastor and lay leaders tend to hurt in this area. Too much work for God; too little time with God. The more the organizational dimension inflates, the more the organismic dimension deflates; yet I have tried to show that they are not in conflict but rather positive transaction and *balance*. If you sense a certain shallowness in your own spiritual life, how foolish it would be to stop any professional reading, stop going to any committee meetings, stop reading your mail, and cancel all engagements for the next three months. In some extreme cases of total burnout that might be necessary. But the more logical response is to get things back in balance.

Part of the problem is popularity in the ministry (though some readers will scoff at such a suggestion). People who do not participate in ministry but merely enter and exit Sunday morning after Sunday morning (occupying different pews so they won't be recognized as regulars) rarely feel the pressure of ministry. But the Sunday School superintendent, music director, chairman of the Christian Education Committee—these people stand in the hot spotlight of visibility. Such popularity, though it may seem exhilarating, soon becomes very much a part of the problem, adding unnecessary phone calls and meetings to an already intolerable schedule. The rookie leader may bathe in his newfound recognition; the veteran pleads for anonymity, a relief from the *pressure of popularity*.

The *pressure of success* compounds the pressure of popularity. Our society refuses to permit failure whether in athletics or ministry. This materialistic spirit, born of sinful egoism has also crippled the church. Vernon Grounds writes:

Do we have faith to face failure? Do we really believe that worldly successes are wood, hay, and stubble? We need to remember how often the church will judge us the way the world does. Before anyone decides on a full-time ministry, for example, they must realize that God may be calling him or her to a ministry of tedious mediocrity. Regardless, God's approval is the important point. It is far more important to follow God's blueprint for your life than to be another Billy Graham or Hal Lindsey or Robert Schuller or Bill Bright. Each of us needs the faith to cling to biblical principles of success despite possible worldly failure. And each of us must have the faith to keep serving even if unappreciated, unsung, and unapplauded—in short, we need the faith to face failure.[11]

Part of the problem stems from our all-too-eager willingness to take burdens ourselves as though we somehow thrust ourselves into ministry (review 2 Cor. 3–4, particularly 4:7). Confidence in the sovereignty of God, His gifting, and His calling offers an absolute requirement for effectiveness in Christian leadership. Yet the simplicity of faithful living in the light of what God has promised is too easy to talk about and so difficult to practice. Of all people, Christian leaders have the most to gain by long periods of concentrated prayer; but of all people we have the least time to pray (or so it seems) and the greatest fleshly tendency to trust in ourselves.

We forget that our service is intended neither to please each other nor to draw applause but rather to glorify God. "Kierkegaard reminded his fellow worshippers that, when they come together for worship, the congregation are the performers, the leaders (ministers) are prompters, and God is the audience and judge."[12]

One beautiful passage describing the balance between meditation and ministry is the one Luke used to describe our Lord.

> While Jesus was in one of the towns, a man came along who was covered with leprosy. When he saw Jesus, he fell with his face to the ground and begged Him, "Lord, if You are willing, You can make me clean."
>
> Jesus reached out His hand and touched the man. "I am willing," He said. "Be clean!" And immediately the leprosy left him. Then Jesus ordered him, "Don't tell anyone, but go, show yourself to the priest and offer the sacrifices that Moses commanded for your cleansing, as a testimony to them."
>
> Yet the news about Him spread all the more, so that crowds of people came to hear Him and to be healed of their sicknesses. But Jesus often withdrew to lonely places and prayed (Luke 5:12-16).

The early verses of our passage describe a harried minister rushing from place to place, besieged by people, carrying out popular procedures. Then we see the Lord decide to "take a break." He doesn't leave the ministry; He doesn't quit; He doesn't stomp off in anger; He doesn't vow never to serve on another committee; He doesn't leave the church and start a new church; He simply takes a break for meditation. He goes away from the people who besiege Him and spends quiet time with the Father. Any leader who wants to reproduce leaders who reproduce must learn that balance.

Dear Lord and Father of mankind, forgive our foolish ways!
Reclothe us in our rightful mind; in purer lives thy service find,
In deeper reverence, praise.

In simple trust like theirs who heard beside the Syrian Sea,
The gracious calling of the Lord, let us, like them, without a word,
Rise up and follow Thee.

Drop Thy still dews of quietness 'till all our strivings ccase;
Take from our souls the strain and stress, and lct our ordered lives confess
The beauty of Thy peace. [13]

## STUDY QUESTIONS

**1.** Answer, for your church, the question that opens the chapter. What can you do about it?

**2.** What must be done in order to "adapt to out-of-step staff"?

**3.** How can a leader develop accountability in staff?

**4.** Review the two lists of "stressors." Do any apply to you? Your friends? Your pastor?

**5.** How do *you* balance "expectation and reality"?

## ENDNOTES

**1.** Win Arn, "Where Are You on the Church Growth Development Scale?" *Church Growth Resource News* (Winter 1985), pp. 1–3.

**2.** David Kornfield, "An Evaluation of the Early Church Model of Training for the Ministry" (Unpublished research paper, institution unknown, 1980).

**3.** Ted W. Engstrom and Edward R. Dayton, "Hiring," *Christian Leadership Letter* (June 1987), p. 2.

**4.** D. Swan Haworth, "How Church Staff Members Relate," *Church Administration Reprint* (Nashville: n.d.), p. 4.

**5.** Larry Maddox, "Train Your Committees," *Church Administration* (August 1987), pp. 14–15.

**6.** John J. Gleason, "Perception of Stress Among Clergy and Their Spouses," *The Journal of Pastoral Care* (December 1977), pp. 248–49.

**7.** Paul Robbins, "Clergy Compensation: A Survey," *Leadership* (Spring 1981), pp. 35–45.

**8.** Craig W. Ellison and William S. Mattila, "The Needs of Evangelical Leaders in the United States," *The Journal of Psychology and Theology* (1983, Vol. 11, No. 1), pp. 31–2.

**9.** Donald D. Huddle, "How to Live with Stress on the Job," *Personnel Magazine* (Mar.–Apr. 1967), p. 7.

**10.** Carl F. George, "Recruitment's Missing Link," *Leadership* (Summer 1982), p. 84.

**11.** Vernon C. Grounds, "Faith to Face Failure," *Christianity Today* (December 9, 1977), p. 13.

**12.** Soren Kierkegaard, *Purity of Heart* (New York: Harper & Bros., 1938), p. 173.

**13.** John G. Whittier, 1807–1892, (text), Frederick C. Maker, 1844–1927 (tune).

# BIBLIOGRAPHY

Adams, A.M. *Effective Leadership for Today's Church*. Philadelphia: The Westminster Press, 1978.

Adams, Jay E. *Pastoral Leadership*. Grand Rapids: Baker Book House, 1976.

Alexander, John W. *Managing Our Work*, Rev. Ed. Downers Grove, Ill.: InterVarsity Press, 1975.

Allred, Thurman, ed. *Basic Small Church Administration*. Nashville: Convention Press, 1981.

Anderson, Carl R. *Management*. Dubuque, Iowa: Wm. C. Brown, 1984.

Armerding, Hudson T. *Leadership*. Wheaton, Ill.: Tyndale, 1978.

Barrs, Jerram. *Shepherds and Sheep*. Downers Grove, Ill.: InterVarsity Press, 1983.

Bedell, Kenneth, and Parker Rossman. *Computers: New Opportunities for Personalized Ministry*. Valley Forge, Pa.: Judson, 1984.

Berghoef, Gerard, and Lester De Koster. *The Elders Handbook*. Grand Rapids: Christian's Library Press, 1979.

Blanchard, Kenneth, and Spencer Johnson. *The One Minute Manager*. New York: Wm. Morrow, 1982.

Borst, Diane, and Patrick Montana, eds. *Managing Nonprofit Organizations*. New York: AMACOM, 1977.

Bossart, Donald E. *Creative Conflict in Religious Education and Church Administration*. Birmingham, Ala.: Religious Education Press, 1980.

Bower, Robert K. *Administering Christian Education*. Grand Rapids: Eerdmans, 1964.

Bratcher, Edward B. *The Walk-On-Water Syndrome*. Waco, Texas: Word Books, 1984.

Burns, James M. *Leadership*. New York: Harper and Row, 1978.

Campbell, Donald K. *Nehemiah: Man in Charge*. Wheaton, Ill.: Victor Books, 1979.

Campbell, Thomas C., and Gary B. Reierson. *The Gift of Administration*. Philadelphia: Westminster, 1981.

Cedar, Paul. *Strength in Servant Leadership*, Waco, Texas: Word, 1987.

*Church Leadership Development*. Glen Ellyn, Ill.: Scripture Press Ministries, 1977.

Dale, Robert D. *Ministers as Leaders*. Nashville: Broadman, 1984.

_____. *Surviving Difficult Church Members*. Nashville: Abingdon Press, 1984.

Dayton, Edward R. *Tools for Time Management*. Grand Rapids: Zondervan Publishing House, 1974.

Dayton, Edward R., and Ted W. Engstrom. *Strategy for Leadership*. Old Tappan, N.J.: Fleming H. Revell, 1979.

Detwiler-Zapp, Diane, and William Caveness Dixon. *Lay Caregiving*. Philadelphia: Fortress Press, 1982.

Drucker, Peter F. *The Effective Executive*. New York: Harper & Row, 1967.

Dudley, Carl S. *Building Effective Ministry*. San Francisco: Harper & Row, 1983.

Eims, Leroy. *Be a Motivational Leader*. Wheaton, Ill.: Victor Books, 1982.

_____. *Be the Leader You Were Meant to Be*. Wheaton, Ill.: Victor Books, 1975.

Ellis, Joe S. *The Church on Purpose*. Cincinnati: Standard Publishing, 1982.

Ellis, Lovdell O. *Church Treasurer's Handbook*. Valley Forge, Pa.: Judson Press, 1978.

Engstrom, Ted W. *The Making of a Christian Leader*. Grand Rapids: Zondervan, 1976.

Engstrom, Ted W., and Edward R. Dayton. *60-Second Management Guide*. Waco, Texas: Word, 1984.

————. *Strategy for Leadership*. Old Tappan, N.J.: Revell, 1979.

————. *The Christian Executive*. Waco, Texas: Word Books, 1979.

Engstrom, Ted W., and David J. Juroe. *The Work Trap*. Old Tappan, N.J.: Fleming H. Revell, 1979.

Engstrom, Ted W., and R. Alec McKenzie. *Managing Your Life*. Grand Rapids: Zondervan, 1967.

Faulkner, Brooks R. *Burnout in Ministry*. Nashville: Broadman, 1981.

Fidler, James E. *Our Church Plans for Leadership Education*. Valley Forge, Pa.: The Judson Press, 1962.

Gangel, Kenneth O. *Building Leaders for Church Education*. Chicago: Moody Press, 1981.

————. *Church Education Handbook*. Wheaton, Ill.: Victor Books, 1985.

————. *Lessons in Leadership from the Bible*. Winona Lake, Ind.: BMH Books, 1980.

————. *So You Want to Be a Leader!* Harrisburg, Pa.: Christian Publications, 1973.

Gerig, Donald. *Leadership in Crisis*. Glendale, Calif.: Regal, 1981.

Getz, Gene A. *Sharpening the Focus of the Church*. Wheaton, Ill.: Victor Books, 1984.

Goodwin, Bennie E. *The Effective Leader*. Downers Grove, Ill.: InterVarsity Press, 1981.

Gray, Robert N. *Managing the Church*, Vol. I: Business Administration. Kansas City: National Institute on Church Management, 1971.

————. *Managing the Church*, Vol. II: Business Methods. Kansas City: National Institute on Church Management, 1970.

Greenleaf, Robert K. *Servant Leadership*. New York: Paulist Press, 1977.

Griffin, Emory A. *Getting Together*. Downers Grove, Ill.: InterVarsity Press, 1982.

Guskin, Alan E. *The Administrator's Role in Effective Teaching*. San Francisco: Jossey-Bass, 1986.

Haggai, John. *Lead On!* Waco, Texas: Word Books, 1986.

Halpin, Andrew W. *Theory and Research in Administration*. New York: MacMillan, 1966.

Harris, Maria. *The D.R.E. Book*. New York: Paulist Press, 1976.

Henricksen, Walter A., and William N. Garrison. *Layman, Look Up!* Grand Rapids: Zondervan, 1983.

Hersey, Paul. *The Situational Leader*. New York: Warner, 1984.

Hocking, David L. *Be a Leader People Follow*. Glendale, Calif.: Regal, 1979.

Johnson, Douglas W. *The Care and Feeding of Volunteers*. Nashville: Abingdon Press, 1978.

Judy, Marvin T. *The Parish Development Process*. Nashville: Abingdon, 1973.

Keating, Charles J. *The Leadership Book*. New York: Paulist Press, 1982.

Kilinski, Kenneth K., and Jerry C. Wofford. *Organization and Leadership in the Local Church*. Grand Rapids: Zondervan, 1973.

Leas, Speed B. *Leadership and Conflict*. Nashville: Abingdon, 1982.

————. *Time Management*. Nashville: Abingdon, 1978.

LePeau, Andrew T. *Paths of Leadership*. Downers Grove, Ill.: InterVarsity Press, 1983.

Lindgren, Alvin J., and Norman Shawchuck. *Let My People Go: Empowering Laity for Ministry*. Nashville: Abingdon, 1980.

————. *Management for Your Church*. Nashville: Abingdon, 1976.

Lovorn, Tom and Janie. *Building a Caring Church*. Wheaton, Ill.: Victor Books, 1986.

Luecke, David, and Samuel Southard. *Pastoral Administration*. Waco, Texas: Word Books, 1986.

McConnell, William T. *The Gift of Time*. Downers Grove, Ill.: InterVarsity Press, 1983.

McDonough, Reginald M. *Leading Your Church in Long-Range Planning*. Nashville: Convention Press, 1985.

McKenzie, R. Alec. *The Time Trap*. New York: McGraw-Hill, 1975.

McSwain, Larry L., and William C. Treadwell. *Conflict Ministry in the Church*. Nashville: Broadman, 1981.

Mason, David E. *Voluntary Non-Profit Enterprise Management*. New York: Plenum Press, 1984.

Menking, Stanley J. *Helping Laity Help Others*. Philadelphia: The Westminster Press, 1984.

Myers, Marvin. *Managing the Business Affairs of the Church*. Nashville: Convention Press, 1981.

Naisbitt, John. *Megatrends*. New York: Warner, 1982.

Pattison, E. Mansell. *Pastor and Parish: A Systems Approach*. Philadelphia: Fortress, 1977.

Perry, Lloyd M. *Churches in Crisis*. Chicago: Moody, 1981.

_____. *Getting the Church on Target*. Chicago, Moody 1977.

Powers, Bruce P. *Christian Leadership*. Nashville: Broadman, 1979.

_____, ed. *Church Administration Handbook*. Nashville: Broadman, 1985.

Richards, Lawrence O. *A Theology of Church Leadership*. Grand Rapids: Zondervan, 1980.

Rosenbach, William E., and Robert L. Taylor, eds. *Contemporary Issues in Leadership*. Boulder, Colo.: Westview Press, 1984.

Rusbuldt, Richard E. *Basic Leader Skills*. Valley Forge, Pa.: Judson, 1981.

Rusbuldt, Richard E., et. al. *Local Church Planning Manual*. Valley Forge, Pa.: Judson, 1977.

Rush, Myron. *Management: a Biblical Approach*. Wheaton, Ill.: Victor Books, 1983.

Schaller, Lyle E. *Activating the Passive Church*. Nashville: Abingdon, 1981.

327

————. *Effective Church Planning*. Nashville: Abingdon, 1979.

————. *The Change Agent*. Nashville: Abingdon, 1972.

————. *The Decision-Makers*. Nashville: Abingdon, 1972.

————. *The Multiple Staff and the Larger Church*. Nashville: Abingdon, 1980.

————. *The Pastor and the People*. Nashville: Abingdon, 1973.

Schaller, Lyle E., and Charles A. Tidwell. *Creative Church Administration*. Nashville: Abingdon, 1975.

Schmidt, Richard F. *Legal Aspects of Church Management*. Los Angeles: Financial Executives of Christian Organizations, 1980.

Senter, Mark. *The Art of Recruiting Volunteers*. Wheaton, Ill.: Victor Books, 1983.

Shawchuck, Norman, and Lloyd M. Perry. *Revitalizing the Twentieth-Century Church*. Chicago: Moody Press, 1982.

Stacker, Joe R., and Bruce Grubbs. *Shared Ministry*. Nashville: Convention Press, 1985.

Stanton, Erwin W. *Reality-Centered People Management*. New York: AMACOM, 1982.

Staton, Knofel. *God's Plan for Church Leadership*. Cincinnati: Standard, 1982.

Stone, Howard W. *The Caring Church*. San Francisco: Harper & Row Publishers, 1983.

Sudgen, Howard F., and Warren Wiersbe. *Confident Pastoral Leadership*. Chicago: Moody Press, 1981.

Taylor, Robert R. *The Elder and His Work*. Shreveport, La.: Lambert Books, 1978.

Tidwell, Charles A. *Effective Leadership for Ministry*. Nashville: Broadman, 1985.

————. *Educational Ministry of a Church*. Nashville: Broadman, 1982.

Wallace, John. *Control in Conflict*. Nashville: Broadman, 1982.

Wedel, Leonard E. *Building and Maintaining a Church Staff*. Nashville: Broadman, 1967.

————. *Church Staff Administration: Practical Approaches*. Nashville: Broadman, 1978.

Westing, Harold J. *Evaluate and Grow*. Wheaton, Ill.: Victor Books, 1984.

_____. *Multiple Church Staff Handbook*. Grand Rapids: Kregel, 1985.

Wilson, Marlene. *How to Mobilize Church Volunteers*. Minneapolis: Augsburg, 1983.

Youssef, Michael. *The Leadership Style of Jesus*. Wheaton, Ill.: Victor Books, 1986.

Zaleznik, Abraham. *Human Dilemmas of Leadership*. New York: Harper & Row, 1966.

# SUBJECT INDEX

331

# SCRIPTURE INDEX